"This book is the perfect prescription for anyone suffering from SEO overwhelm. Rognerud's approach breaks down SEO in a simple-to-understand way then builds on visibility breakthrough concepts. I ultimately love this holistic approach to SEO. His strategic approach teaches how to get people TO a site but it also helps plan ways to get them THROUGH it to maximize ROI."

—Lorrie Thomas Ross, M.A., Author, *The McGraw-Hill 36-Hour Course to Online Marketing*
www.lorriethomas.com

"Mr. Rognerud is a master in search engine optimization and internet marketing. The tips and suggestions that he offers in his book are easy to understand and to implement even for the novice. He also offers many other powerful strategies that even an old pro like me finds insightful. *Ultimate Guide to Search Engine Optimization* is one of the few books that I recommend to students at our SEO workshops."

—"Radar" Roy Reyer, Certified Advanced SEO—Search Engine Academy,
SEOtrainingSW.com

"Jon Rognerud has a long history in technology, business consulting, and web development. His new book reflects that knowledge and experience in the search marketing field. He is a smart guy, and for folks starting in SEO, I suggest you pick up a copy."

—Andy Beal, MarketingPilgrim.com

"This is the best treatment of SEO I've seen—get this book! It's the first SEO reference that also covers the latest in social and local search. At over 300 pages, you can brush up on your skills or just put it on your bookshelf to impress your colleagues!"

—Dennis Yu, Chief Executive Officer, BlitzLocal

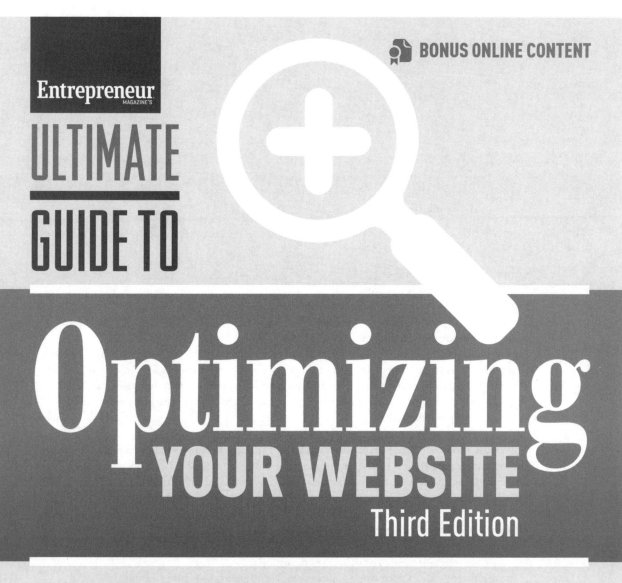

BONUS ONLINE CONTENT

Entrepreneur
MAGAZINE'S

ULTIMATE
GUIDE TO
Optimizing
YOUR WEBSITE
Third Edition

- Build a High-Performance Website
- Get **Top Ranking on All Search Engines**
- Drive Quality Local, Social, and Mobile Traffic

Entrepreneur
PRESS®

JON ROGNERUD

Entrepreneur Press, Publisher
Cover Design: Andrew Welyczko
Production and Composition: Eliot House Productions

This publication is designed to provide accurate and authoritative information in regard to the
subject matter covered. It is sold with the understanding that the publisher is not engaged in
rendering legal, accounting, or other professional services. If legal advice or other expert assistance is
required, the services of a competent professional person should be sought.

Library of Congress Cataloging-in-Publication Data
Rognerud, Jon.
    [Ultimate guide to search engine optimization]
    Ultimate guide to optimizing your website/Jon Rognerud.—[Third edition].
    pages   cm.
    Revised edition of the author's Ultimate guide to search engine optimization.
    ISBN-13: 978-1-59918-520-0 (pbk.)
    ISBN-10: 1-59918-520-2 (pbk.)
    1. Internet marketing. 2. Internet advertising. 3. Search engines. 4. Web sites—Design. I. Title.
HF5415.1265.R64 2013
658.8'72—dc23   2013037977

Printed in the United States of America

18 17 16 15 14   10 9 8 7 6 5 4 3 2 1

Contents

Acknowledgments

This book is dedicated to Eilif (Dad) and Patricia (Mum) for bringing me into this wondrous world and Ana (my wife) for being the most loving, patient, and strongest person I have ever met. When I met her, my search (no pun intended) stopped. She brought me three incredible offspring: Victoria Maria (10), twin brothers Jon-Phillip and Jon-Anthony (7), and I thank God every day for sharing them with me. Of course, without my brothers Nils and Per, and my younger sister, Anne-Karin, life would not have meant or been the same.

People I Want to Thank

I want to thank all the professionals at Entrepreneur Press, and all the amazing and directed support I have received. I also send thanks to all the incredible people in the internet marketing business, from small business owners to the larger corporations that I work with daily. This includes all the coaches and trainers of internet marketing, SEO, PPC, social media, analytics, email, usability, testing, and conversion specialists, many whom I've met online and also at the various business conferences. They give me constant fresh learning, challenges, and insights to their businesses, allowing me to work directly on strategies and building out tactical plans. The fact that they have an open mind, are willing to test everything, and will try new things for their businesses is huge.

Why Optimizing Your Website Matters

This next edition of my book is an updated compilation of not only recent strategies and tactics for SEO (search engine optimization), but also of local SEO, analytics tracking, search-engine friendly blogs, and expansion of the social search and social media phenomenon. Central to SEO is website development from content to links. SEO strategies have not changed much since the mid-'90s when I starting writing HTML, but the tools sure have! We now have social media and massive social networks (Facebook) to leverage visibility, which can be significant. While social media by itself is not an ultimate SEO strategy, the effects of it certainly can and will help. As links get generated over time from the "real" linkerati—journalists, top bloggers, and business pundits (moz.com/blog/identifying-the-linkerati)—you can build what you want: authority and trust for your domain(s).

Let me tell you a little about me.

I came to this country over 20 years ago as a recent graduate in business and computers. From that time until now, I have learned a fair share about things that work and don't work in business and online. The United States provided fertile ground for entrepreneurial thoughts and activities. I have had such a ride, and it keeps going and going.

The business knowledge was easily transferable to the web. For my technical compatriots, allow me to share a little about how I got from there to here. My own web journey can be traced back to a turning point in July 1996, when I wrote my first HTML page. It was my brother who told me to try it and see how I felt about it. He was not as heavily into software as I was at the time, but we both felt that this "internet thing" was worth a look. I probably have the code somewhere on a floppy drive (it seems that long ago), but it was simple: an input form to type your name and email plus a submit button. Once this submit button was pressed, it would push the content to a second page for confirmation, and then write out all the information on the third page.

At that time, the movie *Independence Day* with Will Smith was the rage at the movie theaters and a friend had just showed me something called ActiveX from Microsoft. This was a 3-D or 360-degree view inside a Mercedes Benz, and it was all online in a browser. I thought it was a little beneath me, to be frank, and I was not impressed. I mean: a text form and an ActiveX showing a video from inside a car?

No, for me it was about COM, Visual Basic 4.0, and SQL Server, 4.81 and 6.0. I had come from years in Compiler Design and Construction (Clipper from Nantucket), and I was not going to be lessened by something not related to "strict" computer science nomenclature and approach.

Fast forward a few years to the dot-bomb craze. Thousands of businesses launched and burned with billions into and out of the economy, and faster than I could say *cake* (that's actually old technology now!), I never looked back.

I really took off with a web application using IDC and HTX (precursor to ASP and ASP.NET) and using HTML, Javascript for Netscape 3.0, and IE 3.0. Talk about cross-browser complications—this was it! With managers breathing down my neck to have it "pixel-correct," I realized that I was either really close to something spectacular or I shortly would be exiting back into music, this time doing it professionally. (Yes, I had a top ten hit a few years earlier in my home country.)

As you can see, my online journey did not (thankfully) crash and burn. However, I could not have predicted my foray into search marketing, or how influential the technology of search would become.

The internet has changed the course of history and fast forwarded the next generation's industrial (internet) revolution. If you know how to implement SEO and social activities, you are in fact joining in this change, globally as well as locally.

It's this continuous implementation and testing, being in the field every day, and receiving input from people, tools, and the ever-changing internet landscape that keeps me fresh and alive. I would not want this any other way.

I dedicate this book to others who want to make money online. I started online in 1996, but it really wasn't until 2003 when I started at Overture Services (now Yahoo!) that I realized the power of all the knowledge, tools, and personal friends and networks that could help me. Friends asked me: "Is it possible to make money online?" "How fast can you get rich on the internet?" or said, "I don't think I can do it—it's too technical." I wanted to find a way to break through some of these questions for myself, but also felt a deep and growing need to teach and develop programs to show others how they could do it. My approaches and results from testing many programs have provided the foundation for this book. I tell my friends and others, and most of all, our newbies to the internet who want to make money online, that it's hard work, like any other business. It's basic Business 101—how to create and launch your own business. And, depending on the niche marketplace you are in, it may require more than your full-time attention. This is not just a 40-hour workweek.

Coupled with information products such as ebooks and DVDs, the "automation" power that an autoresponder email list-building system can bring is beyond exciting. However, many get caught up in the simplicity and promises of quick wealth, and buy courses from people who may con you into thinking it's easy, that by buying their ebook or DVD, it makes you an "insider." That is not true. You need to spend time, energy, and focus as with anything in life. Doing something you are passionate and knowledgeable about helps (a lot!)—and so does trying to make a difference. It's fine to start out with pushing other people's products as an affiliate marketer, for example, but you need to create your own products and differentiation to take it to the mountain top. In my business, we created a blueprint service, which uses tools found in this book plus some of my own designs and technology, and we now sell this for anywhere from $2,500 to $3,500 as a one-time fee. Imagine, a few years ago I would create these (in paper form) for only $500. The technology and value added is significant, and it's a living product and service for companies that choose a full-featured SEM campaign. Some say another business model might offer it for free (to upsell other services along the way for much bigger gains) or sell it for $6,000 to 8,000 and promise more beyond that. I believe in more value up front and presenting opportunities over the "lifetime visitor" to grow a sustainable business.

Reading this book will help you with SEO, teach you how to optimize your websites, drive traffic, and increase conversions. It is search marketing, internet marketing, and the "Business of . . ."—teaching you fundamentals of not only business planning but also execution. Do you know that many who sell info products online offer long periods of guarantees ("100 percent money-back, 90-day guarantee if not satisfied")? It sounds like an "irresistible offer" for you—but they are betting that more than half of you will never pick up the book or ever complete the exercises. Health clubs are an example of this business model. The health clubs know that many will pay for the membership but only a small percentage ever shows up. The same is true of internet marketing. I don't like that approach (even though it makes money for the internet marketer) because it does not provide a "differentiation" and "changing" experience. I wrote this book and the accompanying member site so you can learn. I also created a place where you could keep coming back and learn from other like-minded people. There are many people who have tried, tried, tried, and failed, failed, failed but found that the answers were not far away. I hope to help you shorten that curve by providing a continuous learning community that will offer support to help you execute your plan and achieve success (and money in your pocket).

You will see references to "Bob" in my book. He is a typical avatar (persona) I'm using as an example. He owns a small business, is learning SEO/M, and studies website optimization and business process improvement. He's continually learning, and keeps an open mind. Hopefully you can identify with him. I don't want to offend anyone here. Bob represents a human, I had to pick the sex. You'll see his face throughout the book. He has a positive outlook and has needs, wants, and goals for his life and business. He mirrors what we all want. However, he really pushes himself, and wants to learn to optimize his business at all levels. His spirit for learning and self-development sets the stage for you, too, I hope.

Another thing that has worked well for many before me—and a model I have adapted—is "help others get what they want, and you will have ANYTHING you want." This model was adapted from a Zig Ziglar quote, "You can have everything in life that you want if you will just help enough other people get what they want." It makes a world of sense—and you must know that I'm here to help you. Please send information directly to me at contact@jonrognerud.com, and I will answer your questions. I look forward to learning from you as well.

I do believe that succeeding on the web is about attitude, the right attitude, and not whining about where you are failing. Get the information, apply it, and you are 99 percent ahead. Focus on the things you are doing right, believe in yourself, read voraciously, and have fun. It will happen for you, too. I got a book deal! On that fateful day in 1996 I could have never anticipated the wonderful, fulfilling journey that lay ahead. What's ahead for you? Enjoy the adventure on the road to your own personal best.

Lastly, keep this in mind. It's a simple, but effective trick. When dealing with the search engines, write for users first, search engines second. What's good for a user is good for search engines—you'll easily create stickiness, bookmarking, and visitors will tell and share with their friends. If you do that, you're well on your way. Ask someone else, do they think your site or page has value? Is it clear what the page is about? It is amazing how this simple secret can work in your favor. If you also pretend you are a competitor, would you still say it provides good benefits?

Chapters reference areas of the online membership portal. This area is always under development, and you can access it inside the book (www.jonrognerud.com/ optimizationbook).

You should also make sure to get more information and join the community at your first level free membership at www.jonrognerud.com/optimizationbook or visit jonrognerud.com (new).

This book contains the most recent updates for optimizing your website for users and search engines. The experience of visiting your website and its pages must be a good one. If not, users and search engines will not come to visit, or worse yet, not come back. Website optimization and search engine optimization are therefore critical to your online success. The traffic, content, and conversion rates (how many take action, i.e., "do something" when they visit) will be very important. SEO has not really changed much over the years, but has become more full-featured. Consider yourself an inbound marketer. While this book is written with a non-technical approach in mind, technical aspects matter, including your pages' loading speeds. However, with current technological advancements and with the power of content management systems and website generation tools like the WordPress platform, you should not be bogged down by technical issues. I've made this an easy-to-read book for the less techno-savvy.

Finally—I'm paraphrasing the late Jim Rohn here—if your goal is to make a million dollars, you first have to become a millionaire. Think about how you can change from the inside first. Then, you'll enjoy success no matter what you do.

—Jon Rognerud, Manhattan Beach, California
America's #1 Small Business Website Optimization Expert

Chapter 1

From Then to Now: How Search Came to Be

Search has become such an integral part of our lives, it is difficult to recall that we once used the internet without it. We use search from home, work, and mobile devices to discover information and research choices.

The concept of search engine technology has existed since 1945. Vannevar Bush, an MIT professor, set forth the concept of computers as a flexible storage and retrieval system. Bush's essay "As We May Think" (*The Atlantic Monthly*, July 1945) described his ideas on hypertext and memory. He wrote, "A record, if it is to be useful to science, must be continuously extended, it must be stored, and above all it must be consulted."

Years later, Gerard Salton, professor of computer science at Cornell University, led the teams at Harvard and Cornell who developed the information retrieval system, Salton's Magic Automatic Retriever of Text (SMART). Salton, considered the father of modern-day search, wrote the book *A Theory of Indexing* (Society for Industrial Mathematics, 1987), which offers definitive explanations of many of the tests on which search continues to be based.

According to Wikipedia, British engineer, computer scientist, and MIT Professor Sir Timothy John "Tim" Berners-Lee, OM, KBE, FRS, FREng, FRSA, is credited with inventing the World Wide Web, making the first proposal for it in March 1989 (en.wikipedia.org/wiki/Tim_Berners-Lee). On

December 25, 1990, with the help of Robert Cailliau and a young student at CERN, he implemented the first successful communication between an HTTP client and server via the internet. The first website, info.cern.ch, was built at CERN and put on line August 6, 1991. The first web page address was info.cern.ch/hypertext/WWW/TheProject.html, and provided information regarding the WWW project.

The first web robot was introduced in 1993 by creator Matthew Gray. Aptly named the World Wide Web Wanderer, it evolved from counting active web servers to capturing active URLs. According to Wikipedia (en.wikipedia.org/wiki/World_ Wide_ Web_Wanderer), it was initially deployed to measure the size of the World Wide Web. Later in 1993, it was used to generate an index called the "Wandex," which effectively provided the first search engine on the web. It should come as no surprise that Matthew Gray joined the Google team as a software engineer in 2007.

Search engine technology has grown significantly since the days of the Wanderer. With each new addition—Excite, Look Smart, Ask, Yahoo!, etc.—an increasingly competitive market drove improvements in automated search algorithms.

As internet use increased, so did the need to logically organize the vast amount of information. The search engine facilitated the ability to logically find specific information from the mass quantity available. Search technology has continued to evolve, fine-tuning the quality of results and incorporating other elements such as video, real-time search, and social search.

THE GOOGLE INFLUENCE

A discussion of search would not be complete without talking about Google. Google has so completely dominated the search market that it has become synonymous with search. "Google it" has become the answer to our daily questions of what, why, where, who, and how. In many statistical analyses of the market, Google is individually categorized as no other engine comes close to its market share. Today, the "Big Three" in search (Google, Bing, and Yahoo!) dominate 90 percent of the search market with the next closest competitors, Ask network at 2.7 percent and AOL claiming only 1.3 percent of searches.

SMALL GOAL, BIG RESULTS

"Our main goal is to improve the quality of web search engines," wrote Sergey Brin and Lawrence Page in the paper that first presented Google. ("The Anatomy of a Large Scale Hypertextual Search Engine")

In 1998 when Google founders Larry Page and Sergey Brin were searching for buyers for their new search technology, one portal CEO told them, "As long as we're 80 percent as good as our competitors, that's good enough. Our users don't really care about search."

Either the CEO was wrong or Page and Brin foresaw a need that had not yet manifested in the market. Google officially opened its door in September 1998, and while still in beta, it was answering 10,000 search queries each day. In fact, by the time the beta label came off in September 1999, Google had been named one of the top 100 Websites and Search Engines for 1998 by *PC* magazine. Today, Google continues to be a dominant player in search. The company employs more than 30,000 people around the globe and is one of the top five popular sites on the internet ("Google Quarterly Earnings Report, Q1 2010," investor.google.com/financial /tables.html). According to comScore, a company that "measures the digital world," in December 2009 Google's websites had 65.7 percent of the United States search market, up 22 percentage points from the previous year (comScore, "qSearch Analysis," May 2007). The report also noted that the U.S. core search market grew 16 percent overall in 2009 with a 6 percent gain in unique searchers and 10 percent gain in searches per searcher. While Google maintains a strong lead and will likely remain a major influence in search technology, Microsoft (Bing) gained traction with the introduction of Bing in June 2009. Bing sites increased their share of search from 8.3 percent to 10.7 percent, with much of the growth coming in the second half of the year.

SEARCH AND MARKETING

Today, 85 percent of American adults go online (Pew Internet & American Life Project Tracking Surveys). Internet users no longer search, they "Google" even when they "Bing." Yet users don't really understand the technology that drives search and neither do most advertisers.

ONLINE RESOURCE

Ninety-one percent of internet users use a search engine to find information (Pew Internet & American Life Project Tracking Survey).

As search technology evolved, savvy marketers sought ways to improve their search engine position. After all, users typically only view the first page of returned results, viewing those as most relevant. If you're on page two or beyond of returned results, chances are consumers will never find your product or service. Rather than scroll through pages of returned results, if the first page doesn't deliver what they were looking for, users will refine their search phrase and search again.

The search landscape grows even more complex as additional elements have been added, such as images, video, real time results from social networking sites, and personalized results from searchers' social networks. The exponential growth, use, and impact of social platforms like Facebook, Twitter, Linkedin, YouTube, and Google+ are not missed by anybody. Add to this the "social signals" effect that now are used in Google's own algorithm, and you have a powerful toolset to get your website positioned well for search and social. In effect, a well-optimized site could get outranked by the results from a searcher's Twitter and Facebook friends.

In 2009, Hitwise®, an Experian company, issued a news release that indicated longer search queries, averaging searches of five-plus words in length, had increased by 10 percent when comparing January 2009 to January 2008 (hitwise.com/data center) while in the same period shorter search queries averaging one to four words had decreased by 2 percent.

> **INSIDER TIP**
>
> Being found for a search term in the top five listings on page one of search engines is considered the hot zone for traffic. Most searchers will click in this area, considered to be the most relevant and trusted of all results.

The battle to win the top ten forced search companies and marketers to come up with innovative ways to satisfy an insatiable market. Pay-per-click advertising (PPC) was created as a method to monetize search engines. While search was becoming an integral part of the internet experience, it was not generating revenues for the search engine. Instead, it was considered cool technology but was difficult to figure how to make money from it. PPC helped the search engines become revenue powerhouses and became a way for companies to buy their way into high visibility spots. With $26.5 billion sitting in cash, cash equivalents, and short-term marketable securities, Google has more cash on hand than many countries. The company has well over $50 billion in 2013.

PPC is also an advancement credited to a startup company. It was introduced by Jeffrey Brewer of GoTo.com (which later became Overture and now is part of Yahoo!). Brewer presented a PPC search engine proof of concept to the TED8 conference in February 1998. In 2007, global search was a $21.9 billion market with North America

Percentage of U.S. searches among leading search engine providers					
Domain	May 2011	April 2012	May 2012	Month-over-month percentage change	Year-over-year percentage change
www.google.com	68.11%	65.24%	65.02%	0%	-5%
Bing-powered search	26.79%	28.25%	28.12%	0%	5%
search.yahoo.com	14.50%	14.74%	14.95%	1%	3%
bing.com*	12.29%	13.51%	13.17%	-2%	7%
Note: Data is based on four-week rolling periods (ending June 2, 2012, April 28, 2012 and May 28, 2011) from the Hitwise sample of 10 million U.S. Internet users. Figures are for Web searches only.					
Source: Experian Hitwise					

FIGURE 1–1. Percentages of U.S. searches among leading search engine providers.

predicted to reach $29.2 billion by 2011. Today we have keyword and content PPC advertising. Universal search, which provides integrated search results from all content sources including websites, video, and news all on one page, is now available to PC and mobile users.

Search Is Getting Personal

Personalized search is certain to become more intelligent, especially in light of the dynamics of the new market where all media (music, video, television, news) seem to intersect online. Where personalized search was once limited to an integration of your search history and preferences, it now integrates universal, local, and social search, serving up personalized options.

TECHNOLOGICAL SHIFT

"The idea that the world is in transition is not new, but we can see much more clearly the dimensions of change in technology, society, geopolitics, and economics, and the consequences for business."

—Ged Davis, managing director and head of the
Centre for Strategic Insight at the World Economic Forum

Google offers free account setup and logins for its suite of products and services. In fact, if you check right now, you're likely logged in. When you search, those results are matched to your personal preferences, and with Google+ (you are using it, aren't you?), you'll see references and links from your circle of friends as you search for information. Google has introduced Authorship, which allows the user flexibility and power in setting up profiles and "home" domains. When you see a friendly face next to a search result, you know that user is leveraging Authorship. It may even be one of your friends or a familiar face from your network.

 Bob made a note to research Google Authorship and AuthorRank, and to make sure he sets up a profile and picture of himself. He also will research WordPress Authorship plugins and add his blog to this configuration.

Search technology and search marketing continue to evolve. As new technologies emerge, search experts seek ways to incorporate those elements into a comprehensive user experience. And as competition for those users increases, search marketers will continue to innovate ways to dominate the race for space.

Yet with all the advancements and competition, the majority of website owners remain clueless about search engine technology, optimization, and marketing! They put up a cyber storefront and have no idea how to tell people they exist. Furthermore, they don't create a strong positioning statement, a unique selling proposition (USP), even if one were found. We'll discuss the importance of the USP later in the book.

It's not surprising that internet users and businesses are confused. The industry itself cannot agree on terms, often using SEO, SEM, or just "search marketing" interchangeably. Some would argue the technical differences while consumers who fancy themselves experts simply refer to this art/science as SEO/SEM in an attempt to demonstrate their above-average knowledge of technology. More and more, you see the term *inbound marketing*. It makes sense. It's what you do to serve your audience with findable assets that they themselves take action on. You benefit by their clicks and visits.

An entire industry has been created around search optimization and search marketing, and with good reason; the effort is well worth the payback. The internet is a key step in the buying process for consumers. In a survey that asked users about their internet activities, 78 percent responded that they use the internet to research a product or service before buying it, and 70 percent use the internet to buy a product.

According to Marketing Sherpa, marketers who optimize their websites saw a 38 percent lift after six months of optimization (from its popular "Search Marketing Benchmark Guide").

How Important Is Search Marketing to Your Business?

If you have a web presence (and you must), it is worth the effort to learn and implement SEO techniques. Failing to invest time and effort in SEO is a bit like throwing a party but rather than send invitations, you're crossing your fingers and hoping that people will hear about it and decide to come!

In fact, SEO has rightfully become an integral part of PR and marketing activities. Content across digital properties is optimized for a business's targeted keywords and phrases. Image tags, video descriptions, blog posts, press releases, and website content all integrate SEO into the process. *Note*: In 2013, Google made it clear that using press-release services purely for obtaining links for SEO would no longer work.

We tend to make the web much more complicated than necessary. Years ago it was expensive and time consuming to design and get a website online. Today, a business can purchase a domain and by using a content management system such as WordPress, be up and running in less than a week without having significant technology skills. Not too long ago, you might have sought out investment money to launch your website with custom software and hardware installation, staff, and more. Today, you can get this done for just a few thousand dollars (or even less) to start. Yet one thing remains constant, whether online or offline: without marketing, people will not know about your product or service. Search marketing employs different technology and tools, but at the center of it all is good old-fashioned marketing.

A Local Business Story: What Not to Do

Last month I visited a neighborhood pizza place. The pizzeria is in a strip mall in between a nail salon, surf shop, and a drycleaners. My first visit was a delight. It was decorated to look like New York, complete with the Brooklyn Bridge extending over the ceiling. Every wall had black and white prints of old New York and enough memorabilia on the walls and ceiling to keep you occupied for hours. The service and food were excellent. The place had been open for several months, but I never knew it existed. By contrast, a restaurant across the street had remodeled, put up new signage, and captured local search traffic by placing the business listing on Google+ Local. The food was OK—not spectacular—but the lot was filled from opening to closing. They leveraged their website, and optimized it for search as well as local and mobile viewing and sharing. They fully used mobile marketing with coupons, quick response (QR) codes, and personal messaging (SMS). They had posted Foursquare and Facebook links at the entrance, on their business cards and menus. It was made fun and interactive, and people shared their experiences online and via Yelp, a popular local review and listings site.

DO YOU BELIEVE?

Marketing begins with a belief in your own product or service. If you have something great to offer—tell people! You may gain a few customers who happen upon your site but accidental marketing will only lead to accidental profits.

The pizzeria offered great atmosphere, excellent service, and food but it had fewer customers because no one knew it was there. The owners didn't believe in all the new technical wizardry, and had virtually no digital exposure. Are you making the same mistake with your business? Do you have an optimal user experience online, and in the local search engines?

In the past, brick-and-mortar businesses designed websites with little if any regard to search engine marketing. These businesses did not use their websites for lead generation but to serve existing customers. Today search engine marketing and social media are critical to branding. Even well-known brands can dilute their branding efforts if they do not come up in key searches. A successful SEM strategy begins with a successful marketing strategy. Technology is a tool, not a replacement for marketing strategy. The basic principles of marketing apply to both online and offline efforts. While there may be specific tactics that differ with the marketing channel, the underlying principles of the marketing discipline do not change.

The first component critical to success is to have a plan! Part of the planning phase is researching the competitive landscape, your existing market, and your target market potential. Once you have identified your strengths, weaknesses, opportunities, and threats (known as a SWOT analysis) and know your target, you can develop a well-thought-out plan.

Know Your Target Market

Knowing your target market enables you to precisely tailor your plan to capture your desired audience. Your marketing message should address the needs and preference of your target market. All too often, SEM efforts fail because the message was targeted at everyone. You can hire the best copywriters, web designers, and SEM firms, but their efforts will be in vain if you're not clear about whom you desire to reach. SEM is only as good as the plan that drives it! In fact, all media must use the principles of proper messaging, addressing the right market, and testing of these within different media (social, paid, organic). That also holds true for online and offline activities that drive prospects to your bottom-line profits. Chapter 6 on the psychology of your market addresses this important topic.

Where We Are Today

Now that we understand the importance of search and social media, what are our options? Online advertising has come a long way from banner and pop-up advertising. As search technology improved, consumers utilized search engines to find products and services. This in turn led to search engine listings driving significant volumes of targeted traffic to websites. In response, search engine optimization became a bona fide marketing strategy. This is not to say that SEO should replace all other efforts, but it should be integrated into a comprehensive marketing strategy. The success of page ranking and driving site traffic is still largely dependent on targeted, relevant messaging, and that should be consistent across all media.

Search Engine Results Page (SERP) listings have become the new battleground for domination. Reminiscent of the traditional Yellow Pages, businesses seek to be in the top listings, and the answer lies in a combination of optimization and marketing. We will discuss the specifics later in the book.

 Bob is a web designer and self-taught webmaster, and has been running his own business for 15 years, initially offering graphic design. At the nexus of the online movement, he began offering services to internet startups and later moved into web design, hosting, and maintenance. His business has been very solid, and he has many long-term clients. However, in the past two years he has seen a slowdown in new growth and the loss of a few long-term clients. His site designs are top notch. Clients really appreciate the responsive service, but Bob is not an expert in driving site traffic. He feels his business services should include more search and social-driven offers. Bob has decided to take some time to become more proficient at offering his customers a full-service digital marketing firm. In the past he just couldn't seem to find the time, but it has now become a business necessity. Bob is tech savvy, but even he needs help with SEO and SEM. We'll check on Bob's progress and journey throughout the book.

How to Leverage Search Traffic

There are many ways to take advantage of search traffic, both direct and indirect. For example, you may choose to advertise on a high-ranking site. This option is very similar to traditional advertising. In traditional advertising you would place an ad in a publication that is read by your target audience. The publication could be a magazine, newspaper, trade journal, or even a newsletter, but your goal is to meet your audience where they gather. In this same way, you would choose an online site that matches you to your audience. Not all sites offer advertising opportunities, but for those that do, they will provide you with a media kit that details their demographics and success rates.

The indirect method allows you to catch a ride on someone else's traffic. It is not exclusive and can be used in conjunction with direct SEM. AdSense, which is a Google program, is another indirect method. Other options are available, both inside the Google advertising platform and via other providers (TrafficVance.com, LeadImpact. com, for example).

For Google, you may now choose retargeting/remarketing options. Once you sign up (many vendors are in this advertising toolset, including Retargeter.com, Adroll.com as examples) a website visitor receives a "cookie" upon the first visit to your page. When they visit other partner sites, and completely separate from your website, your ads will "follow" them around. Ads, banners, and videos can be displayed to the user. They appear to be personally driven and give you a brand and visibility lift. While click-through rates are typically lower, you'll receive targeted clicks for the work. For Google AdSense, for example, you are paying to have your ad run on contextually comparable sites. Your ad runs on a site that targets your audience, providing you visibility via another site's traffic. Later in the book we'll examine strategies to drive traffic in greater detail.

TRENDS AND THE MARKETPLACE

It is an exciting time in search! As the internet has become an accepted standard, big business and traditional media have shifted their attention and diverted bigger portions of their budget spend to the digital space. The increased competition has also created many innovations that mirror the way we live and put the focus once again on quality messaging as we move away from the one-way broadcast messaging that dominated traditional media.

Search expands into your personal life in many ways, and perhaps most directly today, the mobile space. We talk about the revolution in mobile marketing and social search in the next section.

We'll also discuss the keys to website and search optimization for mobile users. Google announced in June 2013 that optimizing search results for mobile users has become a factor in rankings (http://googlewebmastercentral.blogspot.com/2013/06/changes-in-rankings-of-smartphone_11.html).

The Revolution of Mobile Marketing

Recent technological advancements have paved the way for effective usage of mobile phones in marketing. Although there is no standard definition of mobile marketing from industrial and academic perspectives, the concept is widely understood as the use of the mobile medium to pass information between a brand and the targeted user (eDigital Research, 2012). This marketing strategy has its roots in the popular text messages or SMS of European and Asian businesses. However, the rapid innovation of smartphones and other high-tech mobile devices has resulted in the development of more intelligent and interactive mobile marketing strategies. Here, we provide an evaluation of the importance of mobile marketing, industrial perspectives, implementation, services, and models available to a small business. And, finally, we'll look at the impact of mobile marketing to businesses.

Mobile technology has had a spectacular rate of penetration in both developing and developed countries. Although there are some challenges (such as lack of electricity and poor road networks) in the developing economies, a study showed that the rate of mobile phone subscription increased by 47 percent from 2002 to 2007 in these economies (Ofosu, 2012). This is one effective example that implies that mobile marketers can now reach potential customers from nearly all parts of the world. In addition, a study shows that 54 percent of subscribers with smartphones use their phones to navigate through the website while 38 percent make online purchases (eDigital Research, 2012). The study also indicated an increase of smartphone market penetration by 51 percent by 2012. The high rate of adoption of mobile marketing and technological advancement increases the potential for businesses to reach consumers faster and at a low cost. The interactive features of mobile marketing provide an opportunity for consumers to search for products preferred via internet enhanced services.

The progress achieved in mobile marketing has resulted from the concerted efforts of key players in the mobile industry, including mobile phone manufacturers, business firms, and consumers. Most importantly, all the stakeholders have a positive perspective toward mobile marketing because of the large number of associated benefits. According to El-Darwiche (2012), mobile phone manufacturers are producing digitalized gadgets (such as smartphones and tablets) with more functionality to meet the rapidly growing demand. Mobile marketers perceive that the increase in production of interactive mobiles and consumer adoption of internet buying provides suitable ground for mobile marketing to flourish. This is because mobile marketing is one of the most personal and interactive media that promises competitive advantages to business that utilize mobile apps (Martin, 2012).

Currently, mobile marketing has become an effective tool for solving socioeconomic challenges in the developing countries and among small scale business operators across the globe. According to Ofosu (2012), mobile phones are currently used for facilitating money transfer, sending text messages about the latest market prices, planning for sales deliveries, and browsing for product specifications, among other services.

Mobile marketing has gained popularity especially among firms targeting young people. Currently, small business can use a wide variety of strategies to achieve mobile marketing. Criteria for selection of suitable strategy depend on several factors, including the targeted market segment, efficiency of the strategy selected, and mobile application features available for the business owner. Similarly, implementation of the mobile marketing strategy varies with companies. However, there are three basic considerations for business firms wishing to use mobile marketing.

First, the firm should focus on establishing a relationship with clients and follow up the implementation process to ensure that the adopted strategies are effective.

Second, the firm should work closely with technical vendors to ensure that the adopted mobile marketing strategies attract the target market segment.

Third, the firm should focus on specified aspects of marketing, such as attaining customer loyalty or acquisition of new clients (Lely, 2013).

John Morris, a small business owner on Prince Edward Island, Canada, is an entrepreneur who has reaped the benefits of mobile marketing. Morris owns three businesses: Morris Code, HG Mobile Marketing, and Lens Make a Picture. From his firsthand knowledge about the benefits of mobile marketing, Morris acknowledged the rapid technological advancement experienced in the mobile industry by suggesting that there is something new every year (Beal, 2013).

Lens Make a Picture produces pictures in the forms of prints, postcards, magnets, and stock photography, which are posted by the partner company, HG Mobile. HG Mobile provides an interactive interface that allows clients to view the exhibits and vote for their favorite. This is one of the strategies that allows Morris to establish a relationship with distant clients. In addition, Morris uses QR codes to draw viewers' attention to the photographs. This helps visitors to scan the QR code using their mobile phones, which leads them to a YouTube video link. Morris claimed the integration of art and mobile marketing has attracted more clients to his exhibits, especially because of the interactive feature of the gallery. His potential clients can also purchase the exhibits using their mobile devices.

Technological advancement has allowed companies to invent different marketing services that can be offered via mobile devices. SMS and multimedia messaging service (MMS) marketing are some of the initial strategies but have been overtaken by more interactive and cost-effective strategies. For example, the email marketing company MailChimp has developed advanced features that allow mobile marketers to view their email campaign statistics by noting the end users who are tweeting them.

Mobile marketers can also manage the list and subscribers using their mobile phone devices (Lely, 2013). Moreover, marketers can upload their newsletters that are accessible to end users using smart phones. This makes the marketing strategies more interactive and comprehensive.

Facebook is a social site that is currently making significant progress in mobile marketing. It is a massive platform where mobile marketers can reach and engage target clients using features such as Promoted Posts and Facebook virtual coupons. A wide range of mobile marketing services is coming up in the industry, each with added advantages and with slight differentiation.

Most important, the marketing model adopted by the mobile marketer has two main features. First, the marketer should target specific consumers, which can be achieved using mobile search rankings. Second, marketers should decide on the most opportune moments to launch the campaigns (Segal, 2013).

Mobile marketing has a significant impact on the way business owners operate their businesses. The adoption of mobile marketing results in increased business and growth rate. This is because mobile marketing allows business operators to reach more consumers faster and at lower cost than other media. In addition, the advancement in technology has resulted in the development of mobile devices (such as smartphones and tablets) that help consumers in searching for products and services without traveling to producers or retail outlets. This implies that mobile marketing has benefits to business and consumers. Moreover, the increasing number of mobile phone users searching for useful information before making their purchases makes mobile marketing a promising tool for rapid growth of small businesses.

What Is Social Search?

Social search is a relatively new term, although the concept has existed since the early 1990s. Social search is powered by human judgment rather than computer-matched results. This taps into the very old but once again very hot trend of "viral marketing," or word-of-mouth marketing. In 1990 the first "social" guide was created by Tim Berners-Lee (to date it is still online) who created a page with links to his favorite sites. Many people relied on these types of pages to find things on the internet in the pre-search engine days. Yahoo! was one of the first to have a directory of websites. Those sites were created not by computers but a real live team of human editors who surfed the web and then wrote descriptions of the websites. Many other directory sites were also created by people, including The Open Directory Project (DMOZ) and the Librarians' Index of the Internet.

The social search movement's latest evolution can be traced to social networking. As social sites such as MySpace, Facebook, Twitter, and LinkedIn have revolutionized the web, we realized that in spite of our tech-savvy society we still like communicating with people! This "revelation" caused yet another evolution in which people became a key element in web marketing. The new buzzwords were *viral marketing, user-generated content,* and *folksonomy* (sites are collaboratively categorized using freely chosen keywords, referred to as tags).

As marketers began utilizing social networking sites to drive traffic and generate leads, new terminology emerged as well. Social media, initially used to describe the tools of social networking, has now become a catchall term for all things social—social networking sites, social bookmarking, and social media applications. Social media marketing, a discipline that did not exist ten years ago, focuses on marketing via social media channels. However it, too, is evolving; rather than a distinct discipline, it is a component of integrated marketing that combines offline and online marketing strategies.

In the new era of social media, people vote on or "tag" sites, articles, blogs, or other web content. For example, you may be reading a *USA Today* news article online and at the bottom you'll see items such as Share This, Like It, and Tweet This. Using these tools, you are "tagging" or recommending the article to other web visitors. You can like, buzz, tweet, and more to your heart's content.

The tags concept is not new. Meta tags were standard in 1996 and were used to describe web pages and what the search engines thought that they were about. As with all good things, spammers got into it and started tweaking, and it became a disaster. As we'll see in the world of search when something is overused or overdone, the search engines catch on and simply change the rules. Search engines are working hard to keep the competitive landscape fair, and webmasters are busy trying to compete. Overuse diminished the importance of meta tags. They were once a key consideration, but today they are largely ignored.

While many debate social search, the trend toward personalized search results will continue as search engines seek to improve relevance. It is an important element to look at for optimization techniques.

Why now? Algorithms have reached a plateau, and at the end of the day humans are still better than computers. A new generation of web users is doing things that are much more dynamic than any computer. Leveraging the work of volunteers, there is an infusion of talent to make content powered by people. An example of this is Wikipedia and other wikis, which are user-generated content.

What are these services? I've mentioned a few, but social search is a broad category that includes:

- Social networking—Twitter, Facebook, LinkedIn, Ning
- Shared bookmarks and web pages—Del.icio.us, Digg
- Tag engines, blogs, and RSS—blog content and seed content, technorati, bloglines
- Collaborative directories (volunteers)—ODP, Wikipedia

FIGURE 1–2. Page with social sharing buttons and tags—Facebook, Twitter, email, and more.

- Personalized vertical search—Google custom search engine (google.com/coop /cse/)
- Social Q&A sites—Yahoo! Answers, Answerbag
- Collaborative harvesters—Digg, Reddit, Popurls (aggregator)

Added to all of this, you have a hybrid of computer algorithm and human content. Examples of these hybrid social sites are:

- Craigslist
- Judy's Book
- Insider Pages
- Yelp

The social sites like those listed above are focused on local events and services, relying on the user community for fresh content. These sites are not only a source of social interaction but can be another opportunity for traffic, which has attracted a lot of interest and opportunity for search marketers. All social search shares the element of human involvement. People contribute to the content, drive content, or are sharing content.

Social search is not without its challenges. Unlike algorithmic search engines, social search is not able to keep up with the sheer volume of information. Additionally, while traditional search has uniformity built in, social search does not. With social search there is no controlled language or standard, so tags can be inappropriately applied. The reliance on people also opens social search to human laziness, misinformation, and abuse. Spammers or those engaging in unethical SEO (black hat SEO) can manipulate and abuse social search to their advantage. For example, a Wikipedia entry for then Presidential candidate Senator Barack Obama contained nude photos of blacks. The photos were removed two minutes later by another Wikipedia editor. As Wikipedia is dependent on users, people can spin information to suit their perspective or personal agenda. The relevance of social search results has also been argued. Results from those in your "social circle" depend on how much you trust your "friends'" judgment. Many have a large number of followers and fans on social networking sites but no real connection with them.

The solution may lie in a combination of algorithms and people-mediated search. A good example of this is Yahoo! Answers. Questions are posted and answered by real people, but the categorization and management of the data is handled by algorithms.

Blended Search Results to the Rescue

Universal search, also commonly known as blended search, unites all search results (web pages, video or images, news, etc.) on a single platform. Bing.com, for example, also integrates data from Facebook. In a May 16, 2007, press release concerning Google's move to universal search, it is explained this way: "Google's vision for universal search is to ultimately search across all its content sources, compare and rank all the information in real time, and deliver a single, integrated set of search results that offers users precisely what they are looking for." Google updated its toolbar to include navigation tools for images, videos, maps, and Gmail. When you enter your search term, you get the traditional results in the body and can then click on the toolbar for other types of content related to your search.

Universal search is now the standard for all search engines and provides rich opportunities for optimization. No longer confined to optimizing for text, you can view all of your digital assets—images, text, and video as an ecosystem—and design a

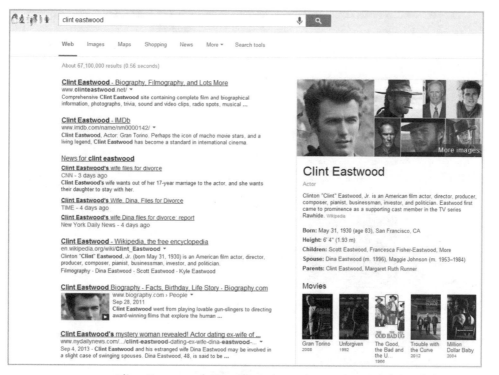

FIGURE 1–3. Clint Eastwood Google universal search results (and the updated knowledge graph).

holistic optimization strategy. Business owners and webmasters using optimized video, for example, may find their video listed before their actual web pages. In 2012, Google introduced the knowledge graph concept. It is an important move to understand and describe people, things, and places. See more on http://searchengineland.com/google-launches-knowledge-graph-121585.

Most recently, Google announced that universal search features included in the desktop version of Google Suggest (a predictive query solution) are available on mobile devices. Prior to universal search, results were limited to text. In the early days of universal search, a Google search would return a two-column page of results. For example, if you entered Clint Eastwood, on the sidebar you would have images of Clint Eastwood and links to blogs, videos, and Wikipedia entries about Clint Eastwood. In the main body of the page were the traditional search results. Today, links, blogs, images, and video are all in the main body, and the sidebar is sponsored links.

If you enter *Clint Eastwood* on Yahoo!, you get a three-column page of results (see Figure 1–4 on page 18). The main body shows Image Results, News Results, Video, and Twitter. The left sidebar shows related people, and the right sidebar contains sponsored results.

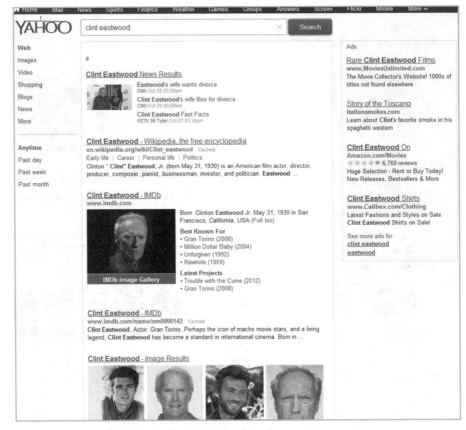

FIGURE 1–4. Clint Eastwood Yahoo! search.

Bing, which markets itself as a "decision engine," offers a three-column layout and has added a few unique features such as hover effects for images and news. By hovering your mouse over the link, you get additional information about the link without having to click on it. The integration of Facebook friends (right column) provides the searcher with useful social engagement data as well.

INSIDER TIP

More than 181.9 million Americans watched 38.8 billion online content videos in April 2013, while the number of video ad views reached an all-time high at 13.2 billion. according to the comScore Video Metrix service (marketingcharts.com/television/americans-watch-312b-online-videos-in-march-'10-12770/).

FIGURE 1–5. Clint Eastwood Bing search.

But let's break down some of the components included in universal search. Video and video search is a fast rising sector. Today, the internet is no longer a separate media but a platform where print, technology, and broadcast intersect. Books, music, television, and magazines can be enjoyed and/or downloaded online. You can watch a rebroadcast of your favorite television show, blog about it, read blogs from the show's writers, watch music videos that were part of the show, and order products associated with the show from one website. It is only natural that search technology would evolve to integrate the multitude of offerings. User-generated video *à la* YouTube initially emerged as entertainment but has gained popularity as a marketing vehicle for businesses. YouTube and the power of viral marketing made businesses and marketers take note as they began to integrate video marketing into blogs and web pages.

In its "2009 Search Marketing Benchmark Guide," Marketing Sherpa noted that 52 percent of people surveyed took action after seeing a video ad; of those watching video, 31 percent checked out the company's website in response to video.

The trend has not been lost on ad agencies. In a survey conducted by BrightRoll, 94 percent of respondents planned to spend more on online video advertising in 2010 than in the previous year (BrightRoll Video Advertising Report, Q1 2010). The report also noted that ad agencies are satisfied with online video's performance, which likely is why

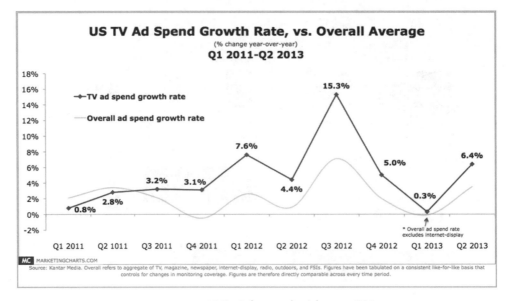

FIGURE 1–6. U.S. Ad spend, video vs. TV.

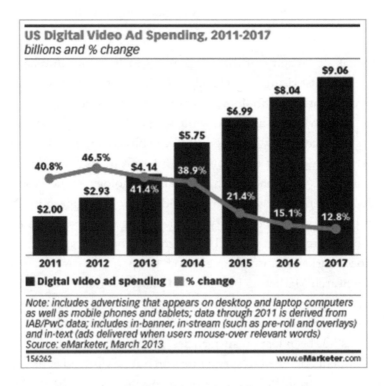

FIGURE 1–7. Online video advertising spending.

budget spend has been increased. More than one-half of respondents considered video more effective than other forms of advertising, and 83 percent claimed they were getting more value for their video advertising dollars than a year ago.

While all the trends in search drive a more dynamic experience for users, they also deliver challenges for search marketing. Search marketing will have to take a wider perspective than it does today to consider the broader platform. We will also be challenged with discovering the right blend of creative media to deliver the highest ROI for our investment dollars and figuring out accurate ways to track and measure those results.

 Bob began his search marketing education in earnest. He now realized that his site designs were largely dependent on the client's perspective and not the end users and that this was a mistake. He also had lots of questions. How do you leverage social search? What structural changes would make the biggest difference in search and traffic conversion? Could videos be optimized and then have spiders read the transcript? What tools were available for the new media? What APIs are available to developers? How could somebody start their own YouTube?

Bob's excitement grew as he embraced search marketing, but he realized there was a lot to learn.

Video Search

Video search, according to various layperson statistics, is driving up to 30 percent of the growth in total search. With *Good Morning America* and other major news outlets featuring YouTube videos, this statistic is entirely believable. Yet opinions are mixed as to how well video search actually works today. Voice-to-text technology has not yet matured, which limits some of the functionality. This limitation is one of the reasons that Google and others have not been able to include podcasts in their universal search algorithms. Certainly as technology advances, we will see the video search engine market grow significantly.

While the Big Three control 90 percent of the traditional search market, there are several players in the video search engine market.

- Vimeo—Popular service with custom options for paid services
- Viddler—Online video solutions for business
- Brightcove—High-definition streaming for corporations and small businesses
- Wistia—New provider with excellent service and deliverability, including detailed tracking and engagement options

Video lends itself especially well to the concept of viral marketing. People tag, share, rate, and comment on videos. Good news for users, not so great for paparazzi-stalked celebrities. As a result of the popularity of user-generated video, news organization now invite viewers to submit "news" via video. This has, of course, opened the market up to new businesses seeking to compete in the news market with their own "from the street" brand of journalism.

The Smartphone Movement and Mobile-Friendly Websites

Mobile computing facilitated by the smartphone movement is sure to be a focus for the search market industry. In a talk at the 2009 Morgan Stanley Technology Conference, Google CEO Eric Schmidt shared his belief that over the next several years Google's revenue from mobile search would eclipse search on the PC. Information technology and research advisory firm Gartner identified the mobile web as one of the Top 10 mobile technologies to watch in 2010 and 2011. According to Gartner, "by 2011, over 85 percent of handsets shipped globally will include some form of browser, and in mature markets, such as Western Europe and Japan, approximately 60 percent of handsets shipped will be smartphones with sophisticated browsing capability and the ability to render conventional HTML sites in some manner."

The fast growing mobile application market, high-resolution imaging, and touch screens will all make it easier than ever for mobile users to access and use the mobile web. The opportunity for marketers becomes even more exciting when you combine mobile and local search with e-commerce capabilities such as mobile coupons, express checkout, mobile reservations, and more.

"Implementing an e-commerce or multichannel technology program will open up many opportunities to drive the business across your company's channels. Work to resolve the conflicts among these channels and functional areas to lay the foundation for new business rules and capabilities. Reconciling conflicting goals, priorities, and projects across these channels and functional groups will pay off in reduced project churn, cost overruns, and delays across the program" ("The Future of the eCommerce Platform," Forrester Research Inc., May 2009).

A mobile-friendly website can further enhance the user experience, and help you gain easier, faster access to potential customers, clients, or patients. Custom applications, called "apps," that serve your audience (on iPhones, Androids) will not only help your brand, visibility, and traffic, but users and search engines have come to expect it. Google sees this as another health indicator for your website, and possible better rankings if implemented correctly. We'll talk about how to implement a mobile-friendly site later in the book.

Chapter 2

Understanding Web Search and How It Works

By now you understand the importance of search marketing, but how in the world does the technology work? In this book we won't get into a deep technical discussion (since this isn't a science book), but rather I will give you a broad understanding of the basics (and some more specialized areas) so that you can apply this knowledge in your online business.

Now let's begin this discussion with a basic definition of a search engine. A search engine is defined as an information retrieval system. In this book we limit our discussion to internet search engines, but there are search engines for desktops, mobile applications, intranets, and more. Think of a search engine as your personal electronic detective—you tell it what you're looking for, and it finds the information that you're seeking. Of course, the more information you provide, the more refined your results are. For example, if you searched for "Clinton" your search might return Clinton, CT; Bill Clinton; Hillary Clinton; book listings, blog posts relating to Clinton, or Oklahoma Clinton. However, a more specific search of "Clinton CT" would return the official homepage for the town, hotels in Clinton, and the Clinton News (Figure 2-1 on page 24).

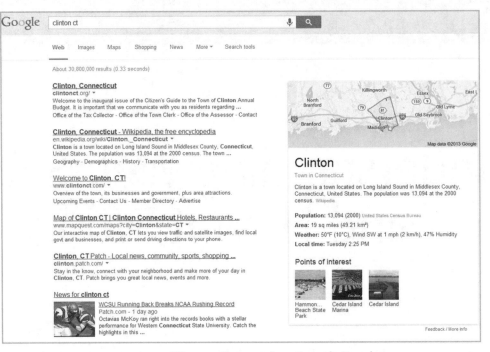

FIGURE 2-1. Clinton, Connecticut Search Results.

There are various search engines on the web that range from general to specialized. General search engines include:

- Alexa (Amazon company)
- Ask
- Exalead
- Gigablast
- Google
- Bing (Microsoft)
- Yahoo! Search

Many users may also use AOL, and others. However, these search functions are powered by other search engines such as Google, Bing, and Yahoo!

These general search engines are used to search for, well, everything. There are also other types of search engines, such as job search engines (i.e., Indeed.com, Monster.com, Craigslist.org), answer-based engines (i.e., Yahoo! Answers [answers.yahoo.com], Answers.com, Ehow.com), open source engines (Swish-E, Dataparksearch, Lucene, lucene.apache.org), blog search engines (Technorati, Bloglines, Blogcatalog, Google Blog search), and more.

> ### INSIDER TIP
>
> Technorati formally stopped tracking blogs by the end of 2007, but is still considered a top blog search engine. Google blogsearch has become very popular and useful in the last few years.

Metasearch engines (Dogpile, Metacrawler—core data used in Wordtracker Keyword research software and used by the top SEOs) are search engines that search multiple search engines. Rather than creating a catalog, a metasearch engine creates a virtual database (en.wikipedia.org/wiki/Metasearch_engine).

A popular search engine among more tech-savvy users is Blekko.com, which allows users to employ custom tags and filters for powerful data retrieval.

> ### SEARCH UNDERGROUND
>
>
>
> Metasearch engines are sometimes called "alternative" search engines. They are typically not as broadly used as Google or the other general search engines, but there are hundreds with really nice features such as ChaCha.com that will "chat" with you until you find what you need.

You type your search term into the meta engine, and it searches several search engines to compile results. Similar to search engines, metasearch engines differ in their results. No two give you the exact same results.

Some metasearch engines look at only major search engines; others query lesser-known engines, newsgroups, and other databases.

Metasearch engines include:

- Bioinformatic Harvester
- Brainboost (answers.com/bb)—Question-answering engine that accepts natural language queries
- Clusty
- Dogpile—Dogpile makes searching the web easy because it has all the best search engines piled into one. Go Fetch!
- Excite—Excite is the leading personalization Web portal, featuring world-class search, content, and functionality

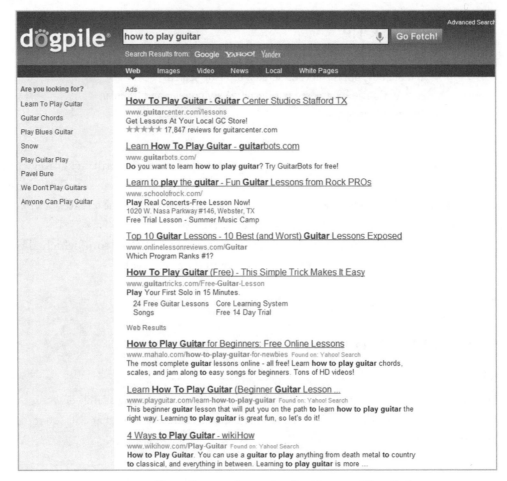

FIGURE 2–2. Dogpile search results for How to Play Guitar.

- HotBot—Powered by Lycos, a long-time search engine.
- Info.com—Allows you to search multiple leading search engines (Google, Yahoo!, Bing, Yandex) at once, returning comprehensive and relevant results fast
- Ixquick—Ixquick search engine provides search results from over the ten best search engines in full privacy
- Mamma—Metasearch tool for web, news, image, video, and Twitter search
- Metacrawler—Search the search engines, including Google, Yahoo!, MSN (now Bing) search
- PolyMeta—Metasearch engine with clustering and advanced linguistic capabilities
- SideStep (Now Kayak.com—travel)—Compare airfares with Kayak, the traveler's search engine, and check out special flight offers for the best deals on airfares

- WebCrawler/80legs.com—Powerful custom webcrawler to extract data from websites you specify

You can search for people, rather than web pages, using people search engines:

- Wink—Free people search at Wink, the world's largest people search engine (includes Facebook, Twitter, Linkedin)
- InfoSpace—Search the web on InfoSpace to get all the best results from leading search engines, plus results from Yellow Pages
- Spock—Intelius People Search is a large people search engine (Intelius bought Spock in 2009)
- YellowPages.com—Find online Yellow Pages business listings, phone numbers, addresses, maps, driving directions, and more in the Yellow Pages
- Zabasearch.com—Honestly free people search. All U.S. postal addresses and telephone numbers revealed free
- ZoomInfo—Founded in 1999, ZoomInfo is a web-based service that extracts information about people and companies from millions of published resources

Answer-based search engines answer questions and include:

- Answers.com—Experts network to ask questions on many different topics and verticals
- AskMe Now—Experts-Exchange.com—Enables people with technology problems to quickly and easily solve their problems by collaborating with experts from around the world
- eHow (ehow.com)—Learn how to do just about everything at eHow (Expertvillage.com is now part of the site)
- Lexxe (lexxe.com)—Processes natural language queries and delivers results in clusters by topic
- Windows Live QnA (answers.microsoft.com)
- Yahoo! Answers (answers.yahoo.com)—A new way to find and share information. You can ask questions on any topic, get answers from real people, and share your insights (one of my favorite sites in this category)

Search engines may be broadly grouped into three categories: crawlers, human-powered, and hybrid. Crawler-based search engines are so named because one of the major elements is a *crawler*, or *spider* (also called a robot or bot), that reads web pages via links. This is what's meant by your site being "spidered," or "crawled." The crawler reads the web page, and follows links within that page to other pages. The web page is crawled on a regular basis to look for changes.

> ### ONLINE RESOURCE
>
> Sign up for a free Google webmaster account today. It will provide a lot of important details on your site, including crawl stats, crawl errors, and overall Google-bot activity. Search for *Google webmasters*.

When the crawler reads the site, the information is indexed. (The index is also referred to as a catalog.) There can be delays between your site being crawled and indexed. Indexing is what makes the pages available to search engine users. Thus, search engines are not really searching the entire web as it exists at the point of your search. Rather, they are searching through what has already been crawled and indexed.

OLDER THAN GOOGLE

The Dewey Decimal System was created by Melville Louis Kossuth Dewey when he was 21 years old, working as a student assistant in a college library. It's now used in more than 135 countries.

To understand this, let's use the analogy of the library. When you go to the library you can use the card catalog (now computerized) to search through the library's collection of books. All the books in the catalog have been processed and entered by the library staff. While you are there performing your search, a new shipment of books arrives. The books are physically present in the library but not yet cataloged and processed for your use. Spiders may have crawled the site, but like the new shipment of books, until they are processed (indexed) the information is not available to you.

The three components of crawler search engines are the spider (bot, robot, or crawler), the index, and the software. The software is a key component, as it's the differentiator of each engine. The software program sorts through the millions of indexed pages to match and rank searches based on relevancy. The software scouts the location and frequency of your requested keywords and phrases, and returns results in order of relevancy. While all crawler-based engines have the same components, they all work a bit differently. For example, Google allegedly has 200-plus factors that support the core search algorithm and the complex crawlers, including linking factors that count into the ranking. For these reasons you may get slightly different results from Google and Yahoo! although both are crawler-based engines.

SAME RESULTS?

According to the USC Beaufort Library (sc.edu/beaufort/library/pages / bones/lesson1.shtml) recent estimates put search engine overlap at approximately 60 percent and unique content at around 40 percent.

Of course, search engine ranking is at the heart of search optimization and marketing efforts (you must also consider click-stream patterns, conversion data [leads, downloads], and page copy optimization), which is why search experts spend so much time trying to analyze how the engines rank sites.

Human-powered search engines depend on human beings for their "catalog." The Open Directory (dmoz.org) is an example of a human-powered search engine. Users submit websites with a short description of each site. When a user types in a search term, the engine searches for matches in the descriptions that have been submitted. DMOZ helps to provide powerful authority and trust for your website when (and if) you get listed.

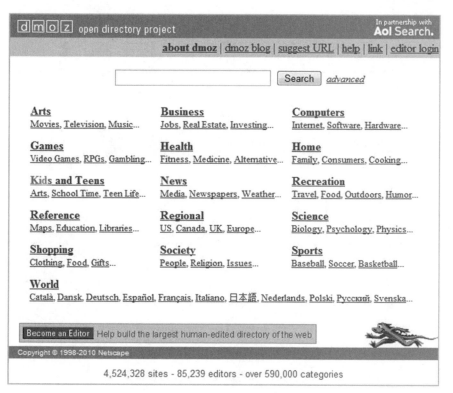

FIGURE 2–3. DMOZ.org, a human-powered search engine.

Hybrid search engines give you crawler and human-powered search results. A good example of a hybrid engine is Bing, although, to be fair, Google also uses human editors and doesn't rely solely on algorithms. This is not a widely known fact, so for the purpose of our discussion, we'll continue to classify Google as a crawler-based, algorithmic search engine.

Most technical professionals are interested in crawler-based search engines as a comprehensive understanding helps them to be more efficient at optimization.

THE HIGHEST TRUSTED CLICK: THE NATURAL WAY

Natural, or organic, search (also referenced as algorithmic search) results are unpaid or non-sponsored links or listings. Achieving a high position in search results "organically" can't be bought and has become the new "holy grail" for search professionals and webmasters. Search engines use an algorithm (and many other signals) to rank the importance and relevance of sites as they pertain to search terms. Higher aggregate

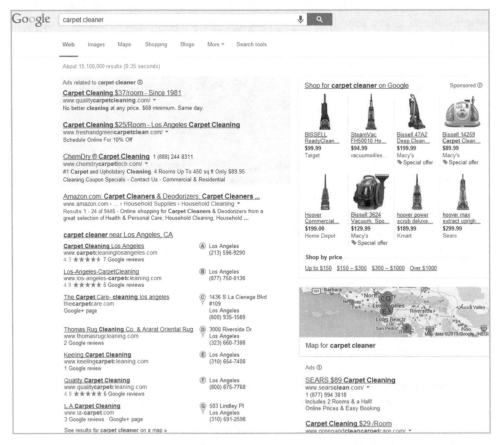

FIGURE 2–4. Paid search listing with local (Los Angeles) paid ads ("Carpet Cleaner").

scores result in higher ranking positions. For example, the search phrase *job search* on Google will show first page results that include Monster, CareerBuilder, Indeed, and SimplyHired in the natural results. Monster also shows up as a paid listing. These sites have heavy traffic and a continuous inflow of new content and links, so are likely to always show up high in natural results.

Paid or sponsored search listings are the result of web owners paying to have their ads shown.

WHAT IS OPTIMIZING YOUR WEBSITE?

So now that we understand a little more about search engines, what on earth is optimization? Search engine optimization is the process of making your website more accessible or visible to search engines via tactics that involve on-page (text, code, links) and off-page (external link development) activities. The goal of optimization is to have the spiders not only find your site and pages but also specifically rank the page relevance so that it appears at the top of the search engine results. The practice of optimization started in the mid-1990s. Initially optimization simply involved the webmaster creating the site, adding a few code tags to the pages, and submitting the site URL or page to the search engine. The spiders would then crawl and index the page.

As search caught on, it became clear that being listed was not enough. When users typed in search terms, they weren't going to continue to scroll through page after page to find what they wanted. So the race for ranking dominance began in earnest. Today the process of optimization requires a holistic approach to the site architecture, content, and links development. It's not a one-time process but requires maintenance, tuning, and continuous testing and monitoring.

Much of this book is devoted to the process of optimization and its overall role in the search engine marketing process. Below is a broad four-step process for a strategy for search engine optimization. Use this as your top-level checklist. We cover each step in more detail, along with tips and tricks, in the following chapters.

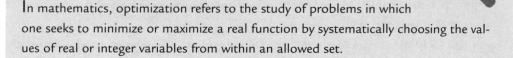

XX X–X* XX < D

In mathematics, optimization refers to the study of problems in which one seeks to minimize or maximize a real function by systematically choosing the values of real or integer variables from within an allowed set.

Step 1: Target Market Business Analysis

■ *Website Analysis.* Analysis of meta sets/keywords, visible text, and code to determine how well you are positioned for search engines. For example: how much code do you have on a page compared to text?

■ *Competitive Analysis.* Examination of content keywords and present engine rankings of competitive websites to determine an effective engine positioning strategy. Pick the top five results in the Google listing results to begin this process. Expand as necessary. Use tools such as Semrush.com and Keywordspy.com.

■ *Initial Keyword Nomination.* Development of a prioritized list of targeted search terms related to your customer base and market segment. Begin with this: What would you type into a search engine to find your business website or page? Then, ask your customers!

Step 2: Keyword Research and Development

■ *Keyword Analysis.* From nomination, further identify a targeted list of keywords and phrases. Review competitive lists and other pertinent industry sources. Use your preliminary list to determine an indicative number of recent search engine queries and how many websites are competing for each keyword. Prioritize keywords and phrases, plurals, singulars, and misspellings. (Misspelled words may be overlooked by many in their keyword strategy, but if search users commonly misspell a keyword, you should identify and use it). Please note that Google will try to correct the term when searching, so use this with care. You can also organize keywords into logical thematic groups for SEO content and advertising campaigns. We'll discuss keywords in depth in Chapter 5.

■ *Baseline Ranking Assessment.* You need to understand where you are now in order to accurately assess your future rankings. You can keep a simple Excel sheet to start the process. Check weekly to begin. (As you get more comfortable, check every 30 to 45 days. You should see improvements in website traffic, a key indicator of progress for your keywords.

Some optimizers will say that rankings are dead. Yes, traffic and conversions are more important, but we use rankings as an indicator. And, if you are a search professional with clients, we see that monthly reports with ranking numbers and search terms are still much wanted by the executives. (Some still even request PageRank as a metric.)

■ *Goals and Objectives.* Clearly define your objectives in advance so you can truly measure your ROI from any programs that you implement. Start simple, but don't skip this step. Example: you may decide to increase website traffic from current baseline of 100 visitors a day to 200 visitors over the next 30 days. Or, you may want to improve your current conversion rate of one percent to two in a specified period. You may begin with top-level, aggregate numbers, but you must drill down into specific pages that can improve products, services, and business sales.

Step 3: Content Optimization and Submission

- *Create Page Titles.* Keyword-based titles help establish page theme and direction for your keywords.
- *Create Meta Tags.* Meta description tags can influence click-throughs, but are not directly used for rankings. (Update: Google does not use the keywords tag anymore, and I have recommended its non-use for competitive [spy] reasons as well). Note: Don't worry about the keywords tags anymore.
- *Place Strategic Search Phrases on Pages.* Integrate selected keywords into your website source code and existing content on designated pages. Make sure to apply a suggested guideline of one to three keywords/phrases per content page and add more pages to complete the list. Ensure that related words are used as a natural inclusion of your keywords. It helps the search engines quickly determine what the page is about. A natural approach to this works best. In the past, 100-300 words on a page was recommended. Each case is different, but many tests show that pages with 800-2,000 words can outperform shorter ones. In the end, the users, the marketplace, content, and links will determine the popularity and ranking numbers.
- *Develop New Sitemaps for Google and Bing.* Make it easier for search engines to index your website. Create both XML and HTML versions. I disagree with some SEOs who say that you don't need XML versions—you do. An HTML version is the first step. XML sitemaps can easily be submitted via Google and Bing webmaster tools.
- *Submit Website to Directories (limited use).* Professional search marketers don't submit the URL to the major search engines, but it's possible to do so. A better and faster way is to get links back to your site naturally. Links get your site indexed by the search engines. However, you should submit your URL to directories such as Yahoo! (paid), Business.com (paid) and DMOZ (free). Tip: Some may choose to include AdSense (google.com/adsense) scripts on a new site to get their Google Media bot to visit. It will likely get your pages indexed quickly. If you review your site logs, you'll see a reference to the "Mediapartners" User Agent, and you'll know it has visited you.

Step 4: Continuous Testing and Measuring

■ *Test and Measure.* Analyze search engine rankings and web traffic to determine the effectiveness of the programs you've implemented, including assessment of individual keyword performance. Test the results of changes, and keep changes tracked in an Excel spreadsheet, or whatever you are comfortable with.

■ *Maintenance.* Ongoing addition and modification of keywords and website content are necessary to continually improve search engine rankings so growth doesn't stall or decline from neglect. You also want to review your link strategy and ensure that your inbound and outbound links are relevant to your business. A blog (WordPress is recommended) can provide you the necessary structure and ease of content addition that you need. Your hosting company can typically help you with the setup/installation of a blog.

 Bob thought that he understood the basics of search optimization and was confident he just needed to learn the tips and tricks of the trade. After a visit to a search discussion forum, Bob realized that he had an intensive learning curve. He thought optimization was being overhyped. After all, he had been putting keywords in meta tags and titles for years. He knew very little about keywords and keyword phrases, links, directories, or even how each of the search engines ranked pages. Determined to turn things around, Bob began his journey in earnest to get educated and renew his credibility with his customers, prospects, and search engines.

OVERVIEW OF SEARCH ENGINE OPTIMIZATION STRATEGIES

The reasons for search optimization and search marketing are simple: to drive traffic to your website and to help you develop tactics to convert this new influx of leads to potentially new business. There are a number of strategies that you can employ to improve your rankings and generate traffic. The search strategies fall into several broad categories: paid search, organic search, paid inclusion, direct marketing, social media (i.e., Twitter, Facebook, LinkedIn, YouTube), and link building.

Organic search strategies refer to natural results without the use of fee-based programs. This strategy relies on organic search traffic. For example, say that you own the one and only feed store in Petaluma, California. Your URL is petalumafeed store. com, and your homepage has content that uses the keywords "Petaluma" and "feed store." Users who type "feed, petaluma" get results that have your site listed at the top. This is an organic result. Needless to say, this isn't the optimal or final search strategy. Search engine algorithms (and your competition!) change frequently, so your ranking results are uncertain. As such, organic search strategy could also be called the "hope and pray" strategy. Therefore, you must be committed to ongoing and long-term success.

DIRECTORY LISTINGS

Directory inclusion can be a good strategy for getting links and in some cases more traffic. Some directories require a submission fee while others are free. Submitting to hundreds of directories is a waste of time and money. Don't do it. Think relevancy, and don't spam.

Paid inclusion means that you pay a fee to be included in search results. Paid inclusion includes annual fee directories (such as Yahoo!) and cost-per-click directories. LookSmart is a major player in the cost-per-click directory market. You can work with it directly or through agencies. LookSmart is important because its directory is syndicated to Bing.

Yahoo! Search Directory (ecom. yahoo.com/dir/submit/intro) is one of the most important directories for submission. Yahoo! charges $299 annually (nonadult content) but is worth the price if your budget can accommodate it. You submit your site along with billing information, and the site is reviewed within seven days by human editors. Your submission should be concise and free of marketing "fluff." The human editors delete any marketing spin and may make other edits. It's wise to wait until your site is completely ready for marketing before submission so that it won't be rejected. The $299 fee is nonrefundable, so rejection can be costly. It's important to note that although you're paying to be included in the directory, you aren't paying for top positioning. In addition to the directory listing, you can pay for higher positioning with Yahoo!'s paid search program, Sponsored Search. You can find the login at marketingsolutions.yahoo.com/ and sign up at advertising.yahoo .com/ smallbusiness/ysm (see Figure 2–5 on page 36).

The Open Directory Project (dmoz.org) is an important directory that also is free. This directory feeds a number of other search directories and is human edited, so inclusion is important.

Directory submissions are reviewed by volunteer editors. The submission process isn't very fast, and if you're rejected, your resubmission may put you back in the regular waiting queue. In fact, as of this writing, I'm waiting for one of my sites to be included— it's already been more than a year.

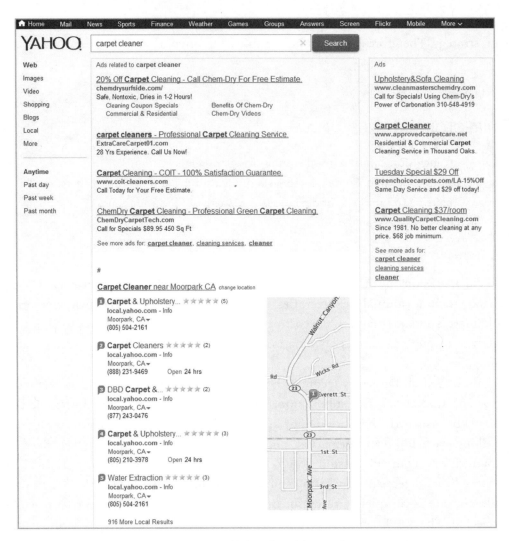

FIGURE 2–5. Yahoo! paid search.

There are countless other directories available, paid and free. Many of the free directories also offer a fee option (with faster review times). There are industry-specific directories and general directories. If we tried to list them all, it would fill ten phone books! However, here are a few paid directories (some have free options) worth considering. I have placed a star next to top priorities in a first phase effort:

- Business.com (business.com, $299 per year)*
- Yahoo! Directory (dir.yahoo.com, $299 per year)*
- Best of the Web (botw.org, $69.95 annually or $199.95 one-time fee)* and consider also local

- UncovertheNet (uncoverthenet.com, $59 to $199 annually)
- Directory @ v7n (directory.v7n.com, $49.95 one-time fee)*
- JoeAnt (joeant.com, $39.99 one-time fee)*
- ExactSeek (exactseek.com, free or $14 for top listing)
- WoW Directory (wowdirectory.com, $43 for an express review, $65 sponsored)
- Gimpsy (gimpsy.com, free to $49 one-time fee)*
- InCrawler (incrawler.com, $49.95 one-time fee)
- Jayde (jayde.com, free)

There are also programs that allow you to bulk submit to directories. One such program is SubmitWolf 7.0 from Trellian.com. SubmitWolf costs $199 per year. You may want to use this initially to launch your new or redesigned site, but likely won't need it in subsequent years. Note: Research these tools before you buy or use them. You should be concerned about quality of submissions, not quantity.

There are still directories to which you would manually submit (like Yahoo! and Open Directory), but it can certainly help you with other listings. Just make sure to manage it naturally, and don't spam.

Link building is another important part of your search strategy, but can be a bit tricky. Link building is the process of creating inbound and outbound links. Outbound links are typically easier to control, especially if you are the webmaster. Inbound links (backlinks, incoming links, external citations) can be your biggest channel overall in SEO. To do it well, be sure to work with other relevant sites. Today link relevancy (think "themes" or "topics" matching) is more important than ever. For example, a resume writer might link out to job search sites and would receive inbound links from those same sites. Sometimes just asking for links works. Don't be afraid of doing so. (Question: Who can you ask—right now—in your network? Customers? Partners?)

The tricky part is determining the quantity and quality of the links. For example: if you get one link from an authority site like CNN or BBC (UK), its value would be more important than hundreds of non-relevant links from other, lesser valued sites. Since these sites are considered an authority, it may not matter as much if it isn't relevant, but even better if it is! If you use unethical practices to trick the search engines, your site can be downgraded or worse, banned. Note: we talk about sites of authority, but it is actually the page in question. You should know a little about PageRank already.

However, legitimate and relevant inbound and outbound links are a valuable way to generate traffic. We'll discuss this in depth in Chapter 8 on link building.

When most people think of search marketing, they think of the paid search strategies. Specifically, they may think of Google AdWords or pay-per-click

LINK POLICE

As of this writing a number of popular sites had their PageRank downgraded by Google for link farming (selling links on their sites). Google updates its link graph and quality indicators at intervals it controls. You don't. Recognize that Google is updating often, and with filters like Google Panda, and ongoing Google Penguin, only bad optimizing practices will be penalized.

campaigns across different engines, like Yahoo! and Bing (Bingads.com now handles Bing and Yahoo platforms in one dashboard). Paid online advertising is similar to paid offline advertising. In traditional media you pay to have your ad listed. You have a choice of size, location, and advertising channel. In popular publications, a full-page ad may cost hundreds of dollars, while a smaller publication may charge far less.

In traditional media, you must identify your target audience, develop creative content that captures their attention, and place it where they will see it. Paid online advertising has all the same basic elements. Your two primary media channels for online advertising are websites and search engines. One of the many benefits of working online is the immediacy of results and the ability to make changes quickly. Online you see results in hours whereas in traditional media it may take months to see results. With online campaigns you can test your messages more frequently, allowing you to fine-tune messaging to maximize results.

INSIDER TIP

eMarketer released a study in 2013 showing that brand marketers are putting more emphasis on social, mobile, and video. And, in a similar study, found that landing page optimization and SEO are top tactics and emphasis for agencies and client-side marketers.

Paid Advertising

Traditional paid ads are based on cost-per-thousand impressions (CPM—M is the Roman numeral for thousand). The ad industry group FAST defines an impression as "the count of a delivered basic advertising unit from an ad distribution point." What that means in plain English is that an impression is eyeballs on the advertisement. CPM is used in online and offline media and is helpful to understand in comparing various media buy options.

The following terms are helpful to understand in a discussion of paid advertising:

- *Ad Click.* As defined by the Interactive Advertising Bureau, it's "a measurement of the user-initiated action of responding to (such as clicking on) an ad element causing a re-direct to another web location or another frame or page within the advertisement." The three types of ad clicks are click-throughs (clicking the ad takes user to a different site or frame), unit clicks (user stays in the same site, sometimes called click-downs, click-withins, or click-ups), and mouse-overs (user holds mouse over ad but doesn't click).

- *Click-Through Rate or Ratio (CTR).* CTR is the number of clicks an ad receives divided by the number of times the ad, ad unit, or page is viewed. The higher the CTR, the better the performance of the advertisement. Example: If an ad unit was shown 100 times, and 1 person clicked it, you'd have a 1 percent CTR. We'll get into bidding strategies and return on ad spend in the pay-per-click section in Chapter 10.

- *Click Fraud.* Fraudulent or invalid clicks generated manually or using automatic tools. Fraudulent clicks generate an improper per-click charge that increases a site owner's profits. Google has cracked down heavily on this over the years, and will refund, credit you back, on any proven click fraud schemes.

- *Conversion.* A conversion is when a user takes a specific defined action. For example, if you ran an ad to have people sign up for a webinar, those who signed up converted. Your conversion rate measures the unique number of actions from unique exposures.

- *Pay-per-Click Advertising (PPC).* This is an online advertising model in which you pay only for the clicks on your ad rather than a set fee for the ad itself. With PPC you develop an ad that links back to a specific page on your site. This page is called a landing page. Many site owners create specific landing pages for different ads. This is a smart strategy because people who click the ad are taken right to the content they need. Google has introduced a very important ingredient to success in PPC, called the Quality Score. You can read more about it on adwords.google.com/support/aw/bin/answer.py?hl=en&answer=10215. Now you can start to see how important overall quality across the user experience is, both for users and search engines.

The major players in the PPC market are Google, Yahoo!, and Bing. The per-ad click-through rate is impacted by competitive bids for keywords and the proprietary quality measures of ad and landing page content used by search engines.

> **INSIDER TIP**
>
> At the 2007 Search Marketing Expo, panelists indicated that pay-per-call may convert ten times higher than PPC and can have conversion rates of up to 45 percent (Janssen, Hallie, "Pay Per Call Ads: Living Up to the Promise? Report from SMXLoMo," SearchMarketingStandard.com, October 3, 2007).

- *Pay-Per-Action Advertising (PPA)*. It is a new advertising and pricing model. In this model you pay when users complete a specific action on your site. For example you may run an ad and predefine signing up for a newsletter as the specific action. If 2,000 visitors click the ad but only 500 sign up for the newsletter, you pay for the 500 users who completed the action.
- *Pay-Per-Call Advertising*. It works like the PPC model except, rather than clicking on the ad, the visitors call a unique number for the advertiser. The call redirects to the actual business. Pay-per-call targets local, service-based businesses or companies that may only have brochure websites or aren't online at all. Some of the firms offering pay-per-call advertising include:

  · ZiffLeads—ZiffLeads is the one-stop shop for pay-per-call performance-based advertising
  · Paypercall.yp.com—from Yellow Pages
  · Paypercallinc.com—a popular pay-per-call service

Pay-per-call users have already made the decision to speak with someone rather than continue to surf for information. Hence it makes sense that an interactive phone call would have a fairly high conversion rate. Pay-per-call is still a fairly new model but worth considering as part of a search campaign. Finally, using walk-on people, the personalities you sometimes see entering a web page to present a product or service, should be tested as well. You can try right now to see what it would look like on your website at websitetalkingheads.com. It's like having a virtual salesperson on your page.

This is a broad overview of the search landscape and strategies to be considered. I provide in-depth information in later sections as we delve into the mechanics of driving traffic to your website.

Don't Make Bob's Big Mistake

 Bob had learned from others in the coaching community that he should do a Google AdWords campaign to promote his site. He created an account by going to adwords.google.com and created a campaign with one keyword phrase as a test: "entrepreneur coaching." He chose the keyword phrase because it was close to what he was doing and at the time it was pretty affordable. Bob did not have a separate landing page for the campaign; the ad simply clicked through to his homepage, which said nothing about entrepreneur coaching. Further, the homepage did not offer any action for visitors to take. He added a few more keywords he thought might work and ended up blowing hundreds of dollars in his first few weeks, and without a single sale. He clearly didn't perform the proper keyword research and analysis. We'll learn later in the book how to avoid making the same mistake!

Chapter 3

Starting a Business with a New Website

Rob and Joe had been friends since third grade. Now both in their 30s, they felt the time was right to start their organic dog food business. They conceived of the idea years ago, but the internet made it easy to start and sustain a business while continuing to work at their full-time jobs. They knew that people were searching for it online, because their competition was already there.

Rob was the artistic visionary and Joe was the analytical numbers guy, so they perfectly complemented one another. Rob and Joe wrote and rewrote business and marketing plans, worked through financing, and came up with a solid five-year plan.

Since they had opted to self-finance their venture, they wanted to keep the startup costs at a minimum so that they could heavily invest in marketing and supplies once the business launched. Looking at the to-dos, they decided that building the website was something they could tackle.

Rob had web design software, and Joe opted to learn the basic technical details to help out with programming. They had to pull information from about 25 sources, but together they came up with a plan. Rob purchased a template, and Joe made a few modifications.

It took them six weeks of effort, but finally the site was launched. Looking back on the experience, they don't regret being do-it-yourselfers, but they did miss a few key steps. While they were able to write and develop the site, they didn't know about how to optimize the site layout and content for usability (users), search engines, how to use keywords to maximize their marketing, or even the right elements to include in the site. The missteps cost them time, money, and opportunity.

In this next section we begin digging into the mechanics of optimizing your website, starting with building it. We revisit the topics in the first section in greater depth and provide practical how-to information that you can begin using. In this section you will learn:

- How to create a website with SEO-enriched content
- The best strategies to use for finding the right keywords for search engine submission
- How to determine what market you need to advertise to
- Natural link-building methods
- White hat vs. black hat SEO
- Marketing methods to turn search engine clicks into sales
- And much more!

We also check in on Bob as he progresses through his search marketing journey.

So, what are you waiting for? Go on and get reading, so you can hurry up and get your site listed as high as it can go.

WHAT ARE THE DIFFERENT WEBSITE TYPES?

There are different types of websites based mainly on the purpose of their existence. This is an incomplete list because human imagination is continually spawning new uses for the internet.

- Affiliate sites
- Archive sites
- Auction sites
- Blogs
- Business or brochure websites
- Community websites
- Contest websites
- Corporate sites
- Data collection websites
- Dating websites
- Directory or search sites
- Ecommerce websites

- Entertainment sites
- Game websites
- Government sites
- Java applet sites
- Hosting sites
- Magazine or e-zine sites
- News sites
- Personal sites or homepages
- Political sites
- Polling or survey sites
- Portal sites
- Rating sites
- Review sites
- Traffic websites for advertising
- Website products and support websites

HOW TO CHOOSE A DOMAIN NAME

Choosing a domain name is an extremely important part of designing your website, because that becomes the name (and brand) of your website. Your domain name is the first part of the uniform resource locator, or "URL." There are many things to keep in mind while choosing a suitable domain name.

If you haven't already done so, give some thought as to what your domain name is going to be. For those who are new to the internet, the domain name, also known as a website address, is a word or phrase that a website visitor has to type in to visit your site. It's preceded by http://www, although for modern-day browsers typing this portion is optional. If you have a long domain name, you might consider dropping the www prefix in all your marketing materials and references. The domain name ends with .com, .net, .biz, or a host of other extensions that you'll be exposed to when you're ready to sign up for one.

A DOMAIN BY ANY OTHER NAME

The Domain Name System was introduced in 1984. The U.S. Department of Defense oversaw the system until 1993. Some of the earliest domain names in the system were symbolics.com, mit.edu, think.com, css.gov, and mitre.org.

Domain Search namecheap

DOMAIN NAME	STATUS
✕ peanutbutter.com	TAKEN
MORE CHOICES ▾	
✕ peanutbutter.me	TAKEN
✕ peanutbutter.net	TAKEN
✕ peanutbutter.org	TAKEN
✕ peanutbutter.us	TAKEN
✕ peanutbutter.mobi	TAKEN
– peanutbutter.cm	ERROR
✕ peanutbutter.biz	TAKEN
✕ peanutbutter.info	TAKEN
✕ peanutbutter.tv	TAKEN
✕ peanutbutter.co.uk	TAKEN
☐ peanutbutter.org.uk	AVAILABLE
☐ peanutbutter.me.uk	AVAILABLE

FIGURE 3–1. Namecheap domain results.

I know from personal experience that Google likes .com, .org, and .net domains a lot, even though it states it doesn't matter. This is likely because .info and .biz can often be seen as spam sites or thin affiliates sites.

Stuffing your domain name with keywords isn't going to help much, if at all, unless those keywords naturally make sense. For example, don't pick "peanutbutterandjelly.com" if you're planning to launch a site for fishing supplies. PsychicWhois.com (Figure 3–2) and wordoid.com can both be fun to get ideas from.

Also, avoid abbreviations. Using your whole site name will make your domain name easier to remember. Try to get a ".com" name, as those are the most popular and easiest for most users to remember. However, if this is impossible, don't use .com anywhere in the name if your site is under ".net." Doing so is tacky, and will only cause confusion to potential visitors. Remember to display your site name—prominently. Multiple domains can be a good idea but only when built as a complete strategy. Each domain also requires different content to avoid being penalized by search engines for duplicate content. Note: if you are worried about competition, you can purchase several domains, but you may choose to focus on the .com (main) domain only.

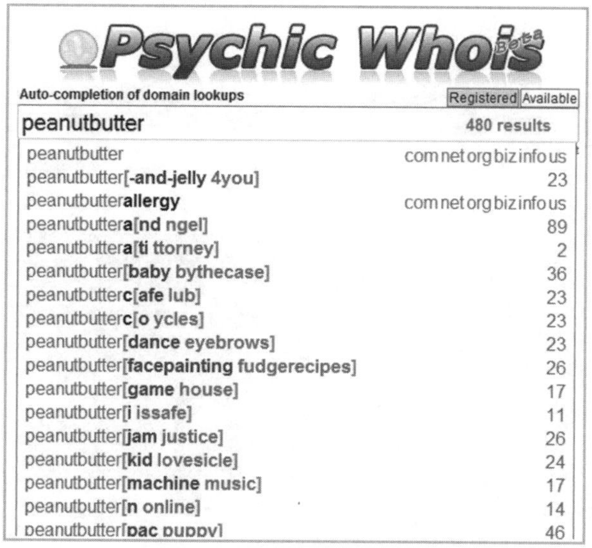

FIGURE 3–2. Psychic Whois domain lookups.

INSIDER TIP

Buying and building several domains within niches in your marketplace is a smart strategy. Try Name-cheap.com or GoDaddy.com to search for domains. GoDaddy has an entire section dedicated to domain auctions. Buying an existing domain can be a smart SEO strategy.

To buy a domain name, you can do so directly from your web hosting provider (which we focus on in the next section) or through a separate domain name service (a recommended option for those who are using their own servers). If you're using a separate domain name service for your server, make sure you choose one such as no-IP. com, which assigns you a static IP address, the numerical address that identifies your computer. If this address is ever-changing (as it is with some internet service providers), you won't be able to successfully assign a domain name to your server. I personally use Register.com, Namecheap.com, or GoDaddy.com. I like the independence that Register. com or similar services provide. Another good strategy is to choose and register your domain in advance of building your site. You then have the comfort of knowing that the name belongs to you. When you register a domain without having a site, typing the name into the browser will bring up a page indicating that it's parked. This means the name is owned by someone but a website has not yet been launched.

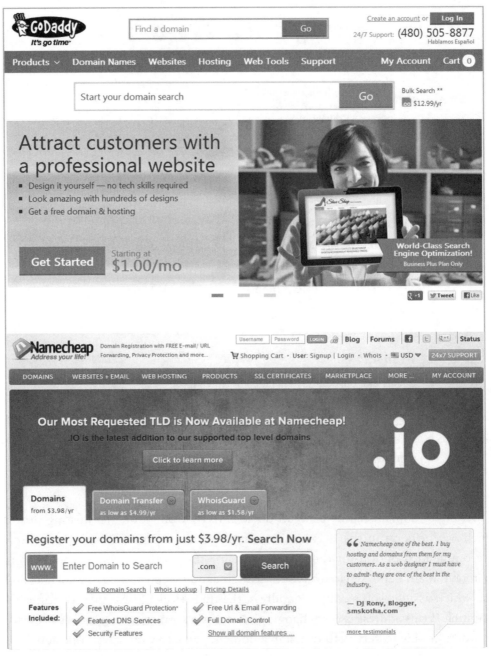

FIGURE 3–3. Screenshots of GoDaddy.com and Namecheap.com.

The process for signing up for a domain name works the same way whether it's through a hosting provider or through a separate domain name service. You'll be asked to enter into a text box the domain name you want to register. The service shows you the extensions you can choose. Generally, you always want to go with .com because this is the most popular domain name extension. In terms of what domain name to use, this is where keyword optimization comes into play. That's right—even your domain name should be keyword optimized. Don't fall into the temptation that many webmasters do and use something catchy and creative for your website. It might be more memorable to potential visitors, especially if you use a lot of offline marketing, but it won't get your site ranked high in search engines. Ultimately, you will want to use keywords to create a domain name that is both memorable and likely to be ranked in the first ten listings of search engine results.

> ## ONLINE RESOURCE
>
> Go to GoDaddy.com/domains/searchbulk.aspx and enter keywords that you are thinking about, and GoDaddy will format them and check the various extensions and names. It will automatically check to see if they are registered and remove ones already taken, leaving you with a list of keyword rich domains that are available for you!

However, keywords in the domain are useful for reasons outside of just ranking by its words. How people link to you and what the description reads in the incoming "backlink," or anchor text, plays a key role. So if you have realestate-mortgage-loans.com, it's better than simply remloans.com. The latter is shorter, but the former yields a better link reputation strategy. Note: Google has taken steps to tighten how exact match domains (EMD) are ranked. In the past, EMDs would almost always rank, depending on the level of competitiveness in the market.

If your desired domain name is taken, the domain name service recommends other selections you could use. This can be helpful, since sometimes it can come up with suggestions that might rank better than your original choice. Or, they could be terrible, especially in terms of their length. Generally, the best domain names are short, contain no hyphens, and offer an excellent one-, two-, or three-word summary of what the site

> ## ONLINE RESOURCE
>
> Nameboy.com helps by offering more combinations of words to review, and providers such as GoDaddy.com and Namecheap.com have advanced search options.

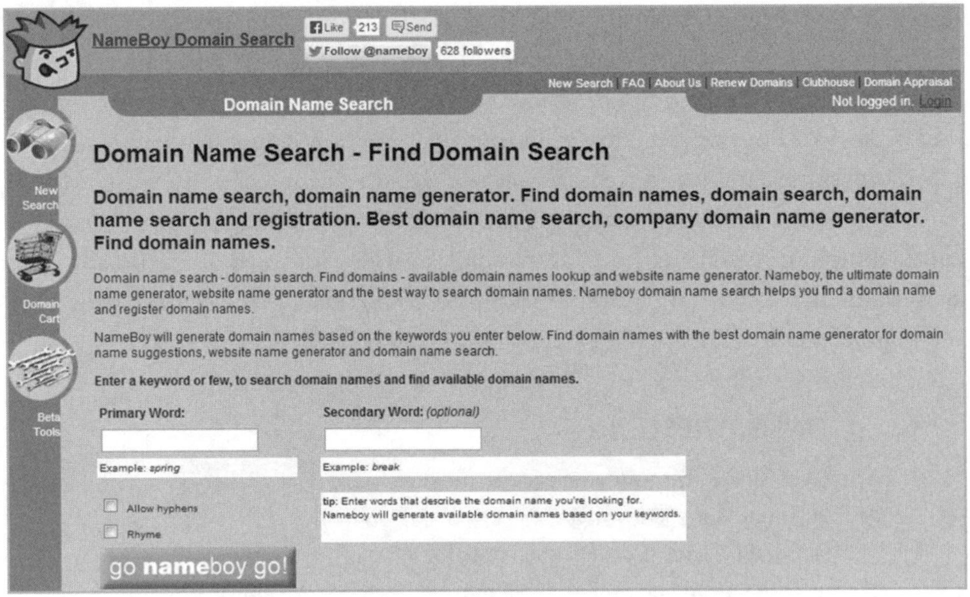

FIGURE 3–4. Nameboy—domain search tool.

is about. An example of an excellent domain name could be cheapknives.com. It's short, contains no hyphens, and, if it's pointing to a website selling affordable knives, perfectly summarizes the main point of the site. One hyphen in a domain is OK, but more than two starts to look a little "shady" (i.e., not search and user friendly).

Another alternative when it comes to domain names is buying one that's already established or expiring. This is a popular tactic used by internet marketers to generate traffic for their websites. You can find these types of domain names anywhere, from eBay to specialized services selling them (they can be found through a general Google search). You could use SnapNames.com to bid on a name that's already taken. On this site you enter your contact and billing information, the domain name of interest, and your bid price. When the name becomes available SnapNames.com will purchase it for you. This eliminates watching and waiting for the name. This is also helpful after you launch your business if you want to snap up similar domain names.

This is a good list of where you can buy/research domains:

- NameJet.com
- Namecheap.com
- SnapNames.com
- Afternic.com
- Pool.com

- Sedo.com
- Flippa.com (look at the previously sold area)
- DomainTools.com (whois.sc)

There are auctions specifically for expired domain names. I've purchased domains both on eBay and Flippa.com. Go there and start searching. You can buy existing domains, sometimes with existing content, and gain the history, traffic, links, and PageRank.

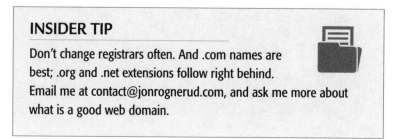

INSIDER TIP

Don't change registrars often. And .com names are best; .org and .net extensions follow right behind. Email me at contact@jonrognerud.com, and ask me more about what is a good web domain.

If you get an admin email account and read the directions on Flippa.com, you can transfer a domain over without losing PageRank and traffic.

Most folks who sell a website/domain will show you traffic charts and money charts. Make sure that it's not inflated and that you can look at it over time. One month is simply not good enough. Make sure you also ask about how traffic has been coming to the site, and ask to see server logs. The way-back machine at web.archive.org will reveal more about the site. Go take a look at what Google looked like in 1998.

Once you've selected your domain name, you need to register it. Be careful whom you select to handle your domain registrations, as losing your domain name could put you out of business. You may want to choose a hosting company before registering your domain name. Many hosting companies will register the name for you when you set up your hosting account.

A little over a decade ago, Network Solutions dominated the domain registration field, charging $100 annually for service. Today, hundreds of registrars exist, which can cause difficulty in choosing one. Use a tool such as RegSelect.com, which can help you compare prices and options of domain registration and hosting companies. All registrars require the name of the company or individual who owns the domain (the registrant), the individual authorized to handle daily matters (the administrative contact), and the person who handles all things technical (the technical contact).

Most registrars have rules against using false names, and you'll run the risk of not receiving important notices if you do so. Whoever possesses the registrar username

```
Registrant:
      Domain Administrator                    ◉ DOMAINTOOLS
      Yahoo! Inc.
      701 First Avenue
       Sunnyvale CA 94089
      US
        domainadmin@yahoo-inc.com  +1.4083493300 Fax: +1.4083493301

   Domain Name: yahoo.com

      Registrar Name: Markmonitor.com
      Registrar Whois: whois.markmonitor.com
      Registrar Homepage: http://www.markmonitor.com

   Administrative Contact:
      Domain Administrator
      Yahoo! Inc.
      701 First Avenue
       Sunnyvale CA 94089
      US
        domainadmin@yahoo-inc.com  +1.4083493300 Fax: +1.4083493301

   Technical Contact, Zone Contact:
      Domain Administrator
      Yahoo! Inc.
      701 First Avenue
       Sunnyvale CA 94089
      US
        domainadmin@yahoo-inc.com  +1.4083493300 Fax: +1.4083493301

   Created on.............: 1995-01-18.
   Expires on.............: 2023-01-18.
   Record last updated on..: 2013-09-06.

   Domain servers in listed order:

   ns3.yahoo.com
   ns2.yahoo.com
   ns5.yahoo.com
   ns1.yahoo.com
   ns4.yahoo.com
```

FIGURE 3–5. Domain owner—Yahoo.com (whois.domaintools.com/yahoo.com).

and password is essentially in control of the domain, despite the fact that the legal owner is the registrant, so be careful. Choose a complex password, as this could protect you from being hacked. Hackers could have the opportunity to change ownership or servers associated with your account. Try to find a registrar that allows you to "lock" your accounts. Finally, avoid registering your domain name with your web hosting service. This could complicate a domain transfer, should you decide to change hosting companies later.

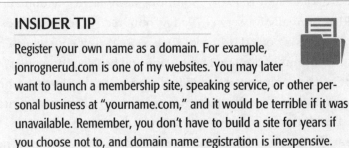

INSIDER TIP

Register your own name as a domain. For example, jonrognerud.com is one of my websites. You may later want to launch a membership site, speaking service, or other personal business at "yourname.com," and it would be terrible if it was unavailable. Remember, you don't have to build a site for years if you choose not to, and domain name registration is inexpensive.

WHO SPEAKS HTML?

Only computers speak HTML (hypertext markup language), which is a kind of text document that web browsers use to show text and graphics, and is the dominant markup language for web pages. HTML text includes tags to create specific formats for the web page represented. You can use Dreamweaver (Adobe) or free downloads like CoffeeCup (coffeecup.com/free-editor/) or kompozer.net/download.php. These are web page editors that are made to automatically generate the code. Whichever method you use, test your site on different platforms and browsers before you launch it. Try BrowserShots.org to see what your web page will look like in 50-plus environments, if you so choose. Avoid tags, plug-ins, and other features that are only available on one type of browser. Remember, you'll want as many people as possible to be able to access your site. Excluding certain users because of exclusive content only available to certain browsers won't help you; it will hurt you.

A recommended and fantastic solution for getting your website up fast is WordPress, a blog publishing system written in PHP and backed by a MySQL database. The system has full World Wide Web Consortium (W3C) standards compliance, which is important for interoperability with other systems and forward compatibility. This open source community platform bills itself as "A semantic personal publishing platform with a focus on aesthetics, web standards, and usability."

ONLINE RESOURCE

Facebook, with over a billion users worldwide, has introduced many tools, one of which is an application to write in FBML, Facebook's own markup language. In June 2012, FBML was transitioned to the use of iFrames.

WordPress has other advantages as well, such as the ability to easily manage nonblog content. Any changes you make to your templates or code entries are immediately reflected on your site. Finally, WordPress comes with a full theme system (wordpress. org/extend/themes/), which simplifies the design process (see Figure 3–6 on page 54). There are thousands of themes and millions of downloads completed. Thus, if you want a different theme every day, you could do it. WordPress is also very search-engine-friendly "out of the box," and I recommend setting up a WordPress blog. There are many resources for WordPress, and I've listed them in the resources section at the end of this book.

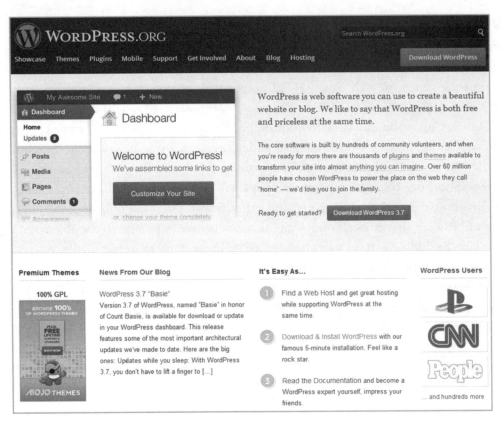

FIGURE 3–6. WordPress.org homepage.

QUICKIE WIKI

A wiki (from the Hawaiian word for *quick*) site is a website whose content is almost completely created by users. Contributions can be organized easily, in addition to the actual content you provide. Wikis can easily be tampered with, however, unless the community of users catch false or malicious content and correct it. Vandalism can be a major problem, and intentional disruption by users (trolling) can go unnoticed for quite a while. In this vein, wikis are generally designed to be easy to create and correct.

PBWorks.com—Online Team Collaboration: shared workspaces for working with colleagues, clients, and partners (formally PBWiki) is a good place to start.

Limiting HTML and cascading style sheets (CSS) can promote consistency, while disabling JavaScript prevents users from implementing code. Most wikis keep records of changes made to pages, and often store all versions of that page. That way, authors can revert to an older version of a page, if necessary.

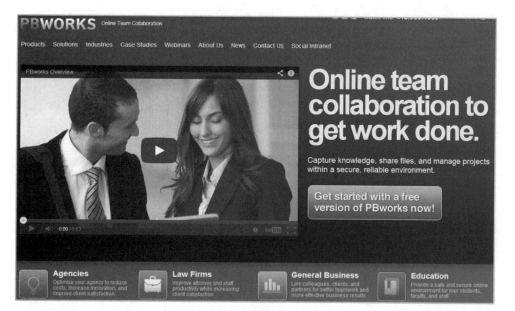

FIGURE 3–7. PBWorks—Wiki.

You have many options when considering your web host and technology. Keep your website in mind when researching, and find out which services you need. Use only what will work best for you, your company, and your website.

THE INS AND OUTS OF WEBSITE CREATION SOFTWARE

To start your journey into website optimization, you must first create a website. This step is as intimidating as it is obvious. Do not think that impressive graphics and animation equate to a well-designed site. While an elegant graphical layout and Flash animations are visually appealing, they won't win over the heart of the website visitor. Rich, useful, and helpful quality content is what does it. As long as you create engaging

---

ONLINE RESOURCE

To get color scheme ideas, visit COLOURlovers.com. This site displays color trends and palettes that can be helpful in choosing the right color mix. The site also has a blog and discussion forum. You will find a quick web usability tip sheet on netmechanic.com/news/vol7/design_no4.htm.

FIGURE 3–8. Example of really bad website layout and design—LingsCars.com.

content, it won't matter as much how your site looks. Of course, this doesn't mean you have a license to produce something tacky. A site that shows no professionalism will drive away traffic, even if the content is good. This is usually the case with layouts with color schemes so awful visitors can't read the content. Ultimately, you want a balance of well-written content and decent layout design. If you are working with an outside design company, make sure they explain their process to handle both designs, content, and optimization for search engines, not just users.

Fortunately, with word processing programs, HTML editors, and web hosting templates, people with any level of web design background can create professional-looking websites. Even if you hire someone to design your site, templates can significantly cut the development cost and save time. The upcoming sections will explain in detail how to use each of these programs, along with determining which one is best for your situation. You can also use outsourced services with sites like elance.com, freelancer. com, and odesk.com.

Word Processing Programs—A Last Resort

If you're low on money, look no further than the word processing program that came with your computer to solve your website creation dilemma. Most current word processors, including Microsoft Word, WordPerfect, and Open Office (a free word processor that can be downloaded from the internet), can create websites because of their "Save As HTML" or "Save As Web Page" option. HTML is the programming format needed to create a web page, so this feature is invaluable to webmasters.

However, one caution in creating pages with these programs: they contain hidden or "junk" HTML code. The hidden code often causes the page to transfer differently from its word processing format. It also adds a lot of other Office code and XML that can be extra overhead to the page. If you've ever copied and pasted from Word to a blog or an online article directory, you're familiar with these quirks. Your perfectly formatted page suddenly has strange breaks in the middle of paragraphs. You may even have to retype the whole thing from scratch because you couldn't fix it. You could teach yourself to do everything in a text editor such as Notepad or WordPad, and copy and paste from that rather than the word processing program.

That said, if it's all you have to use, then by all means use it for a simple website, and check it in various browsers to make sure that what you see is truly what others will see. It may not always provide the cleanest code, but the upside is it makes a site super easy to build!

Ultimately, as long as you remember to save your work in HTML format, you can go about making a web page in the same way you would any other type of document. The what-you-see-is-what-you-get (WYSIWYG) principle most of today's word processing programs observe also applies for web pages, at least to a point. This is because browsers display content differently from other browsers. What looks good in Internet Explorer may look horrible in Firefox. Don't think any knowledge you have of HTML can help fix this problem

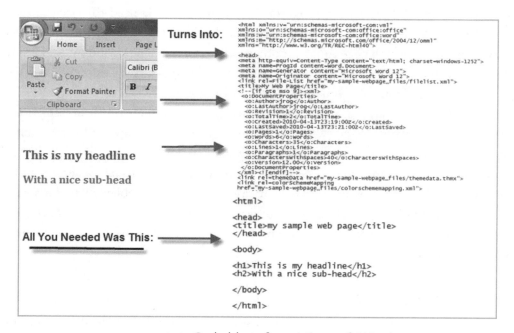

FIGURE 3–9. Code bloat from Microsoft Word.

either, since it is often the result of the junk HTML. You'll have to edit your web page in the word processor, possibly having to take out some of the more advanced features.

For this reason, word processors aren't your answer if you need a more complex website. However, if a site is simple, a word processor should be okay. There are also website templates you can download to use with your word processing program (especially with Microsoft Word). The downside to templates is that some of them are overused, so your site won't be unique, but don't worry about this. Remember, in the overall scheme of things the content matters more.

Wondering what's the best way to go about creating a website in a word processor? First, make sure to use "Web View" if it's available on your word processor. Microsoft Word has an additional "Web Page Preview" that shows you what your web page will look like in Internet Explorer. This is a great resource because it allows you to know as you design your document how it's going to turn out. The navigation is different in Word 2010/13, but the options still apply.

Your next step is to put all your files in the same folder. Your website is essentially a collection of information, and the website looks in that collection for information to load pages. You can't have your homepage in one location and About Us in a different location. Name your first file "index.html" because this is how servers identify your default page (something that will be of importance later when you submit your files to a web hosting service).

When you need to make connections between web pages, you can use the hyperlink feature in your word processing program. For Word, you only need to select "Insert" then "Hyperlink." If you select "Target Frame" within the Hyperlink menu, then select "New Window." The web page you're linking to will display in a new window. Make sure that when you use the hyperlink feature that your web pages already exist. You will get an error message if you try to link to pages you have not yet created.

Another thing to keep in mind when creating websites in a word processor is the use of tables for layout design. With Microsoft Word you can draw a table or insert a table with predefined parameters. But for web page design, you'll want to draw your table. You can create tables within tables for more complex designs. However, the more complex your layout is, the more likely you are to encounter problems when it's time for the website to display in a browser. This is why you'll want to constantly check your work in different browsers as you're doing it so you can make the necessary changes right then and there.

The HTML Editor Is Your Friend

If you're looking to build more complicated sites, consider using an HTML editor. The HTML code that editors produce is cleaner than that of word processors, and you can do a lot more with clean HTML. When using HTML editors, you have three types to choose from: text-based, object-based, and WYSIWYG.

If you're a webmaster and you want to incorporate advanced script programming into your website, then you use text-based or object-based HTML editors. Both of these work through HTML code only, so if your HTML background is not advanced, they won't be a good choice. On the other hand, if your HTML code is up to par, you are at an advantage using these types of software. How much cleaner can code be if you're doing it yourself? If you're familiar with the concept of objects (which in programming refers to segments of code that can serve as an individual unit and can be used with other units throughout the coding process), object-based HTML editors might make things easier for you. You can try Dynamic-HTML-Editor.com.

Most professional editors work with both HTML and CSS. CSS stands for Cascading Style Sheets and is used to style web pages. It's worthwhile to become familiar with both HTML and CSS. You can lay out web pages with style sheets, which saves you coding time and enables you to create faster-loading pages. You'll find many free online tutorials for HTML and CSS. For example, csstutorial.net and w3schools.com/css/default.asp are easy ways to follow the step-by-step guide to CSS.

If you don't have advanced HTML knowledge, you can still use an HTML editor. You would simply have to use the WYSIWYG form of HTML editors. They are similar to word processors, in that you get a clear picture of how your website is going to look

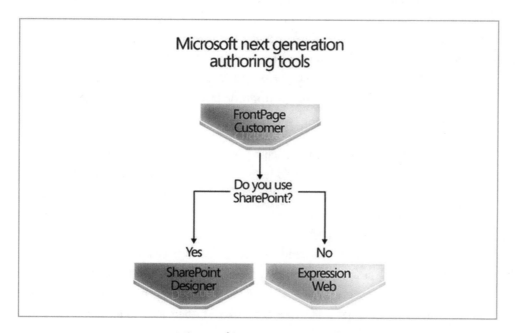

FIGURE 3–10. Microsoft's new HTML and coding tools.

when it's uploaded into a browser. To use them, you type in your text and insert various HTML elements, which can be selected from menus and toolbars. Some examples of popular WYSISYG HTML editors are Dreamweaver, and Microsoft's products. (Note: Frontpage HTML editor is no longer supported.)

How Web Hosting Templates Can Jumpstart Your Website

Many web hosting companies (something that I expand on in upcoming sections) offer templates to help webmasters create their websites. Just as with templates designed for word processing programs, all you have to do is enter the information in the appropriate spots. Granted, the template option isn't an attractive one for advanced webmasters who want more sophisticated features on their website, but for average people who may not have an HTML and web design background, the work is pretty much taken care of.

Generalized templates not associated with a web hosting account can also be used in WYSIWYG HTML editors or (as already mentioned) in word processing programs. On the internet, you'll find hundreds available for download. Some are free; others can be purchased. Sites such as TemplateMonster.com offer a variety of templates, including e-commerce, blogging, and web site. You pay a lower fee to purchase nonexclusive use or a higher fee to retire the template. (It's removed from the gallery and no one else can purchase it.) Both free and paid templates are high-quality when it comes to design, but the free ones tend to be harder to find. Regardless, either can be a suitable option if you don't like the templates available through your web hosting service.

Keep in mind that at some point you will redesign your site. First-generation websites tend to be simpler with fewer pages because you're just starting out. As your business grows or as you become more knowledgeable about the online marketplace, you will probably design a whole new site. So for your first effort, don't worry if it isn't absolutely everything you want—you can upgrade later. In fact, think of website design and development in phases.

 Bob began reviewing sites of online businesses that were doing well. A friend pointed Bob to a site that sold leather goods. The site was black text on a plain white background with no graphics. In fact, it was borderline terrible! The content was also simple and in many places not even grammatically correct. However, it was honest, and it presented the information that buyers wanted. The owner of the business wrote the About Us section and told visitors about himself. Even with its lack of Flash and its grammatical errors, the business was doing over $1 million in sales annually. Bob learned that day the value of knowing your audience. You don't have to have a perfectly designed site, but you do need a perfectly targeted site. Give people what matters most to them and you'll be successful.

Templates are a better option than word processing software. In fact, many web designers routinely use templates to expedite their design time and help lower their costs. They can quickly customize elements without having to create a custom site from scratch.

A good place to start and find general templates is on eBay. I see purchases from people buying over 100 templates for only $9.99. Considering that one template could cost $100 or more, this is an incredible deal. You may not get the flashy graphics and animations you could find with more expensive website templates, but it's still a good buy. If you have some website design experience, you can easily customize a template so that it's not so canned. Remember to also use Google.

ONLINE RESOURCE

You should consider looking at bad web pages to learn what not to do. Go to WebPagesThatSuck.com and be prepared to view the ugly.

Keep in mind, however, the more graphics and animations your site has, the longer it takes to load on your visitors' computers. Google recently announced that speed is another signal in the 200-plus stack of things it includes for ranking. While targeting a small percentage of outliers, you will serve users and search engines well with a fast loading site. Learn more at code.google.com/speed/.

You have to remember that a lot of people may still be connecting through dial-up and/or slower computers (yes, some people still use dial-up!). A fancier site creates a definitive presence, but if your site is slow to load, the site loses its impact, and people will leave quickly. When it comes to website creation, simpler is always better unless you're promoting a service or product where you need a more complex design. If you're promoting and generating business, and clients are happy with your site, you're winning!

ONLINE RESOURCE

WordPress should form the base of your new website development. Look at minimalist themes that can help you get started: sixrevisions.com/wordpress/20-beautiful-minimalist-wordpress-themes/.

HOW TO CREATE THE WEBSITE CONTENT

Once you decide which website creation software you're going to use, it's time to create the content. You have a few options: write it yourself, hire a ghostwriter, transcribing and editing from videos, or buy private-label content. This section explains three options in detail.

Writing the Content Yourself

Obviously, the cheapest option when it comes to content creation is writing it yourself. Don't get scared at the thought of writing, like many people do. The type of writing you do for website is different than the formal writing required for academia. It's a little bit more restrictive than creative writing but only in the sense that you have to write with keyword optimization in mind.

OK . . . if you're a newbie to internet marketing, you might be wondering, "What the heck is *keyword optimization*?" It sounds more complex than it is. Basically, keyword optimization is making sure your content contains enough instances of your keywords, which are words or phrases commonly used in search engines to find what you offer. For example, if you're selling real estate in Florida, your keywords may be "florida real estate," "jacksonville florida real estate," "Orlando Homes For Sale," "Palm Beach Houses For Sale," etc.

You can find keywords by using keyword research tools and analyzers. This is software that tells you each of the combinations used with a particular keyword, along with how many times the original keyword and its combinations have been used. Indeed, keyword analyzers are so important in the SEO process that they by themselves are discussed in detail in the following chapters. If you want information on the specific types of keyword analyzers you should use, go immediately to Chapter 5. This is particularly the case if you want to invest in paid keyword analyzers, which offer significant advantages over free ones. Otherwise, you can just use the popular Google keyword research tool, which is offered for free in the Google AdWords toolset. You can get to this tool by visiting adwords.google.com.

How do you use a keyword analyzer tool? They're all the same: You enter in the desired keyword, and you are given a list of results. Paid keyword analyzers return more specific results, while free ones return more basic information, although Google now provides Power Tools for free, and you may decide to only use those. If you find that your keyword receives a lot of visitors—from 20,000 to 30,000 visitors a month for exact matching terms as a minimum (more on this in the keyword research examples)—these are the keywords you may consider as part of your strategy of head terms, middle-level terms, and long-tail terms.

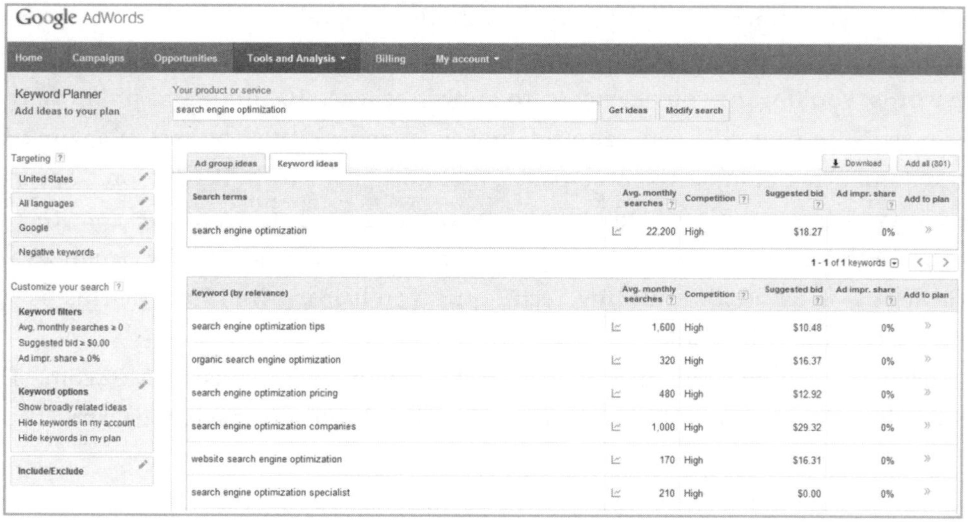

FIGURE 3–11. Google Keyword Planner.

Examples of head, middle and long-tail terms are: "shoes", "shoes for women", "leather cycling shoes for athletic women." Also notice that while "shoes" has a large amount of traffic, it's too generic, and not worth your time trying to optimize for (shoes. com, zappos.com, and dsw.com are top brands listed in the top three already) .

As you review the keywords, think about how you can break them out into logical, related groups. If the site is fairly new, start with the less competitive terms and build out using longer phrases to get some traffic and conversions. Don't lose hope here; you'll not get top traffic for top keywords overnight. SEO is a long-term process. However, keep in mind that extremely general keywords may be more competitive than those that are more specific. For example, the term "mortgage" returns over 124 million results, but if you use additional paid keyword research tools, this expanded research may reveal that there are too many websites competing with it. Therefore, you might want to use a more specific keyword relating to mortgages, such as "arizona interest only mortgage loans." You may decide to combine this with your local city or state, depending on where you operate your business. It could be single or multiple locations. These keywords may not have as many searches per month, but if there are fewer sites using the keyword, you increase your chances of getting a higher ranking on search engines. A well-positioned website will guide the visitor to the most desired action you want. Think about quality, not quantity. Would you rather have 500 visitors a day with nobody acting on your offer, or 100 a day with a 1 percent conversion? That's one person per day.

When you have selected your keywords, you're ready to write your content. Here is where the keyword optimization takes shape. What you need to do is repeat your keyword several times throughout your content. Generally, you want your keyword to appear 2 to 5 percent of the time. For example, if you're writing an article of 500 words, you'll want your keyword to appear at least 10 times and no more than 30 times. Note that this general guideline (it changes) must be tested against the market and other competitive web pages, including your own. If you don't optimize your keywords correctly or inclusively, search engine bots won't be able to pick up your web pages. However, optimizing it too many times actually penalizes you because it is seen as a spamming technique. You'll learn more about this as you progress through this book.

Below is a simple but effective screenshot from my friends at Moz.com. This infographic suggests paths and inclusions of keywords on your page, code, and URL. It is natural and mixed up.

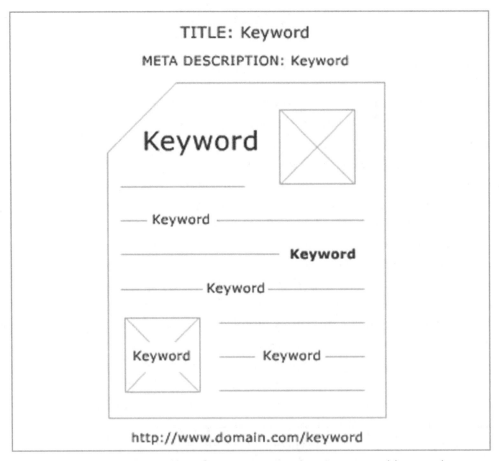

FIGURE 3–12. Screenshot from Moz.com showing natural keyword inclusion on a page.

You might be wondering, "What if the nature of my website can't use keywords 2 to 5 percent of the time?" First of all, remember that I said this is a guide. You should think about your users, and then go back and look it over with a search engine mind. Don't let this override or change your work to the point of being robotic. I see too much scrutiny placed here. This is a little "old school" today. This could be the case for websites with a community theme or those promoting more creative content. You'll have to include separate sections that contain optimized content that still relates to your site. For example, if you're running a site related to "fan fiction," you could create articles that talk about how to create fan fiction (with "fan fiction" being the optimized keyword). However, I might try to think about content ideas first by asking your community and reviewing logs and analytics, and build keyword lists into your posts from there. You could also include articles that while not relating to fan fiction could still be of interest to your audience. Example keywords could be writing novels, writing movie scripts, and self-publishing.

INSIDER TIP

Make sure you write for your users first, search engines second. Write naturally! (When you read your copy aloud, does it sound natural?)

By including optimized content on a website that would otherwise not contain such content, you get the advantage of self-expression while making sure your site gets seen by search engine bots.

As you write your content, make sure that it sounds natural and is an enjoyable read for visitors. Although the goal is to include your desired keyword 2–5 percent of the time (don't lose your breath over it), if you use it in a context that is inappropriate, you turn away visitors. In situations where using your desired keyword would make the read a chore for visitors, you need to substitute another keyword that makes more sense.

Copywriting Tips: Good Copywriting vs. Keyword Stuffing

- *Purpose.* Quality keyword writing is a multipurpose exercise. You're serving the search engines and the readers, but write for the readers first!
- *The Search Engines.* The obvious choice is to rank at the top of the relevant organic listings and avoid being banned.

- *Your Reader.* What is the purpose of your writing for the reader? Do you want your reader to act, such as clicking on a link, visiting your site, submitting an email address, downloading a document, or purchasing a product?
- *Re-examine Your Subject.* Are your subject and purpose well aligned? You might need to adjust or narrow your subject.
- *Total Quantity.* What is the total number of words or pages you expect in your final project?
- *Total Keywords and Phrases.* What are the keywords and phrases you'll incorporate in your project?
- *Density.* Be careful of the keyword lists you take on. Generally speaking, if you have a long keyword list and require many keywords in your text, most search engines will rank the web page low and therefore you may be unable to achieve the results you want. Don't place too much focus on it, but think/write naturally and continue testing.
- *Format.* In what format will you create the project and what formats will you use for the final version?
- *Competitive views.* What layouts, structure, and keywords do your competitors use?

Advertising, Ad Copy, and Copywriting

Writing for the purpose of selling a product or service is advertising copy, also referred to as ad copy or copywriting. Much of web content and SEO use the principles of this type of writing. Articles, blogs, newsletters, and press releases are usually written to elicit an action from the reader. The action might be to return to a website, click on a link to another website, or promote or buy a product or service.

When you understand the laws of copywriting, you'll be able to use them in the other types of writing.

The Laws of Copywriting

There is an abundance of data collected and psychological tactics for copywriting, yet by following a few basic principles, you can be successful. Over the years, I've become very

INSIDER TIP

What's not included in the AIDA graphic in Figure 3–13 is "satisfaction," which is a measure of repeat business and engagement that continues forward. Make sure you serve your customers for the long term with AIDA+S.

FIGURE 3–13. AIDA

interested in and now practice and test copy-written materials on my pages. Most of my clients have bland "corporate-speak" on their websites. Even their blog content (hats off for having a blog!) is boring, not keyword optimized, and with no clear call to action. But it's fairly easy to start fixing this. Continue reading about where to begin. This will become very important for your business as well.

No matter how many millions of dollars are spent and how sophisticated the advertising or website might seem, I have seen few advertisements and pieces of web copy that succeed without adhering to some basic rules. The first rule of copywriting is AIDA (Attention, Interest, Desire, Action).

Always follow this age-old principle for successful results. Keep this in mind whenever you write. Bookmark this page or copy it and tape it up where you can see it while you work. Yes, it's that important. Contrary to the infinite variables of successful business, such as the timing, target, media, content, colors, offer, sense of urgency, ad position, etc., the basic principle of AIDA works. By the way, an often overlooked step is the call to action. Once you've gotten their attention, kindled their interest and enthusiasm for your offer, tell them what to do next! This last step is the call to action (CTA). Tell your clients what they need to do, as well as where and when to do it.

Some of the direct response copywriter pros refer to this simple model taken from John Carlton a master copywriter to start:

1. Tell them what you have, (features, advantages)
2. Tell them what it will do for them, and (benefits)
3. Tell them what to do next. (CTA/offer)

In some ways, it is really that simple.

Figure 3–14 on page 68 is an example of this model in a squeeze-page I tested. Can you spot the two major actions I wanted them to take?

When your content is finished, you can, in one step, figure out your page details for overall consistency. To do this, use a free text analyzer tool (http://www.webconfs.com/keyword-density-checker.php). A more advanced, paid tool is found at http://ranks.nl/tools/spider.html.

Killer Tip: How To Quickly Get Twitter Followers & Smiles - Guaranteed!

Watch This Video Right Now To Discover This Simple, But Powerful Twitter Secret

Simply Enter In Your First Name & Email Address To Get INSTANT Access To Downloads Right Now!

You will be getting the exact Social tips that others also received for free. All you need to do is just enter in your information below so I know where to send your Social SEO Tips & Files...

Name:

Email:

Download Now!

* I will not spam, rent, or loan your information! - JR *

Pass Along This Message - Twitter This Now!   SHARE

FIGURE 3–14. Action/conversion page.

You can use your favorite word processor also. If your content is short, you could use the Find feature of your word processor to see how many times your keyword appears. To access this feature in Word, press the F5 key. Count each time your keyword is found. Divide this number by the number of words in your content (which can be found by using the word count feature of your word processor), and you have your keyword density percentage. Granted, this method is more involved than using a keyword density tool, but you should have other ways of figuring out your keyword density, just in case. When I first started SEO in the mid-'90s, there was a higher focus on the keyword density. These days, just make sure you include it naturally, and go build more quality content and begin to attract earned links instead. Keyword density is just a metric, so don't over obsess.

ONLINE RESOURCE

There are many more tools online at www.jonrognerud.com/optimization book.

Hiring a Ghostwriter

If you don't feel like going through the process of writing your website content yourself, you can hire an SEO ghostwriter. The keyword is "SEO," because ghostwriters used to writing more creative content may not know the importance of keyword density when writing web content. SEO ghostwriters can be cheaper than ghostwriters who specialize in creative writing.

With recent and ongoing changes in Google, quality content is more important than ever. Instead of finding writers that work for $5 per article, consider spending $20 to $80 per post/article, and closer to the 1,000-plus word range. This alone is not enough, you must promote it also. We cover promotional strategies throughout the book, so watch for that also.

What can you expect to pay when hiring an SEO ghostwriter? This depends on the ghostwriter and what you can negotiate. If you find SEO ghostwriters on freelancing sites such as Elance.com, Odesk.com, Guru.com, or Freelancer.com, you might be able to negotiate as low as $1.50 per 350 to 500 words of content. Remember, though, that you get what you pay for, so for that price don't expect customized, original, perfect content. That being said, "average" SEO ghostwriters will expect payment of at least $20 per 500 words of content. A note of caution here: The SEO ghostwriting market is filled with many low-cost providers. If your goal is average content, then paying the average price is fine. If your business requires highly professional content, expect to pay more. Copywriting can range from $0.25 to $4 per word, depending on the type of content.

When using an SEO ghostwriter, make sure you check copy using Copyscape.com. This is a service that helps webmasters determine if the content on their websites has been plagiarized. If there are matches, don't be alarmed—the ghostwriter may have plagiarized accidentally or it may be a common phrase such as "Christmas Day." Still, make sure he or she makes the necessary changes to ensure that your content is 100

INSIDER TIP

The Philippines have provided good writers to me and their English is very good. You should consider looking at Craigslist Manila (and related areas), as well as Onlinejobs.ph.

(Email me at contact@jonrognerud.com if you have questions on how to start this.)

WILL THEY STRIKE?

The average rate internationally for writers is $1 per word and up.
The internet has created opportunities for writers to enter at lower price points while building a portfolio. Internet marketers have the benefit of being able to hire talent at a lower rate. How long will it last? Time will tell.

percent original. You should ask for this service to be included. Services like writeraccess.com will provide Copyscape verified content in their dashboards.

Should You Use Private Label Content?

For individuals who don't want to write their content from scratch or hire a ghostwriter, there is the option of buying private label content. What is private label content? It is prewritten content that allows you the same rights as if you wrote it yourself. These rights can range from branding it with your own name or company logo to altering it, selling it, or giving it away for free. You can buy private label content as individual articles or books, or you can buy it from membership sites. Search also in Google for these terms (PLR), and search in WarriorForum.com to see what people are offering. (Don't go for the hype here, stay level-headed. They make it sound like they have the magic pill—but they don't.)

In terms of what you can expect to pay, private label articles or books individually can range from $0.01 (especially if you buy them from eBay) to as high as $200. More expensive private label content is usually sold exclusively to you, so you won't need to alter it. On the other hand, if you buy private label content from membership sites, you won't have to pay as much. In fact most membership sites of this nature charge less than $50 for access to their content. There is a major disadvantage to this method: you aren't the only one buying the content. The unaltered content loses its uniqueness once it's submitted to search engines. In fact, if other people have already posted the content online, the duplicate content filter of search engines will pick this up and penalize your website. Your website will be filtered out of search engine results, making even the best SEO attempts futile. You may decide to use this content for PPC, tweak it, and rapidly build out targeted content. Make sure to block it from search engines, which you can do with a META ROBOTS tag and a server side directory or page exclude command. See my member section for more information on this at www.jonrognerud.com/optimizationbook.

> ### INSIDER TIP
>
> You can drive traffic to a private label content page/site with pay-per-click programs. Remember that PPC traffic is completely different from SEO/natural search; many are confused about this.

To prevent this problem, you need to alter private label content bought from membership programs. You may think that rewriting the content defeats the purpose of buying it, but even when rewriting, you save a lot of time. When writing website content yourself, you have to do the keyword research on your own—a step that can take too much time, especially if you want to design a large website. Most private label content is already optimized, so you have a general idea of what you should write about. While you won't be able to use private label content from membership programs word for word, you can use it as a source of research, using their ideas, rather than their words.

> ### INSIDER TIP
>
> Some search marketers will pull information from private label rights documents, and use a content spinner (replacing words and phrases), making them their own. You can test this, but a good rule of thumb is this: "If it's easy to get, then it's easy to lose." Ask this: "If Matt Cutts (Google's top spam cop) were watching behind your back, would he be pleased with what you're doing?" I always advocate testing, but I don't use this approach for any of my clients. It's up to you. I should add that if you are into flipping domains and sites, and just building out to get some street credibility and selling it, that can be one option. Ethics and real business models always enter the conversation here.

Duplicate Content Horror Stories

 Bob wanted to have articles written for his site, but had neither the desire nor time to write them himself. On the advice of a colleague he posted a project in an online marketplace, Elance.com. His colleague advised him to pay $2 to $25 per one-page article and to commission 10 to 20 at one time. He followed his friend's advice and posted a project for 20 articles, adding the words "easy project for someone who knows what they are doing." He received bids from 15 writers in the first 3 days. He selected a writer for the project who agreed to write the 20 articles for $100. Bob received the articles one week later. Some were written poorly. He put those aside believing that he could correct them himself. He posted 3 of the articles to test the response. A week later he received a note from the real author asking him to kindly remove them. The writer was nice and shared with Bob how to check for duplicate content using Copyscape.com. Bob took the articles down from his site. He was horrified to find that none of the articles were original! Although he had only spent $100, he had risked his own reputation and could have potentially been sued by the woman whose articles he had inadvertently "stolen."

ONLINE RESOURCE

On the membership site at www.jonrognerud.com/ optimizationbook, there is a tool that can compare one content piece against another and tell you if it's "different enough" and valid for internet/search engines, so you do not get a penalty for duplication.

This action is more typical of lower-cost ghostwriters. This warning is not intended to steer you away from ghostwriters but to caution you to choose wisely. In fact, use them if you don't have enough background knowledge to create the content on your own.

Just make sure you check their work for duplicate content before you post it on your site. Also make sure that the ghostwriter includes confidentiality agreements stating that his work is exclusively yours and won't be shown anywhere else. There are many ghostwriters who are highly professional and well worth using. You will develop relationships over time. So, do not be afraid to try. It's OK to delegate. Figure out the things you are not good at, and plan out the things you can you can work "on" for the business, not "in" the business.

THE POWER OF WEBSITE GRAPHICS

If you want to include graphics in your website content, such as photos, clip art, or animations, you need to create the graphics yourself, buy them, or use free graphics. Consider also building infographics, which combine graphical and textual elements in one easily distributable JPG file. You can try it yourself using a service like infogr.am or visual.ly.

ONLINE RESOURCE

Try 99designs.com to have designers bid on your project. It's affordable, and you can get great designs, logos, and more.

Creating Website Graphics Yourself

You can create graphics yourself by using Adobe's Photoshop, Fireworks, Windows Paint (low-end tool), Techsmith's Snagit (amazing for simple graphic jobs), Google's Picasa (great image search, too!), picmonkey.com, or other graphic-manipulation software. You still need an image that you legally own as a "base" for your artwork, but with the current technology of most graphic software, you can let your imagination run wild when creating your images. For example, with Photoshop, there's an option to turn an average photo into a drawing or a painting. You can also use Photoshop's pen tool to outline parts of a photo to create a new image. Doing this well takes practice, but it lets you create professional-looking images without advanced drawing or art skills. And, with a free service like QuotesCover.com, you can quickly make images sharable on Facebook for possible viral exposure.

If you have no original photos or other types of images to work with, you can always use graphic software to create very fancy text and borders. You can also use text to create .GIF images that incorporate animated effects. Additionally, by using a .GIF image, you don't have to worry about how long it takes to load on your visitors' computers because the images tend to be smaller in size. You can even access Flickr's Creative Commons License, found at flickr.com/creativecommons.

How to Buy Website Graphics

If you decide to buy website graphics, you can purchase them individually, in bundles, or through subscription sites. If you buy individually, expect to pay from $1 to $50. Bundles can be as low as $9.99 to hundreds of dollars. Subscription sites also vary in price, ranging from $20 to $199. A few low-cost sites are Dreamstime and Shutterstock. Photopin.com contains free and paid images. You can buy images for web or print. Most are only $1 per image and there is no subscription fee. Other sites, such as PunchStock (punchstock.com/), are more expensive but have higher-quality images with and without royalty fees. Rights-protected images can cost several hundred dollars and more per photo for limited use (i.e., for one year). Unless you have a business need for exclusive photos, stock photos are a better option.

> ### ONLINE RESOURCE
>
> Log on to my member portal at www.jonrognerud.
> com/optimizationbook and see the Bookmarks sec-
> tion. Check also Resources at the end of this book. It
> has links to some great free sites and paid graphics that you can
> use. Try sxc.hu, a leading free stock photo site. iStockphoto.com is
> another great (paid) service.

How About Using Free Website Graphics?

You can get attractive website graphics for free, but there is a cost. This cost is not money, but advertising space. In order to use free website graphics, you have to provide a link to the site offering them somewhere on your site. This has an advantage and a disadvantage. The advantage: When it comes to SEO, this creates a backlink if using an associated text link (since graphic links are not read by search engines), increasing the chances that search engine bots will notice your site. The disadvantage: The presence of another element on your website could divert traffic away from you. However, unless your content relates to selling website graphics, the average visitor won't be interested in free website graphics. Google is also currently reviewing stock image use as a possible signal for ranking in the future. For video summaries from Google, watch TheShortCutts.com. You'll see the latest videos from Matt Cutts, the head of search quality at Google.

As you determine whether to write your own content or design your own graphics, you must consider the cost factor. How much is your time worth per hour? Is doing it yourself the highest and best use of your time? Sometimes doing it yourself can cost you more than outsourcing the task to a specialist. It's easy to believe that "not spending money" is the cheapest option, but this isn't true. For example, assume your time is worth $100 per hour and it takes you 20 hours to design your site. Your just spent $2,000 for the site. Now, let's say that you could have found a web designer to do the site for $50 an hour and it would have taken 10 hours for a total of $500. Did you really save money? You're faced with this cost-benefit analysis every day in business, so why not here as well?

A WORD ABOUT WEB STRUCTURE

Content is important. Just as key is your navigational structure and page access for users and search engines. Users and search engines get to pages via links, and this layout of information is often called information architecture. Building this correctly should be of primary concern. My friend Bruce Clay has much more information on silos and themes; if you want to go deeper, go to bruceclay.com/newsletter/0906/silos.html.

The easiest way to think about this is as "silos" of information. This forms a logical structure of your site, and creates related and supporting pages of your site. In this approach, related information is grouped into distinct sections within your site.

Not only will users enjoy it, but as you build link profiles on your site using keywords in your links (anchor text), you can do the same externally and build backlinks to the pages deeper in your site—to build strength and authority to your site—over time. If you think of your site's architecture as domains, pages, categories, sections, and media (docs, sounds, videos)—and work on arranging them into logical buckets—you are off to a good start.

In a post in Webmaster World from 2001, its members talk about the "theme pyramid," which is still valuable today. It's the theme pyramid (Figure 3–15) that looks at the site as a whole, and breaks it down into sections. The infographic shows how you can map out a site, starting with broad keywords and drilling into more specific ones. It allows content and links to flow in a much more logical way—both for users and search engines.

Represented in an even simpler way, each theme has a subtopic that includes related words and links to support that theme (see Figure 3–16 on page 76). Send me a note at contact@jonrognerud.com if you have more questions, and I'll try to help you. Yeah, it's that important.

The silo approach could be applied to organize a more logical structure for *power tools* (a broad topic) below, and organized into something like Figure 3–17 on page 76.

#	Seo Value	Site Structure (sub content categories)							
1	No value	Main Site Root Index Page							
2	Low value Primary single kw's On index pages (hallway pages)	Sub Topic A		Sub Topic B		Sub Topic C		Sub Topic D	
3	Medium value Secondary 1-2 word kw's (doorway pages)	kw a1	kw a2	kw b1	kw b2	kw c1	kw c2	kw d1	kw d2
4	High value 2-3 word kw phrases on high content pages	kw a1a | kw a1b | kw a2a | kw a2b		kw b1a | kw b1b | kw b2a | kw b2b		kw c1a | kw c1b | kw c2a | kw c2b		kw d1a | kw d1b | kw d2a | kw d2b	
5	Money! 2-4 word kw phrases on prime targeted pages	$ $ $ $ $ $ $ $		$ $ $ $ $ $ $ $		$ $ $ $ $ $ $ $		$ $ $ $ $ $ $ $	

FIGURE 3–15. Theme pyramid.

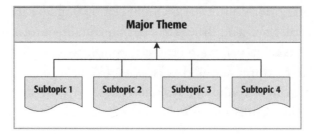

FIGURE 3–16. The silo approach to websites.

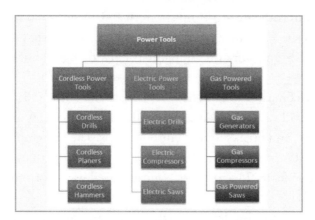

FIGURE 3–17. Power tools silo approach (from my friends at bruceclay.com).

WEBSITE STRATEGIES THAT MAY (NOT) WORK

Cartoons. Animation is annoying on your home or landing pages and should only be used under specific circumstances. For instance, if you're a graphic designer selling animation, you would display samples. It certainly works very well—and still does—for sites like JibJab.com (see jibjab.com/originals).

Movement on the Page Is Distracting. You either have a media site or a content site— don't mix them on the same page. Leave the animation to Looney Tunes and JibJab. Here, less is more.

Sound. Auto-start sound is annoying and deadly. Many people are surfing in the office or in a public environment, and the surprise of a sudden sound track often makes them panic and hit the button to close your site. While sound is a great addition for selling, be sure you point out the "turn sound off" option. This may be true for video also, but you should test this to see what engages more and what gets the responses you are aiming for.

Pop-Ups. While most people dislike them, pop-ups on exit to collect email addresses have been shown to increase email lists. This is about the only time pop-ups should be used, and even in this case sparingly. Lightboxes (popping up a small window, staying on the same page, graying out the background) presented with useful information on an exit, or after a few minutes, and not again for 30 days can be programmed, and work well. Test it.

Background Images. Background images are cheesy and amateurish. Review some of the major sites such as Google, Yahoo!, eBay, Amazon, and Monster. You won't see background images. Also, background images slow down load time, as they can easily be a drain.

Organize Your Site. Content should be organized for:

- Relevance—SEO
- Eye appeal
- Navigation
- Social engagement (include social widgets on your pages, so visitors can easily share them)

Navigation. Make sure your site is easy to navigate by having a navigational bar at the top of each page. Keep the look consistent on each page. You may decide to use a top and left navigation. If you do, don't make it cluttered and hard to read. Use keywords in the links where you can.

If pages require scrolling, a side navigational bar and links at the bottom of the page are useful. Remember that every page on your site is a hair trigger (click) away from execution (visitor leaving).

Splash Pages Are All Wet. A splash page (entry or welcome page) is like someone driving by and hitting a puddle while you are walking along the road. You just want to scream. Why would anyone work so hard to attract website traffic and then make visitors choose whether to enter when they get there? Avoid placing roadblocks on your website.

Click and Scroll, and Rock and Roll. People dance to rock and roll, and that means they keep moving. Imagine every click of a mouse as a roadblock between you and your prospects. Every time you make a visitor click, scroll, or move the mouse, you risk losing that visitor! While you can't eliminate the mouse, you must minimize the number of times a visitor must click and scroll. The last thing you want people to do is rock and roll off your site. Keep mouse clicks from getting between the visitor and your message.

Limit scrolling to article pages and sales pitches. Keep the scrolling on those pages to under eight screens.

There's No Place like Home. An absolute must for every website is having a "Home" link on every page. Visitors often want to return to the homepage, and depending on the depth of your website and how they arrived there, the back button in their browser might not take them to your homepage. Make sure your button or link says (keyword)

"Home Page" or "Back to Home Page." If it makes sense and you have space, maximize your Home button by adding a keyword. For example, if you have a computer supplies business, you could use "Computer Supplies Home."

Include your menu bar on every page.

> **INSIDER TIP**
>
> If you want to provide text/content early in the HTML page (search engines like it), you could cut down all the links/navigation and place them in a Flash object, and use the links at the footer to help spiders find their pages.

Make navigation as easy as changing channels on the television remote control. Your menu choice should appear at the top and bottom of every page.

Don't Get Framed. Some frames are user-friendly, though they come at a hefty sacrifice: First, the name remains the same. The address bar never changes as visitors travel between your pages. This means no one can bookmark or link to any specific page or share a page by emailing the link. Also, when a page in your site other than the frameset appears in search results, visitors will only see the sub-page and not the surrounding frame.

Yes, there are clumsy JavaScript tricks to sidestep this issue, but you're defeating the purpose of using frames in the first place. You can maintain the same elements on your pages with headings and server-side includes. Printing and bookmarking also becomes an issue, and it's not search engine friendly. You may decide to use frames on an intranet site (internal, behind the firewall), that's OK—if you absolutely must.

A Picture's Worth a Thousand Kilobytes (or so). Don't make your visitors wait! A 200k graphic should be compressed to 20k as an example. Use graphics software to compress your pictures to use less disk space and download faster. People don't like to wait. They will leave. Imagine going to the grocery store and finding a 20-minute line just to get inside. Would you even park? Compress your files. There are several inexpensive software programs to do this for you.

Unless you're selling your graphic capabilities, keep the multimedia off your site. However, you should consider including embedded code from streaming video sites such as YouTube and not just images.

Serve Your Text on the Table. Put text in a fixed-width table in the center of the page. Don't make content too wide for viewers with small screens. Content is fluid and expands as window size increases. A way around that is to fix the width of the content, but that poses another problem. Maximum page size should be 770 pixels

ONLINE RESOURCE

Smush.it is easy and quick, and can be used in conjunction with YSlow, a Firefox plugin from Yahoo (addons.mozilla.org/en-US/firefox/addon/5369/).

wide to account for scrollbars. A percentage width or fluid content is usually the best choice. Review your analytics to reveal the broad base of user's screen sizes, and adjust accordingly. Pick a large timeframe for review (12 to 18 months). Google analytics provides this information, and will show data from portable device use, too.

Make Your Text Large Enough and Easy to Read. Backgrounds should contrast with text color. Avoid placing text over images. Use space between lines to make text easier to read. Visit websites and note those you find appealing and easy to read. Mock up the space, background colors, and font colors and sizes.

- Use short bulleted lists.
- Make points in bold.
- Use CAPITAL LETTERS appropriately and exclamation points sparingly!
- Underlining any text other than links only irritates your visitors and makes the text harder to read. Instead, use italics, bold, or color to emphasize. Blue links are good. You can test this, also.
- Web surfers have come to expect all links in content copy to be underlined and blue. Stay consistent within your site.

Links. Place your links in relevant locations. Keep in mind that when a link is incorporated in text, that can cause your reader to leave and possibly not come back. For this reason, use embedded links only when they invoke the action of your content or web page's purpose. While links are important and convenient, be sure you're not placing an exit door right in front of your cash register.

Clearly Identify All Links. If your links aren't self-explanatory (to your visitor), include a brief description. Create links that are keyword rich, and don't worry about a perfect alignment. User action and page/navigation understanding is important.

Open a Window—Just Don't Close the Door. Make your links open in a new window when people are leaving your site. You specify this in HTML with the _blank tag on the href code like this: <a href="..." target="_blank">. This gives them the opportunity to revisit your site and keep you in front of them a bit longer. While closing out windows can be a bit of annoyance, the cost here is minimal compared to the benefit of staying power. Your visitors might have forgotten your URL or failed to bookmark your site, and in these cases you've done them a favor. Remember, sometimes people may be in research

PLAIN AND SIMPLE

Maximize your site experience by using descriptive words and keywords for your links and call to actions like "Click Here."

mode and surfed through a few sites or search terms. (Since you have a link to your home page from every page on your site, your site will be easy to navigate; make internal links to pages within your site open in the same window.)

Be Easily Locatable—Be Incognito. Make sure your contact information or contact link is on every page of your site and easily found. If you're only reachable by email, let visitors know that. Make sure you encrypt your email address to stay hidden from the spam bots. You can do this by creating an image that looks like the email link. Or, you can use this example: contact at jonrognerud dot com, but it is not as good as the image choice.

Be Original or Get Punished. As tempting as it might be, don't copy content from other sites. Copyright infringement is serious, and if the owner or a client doesn't catch you, the search engines could deal with you harshly. Content must be relevant and original to do you any good with organic rankings and prevent identification as a spam site. High-quality original content is the "king" of the internet. I cannot tell you often enough that this is a must with your SEO strategy.

Test-Drive Your Site. Broken links and images make your site look shoddy and appear untrustworthy. Test your site by loading from the internet and test every image and link. View your site from several browsers. Recruit friends and family to help you identify and resolve any problems before you launch. Download the XENU broken link checker tool at home.snafu.de/tilman/xenulink.html. Note: this power tool has many uses, including looking for duplicate content titles, types, sizes of pages, and more.

A Happier Webmaster: Content Management Systems (CMS)

Consider implementing and using a content management system. WordPress is an example of this, although some features are excluded. This allows you to easily maintain your website. Any staff member—with or without an IT background—can use a content management system without a webmaster's help. Make sure your content management system is search engine–friendly, with smart navigation, architecture, and file naming conventions. Can you easily set up a layout described in the section where you learned about information architecture? Look for pages on the company's website that discuss its SEO-compliancy policy to be sure you're making a good choice of companies.

There are two elements to a content management system: the front end and the back end. The front end of a content management system represents the website as it appears when accessed by a user. The back end is the control panel, or the interface with the system's databases and templates that define the look and feel of your website. Access to the back end is password-restricted, and you can provide different levels of authority for those restrictions.

If you have a small website that doesn't need frequent updating, you may not need a content management system. However, rather than relying on external web developers, a content management system could save you money. The system can also reduce the amount of work required from some of your highly trained staff members.

To put your website on the internet, you need to acquire web hosting. Specifically, web hosting is the process that puts websites on the web. It usually works by storing sites on a server, which is a large computer that houses websites and their data. You can buy web hosting or try to establish the service yourself. This section talks about the features you should look for when buying web hosting, why you should avoid free web hosting services, server configurations and setup (if you decide to do web hosting yourself), and finally, how to move your files into your web hosting account.

CMS systems exist for the enterprise, mobile, learning (LMS), web, and document storage.

CMS web systems you should look into are:

- WordPress.org—download and configure on your own server (my favorite)
- WordPress.com—hosted on its platform
- Joomla—popular CMS system—joomla.org
- SharePoint—Microsoft's CMS and collaboration system—sharepoint.com
- Drupal—very good, can be a little technical. Visit drupal.org
- CrownPeak—dynamic platform with great support staff, used more for the enterprise—crownpeak.com
- GoDaddy, Bluehost, HostGator, DreamHost—these top hosting companies all have a CMS options and systems included. You pick the one you want.

GET YOUR WEB HOSTING RIGHT

A web host is a company that can provide you with server space for your website, including pages, graphics, scripts, and files. This is where you'll upload your website.

You should keep certain points in mind when selecting a web host. How many customers does it have? What is its percentage of "uptime"? Your site won't help you at all if your web host's servers are frequently down. Does this web host require advance payment, or does it charge setup fees? Test the web host's customer support, and see how well it fits with your plans. Does it offer fast connections? Your site's visitors will want the fastest connection available. How much daily transfer is allowed? Will you be charged for exceeding its transfer limit? Does the web host offer shopping cart software for your customers, secure servers, and a CGI (Common Gateway Interface) bin? Can you upgrade for free?

There are many basic features you should expect when you look for a suitable web host. You should receive 24/7, reliable support and your own domain name. You'll need at least 10GB of monthly transfer, and a minimum of 20 to 50MB of server space, depending on the size of your site and data acquisition expectations. You'll want unlimited true POP email accounts, unlimited email aliases, and email forwarding; also "htaccess" password protection, SSI (Server Side Includes) support, and the ability to design and upload to your site using HTML editing software. You'll want unlimited access to your server through FTP/Telnet, easy access to log files, and statistics on all visits to your site.

You will also want to make sure that the account manager employed by your web hosting provider has an easy-to-use control panel. A good control panel should give you the ability to manage your email addresses, including adding addresses and deleting old ones. Generally you will want to avoid web hosting providers that require you to do these things through their technical support. You'll also want the ability to modify passwords associated with your account. Both Unix- and Windows-hosted accounts provide good access panels, and cPanel is popular and effective. The popular Fantastico cPanel/PHP web application can be performed by novices and allows set up of files, SQL databases, structure imports, chmods, and more.

FIGURE 3–18. GoDaddy hosting options.

Make sure the web hosting provider can make allowances for complex website features, if this applies for your website. This could include making allowances for advanced scripting, such as PHP or CGI. It could include SSL (secure sockets layer), a protocol that sends data in an encrypted format. It might also have MySQL, a database management program. It may even include a shopping cart, a feature that's important for e-commerce websites.

Don't let these terms confuse or scare you. It's made very simple with today's fantastic technology solution providers.

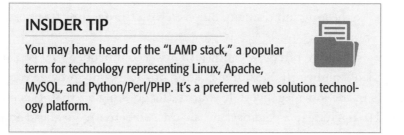

INSIDER TIP

You may have heard of the "LAMP stack," a popular term for technology representing Linux, Apache, MySQL, and Python/Perl/PHP. It's a preferred web solution technology platform.

Finally, you should investigate the operating system used by the servers of your web hosting provider. If you want to use ASP (Active Server Pages, Microsoft scripting language), you'll need to use Windows technologies. If this is not the case, you can choose setups using Unix, Linux, and Apache servers.

With so many options, you'll have to decide which ones are right for you. Will you need an unrestricted CGI bin for dynamic content? Do you plan to do any server-side programming with PHP or Perl? You'll want to make sure support for that is available. Do you need MySQL databases? If so, be careful to make sure you have a backup procedure in place and know what you are doing. Hourly, daily, and weekly backups may be needed. Your requirements may be different, because no business is the same.

Many web hosts charge extra for additional databases past the first. Do some research, and find which web host will serve your website the best.

Why You Should Avoid Free Hosting Services

After evaluating some of the features offered by paid web hosting services, you may feel that they are excessive for you. Therefore, it might be tempting to sign up for a free web hosting service, especially if your site is small and uncomplicated. Resist the temptation. Why? Well, websites that use free hosting tend not to get high rankings from search engines. Search engines want what they perceive to be unique sites with separate domain names. Most free hosting services give you a very long and complicated subdomain name. If you use a redirect URL service, you could try to

REACHING THE WORLD

MySQL is one of the most popular open-source databases in the world. It's even used in Antarctica.

circumvent this problem, as you would be purchasing a legitimate domain name that would "point" to the long sub-domain. But even with this feature, free hosting services aren't worth your while.

Free sites also tend to offer low bandwidth. It's recommended that you allow one to three gigabytes of bandwidth. Most free hosting providers only provide you bandwidth with numbers in the low megabytes. If your traffic goes higher than this number, you will be forced to upgrade to a paid package anyway. So better to go ahead and start with one. Not only will lower-priced web hosting packages provide you with a suitable level of bandwidth, but they will also not put ads on your site, the last major disadvantage to free hosting services. Since you're getting free hosting, free web hosting companies have to get their revenue from other sources, which are advertisers. These ads create more potential for a website visitor to click away from your site, something that you don't want to happen. Further, you can't assume that these ads will offer backlinks for your site, since most search engines ignore free web hosting sites anyway.

Server Configurations and Setup

If you're technically inclined, have aspirations of starting your own web hosting business, need insane amounts of bandwidth, and feel limited by the current choices available for web hosting providers, you may want to use a server of your own. You can even use your own desktop computer for this purpose, though it's not recommended for two reasons: 1) You won't get as much processing power; 2) You don't want your working computer to be exposed to the risks possible when using your own server as a web host. Thus, you may want to buy a professional-grade server. Be prepared to pay a lot of money, though.

ONLINE RESOURCE

Google likely includes "age of domain" as a metric of trust and authority. Therefore, get a standalone domain today. Don't wait. Register it on Namecheap.com.

The minimum cost for servers tends to be a few thousand, while the most elaborate models can be hundreds of thousands. In fact, if you search Google Products, you'll find out about servers and costs very quickly.

Of course, more than likely you won't need these high-end servers, but even the so-called "cheaper" servers may be out of an ordinary person's budget. However, if you're starting a business, you can use your server expense as a deduction on your taxes.

Once you've selected your server, you need to configure it to put your websites on the internet. To do this you have to use a server configuration program. Apache is one of the most popular because it is easy to use and free to download. To download the software, visit Apache.org. After the program is downloaded, you have to use an installer to put Apache on your server.

You should know your network domain, server name, and administration email during the course of installation. Some experts recommend that you say "local host" for network domain and server name and list your email address for the administration email. The exception would be if you have a network administrator you work with; if

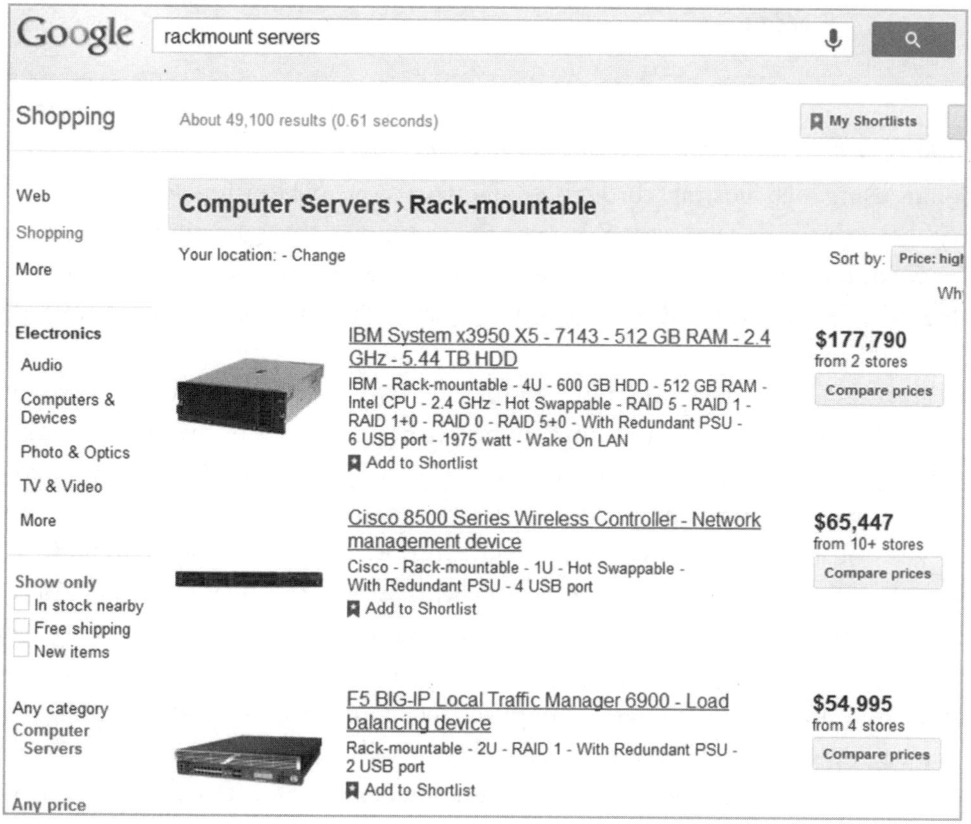

FIGURE 3–19. Google products server search.

so, list his email. If you need a powerful search option, you can even install Google. See Google's search appliance at google.com/enterprise/search/gsa.html.

If you want your server to be viewed by other people, right-click "Network Connections" and select "Properties." From there select the "Advanced" tab, and press the button on the page. A pop-up containing a list of ports appears. Select "Port 80, HTTP," and check the checkbox by clicking on it.

Now you need to set up your website files. Look for the folder HTDOCs (depending on setup) in the Apache folder. Put your website files in this folder. Now your server can place these files onto the internet.

When the configuration and setup of your server are complete, you need to assign it to a domain name. If you've already bought a domain name, then all you have to do is log into your account. You now have to configure the DNS A and CNAME with your server settings; usually this involves just entering in your IP address.

ONLINE RESOURCE

You can use IPChicken.com to find out what your local IP address is.

Moving Your Files into Your Web Hosting Account

If you're using web hosting through your own server, obviously you don't have to worry about this step. However, if you use the services of a web hosting company, you will. Depending on the host that you use, it may already have made this process easier through file managers found in the control panel of your account. If not, you need to use an FTP program.

FTP programs use FTP (file transfer protocol) to transfer files from your computer to your web host server. FTP programs can be free or paid. Some of the most commonly used FTP programs include SmartFTP, a free FTP program, and Filezilla (my personal favorite), a paid FTP program.

When you begin using an FTP program, you need: a host name or IP address, a username, and a password. Your web host provides you with this information. In fact, your username and password may even be the same as that initially used for your account. Check your web hosting company's welcome documentation to make sure. Entering in this information logs you onto the server, making you ready to upload files.

Uploading files from your computer to your web host server is easy. The FTP program displays two panels: the left panel contains the information stored on your computer, while the right panel contains the information stored on the host computer.

To transfer files between computers, all you have to do is select a file, then drag it into the appropriate pane. For example, if you drag a file from the right pane into the left pane, you will have successfully placed one of your files onto the web host server. If you do it in the opposite direction—from right to left—you will have transferred files from your web host onto your computer. Make sure when uploading files that you keep everything within the same folder you were originally working from. If you change folders, this could mess up links you've established between web pages. Additionally, you want to make sure that your homepage is named either "index.htm" or "index.html." Depending on the configuration of the server, you have probably seen default.htm/html as well. They all work the same way.

INSIDER TIP

If you have hired outsourced help, you can easily set up new FTP accounts and give them access to just the directories or files you need.

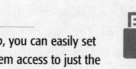

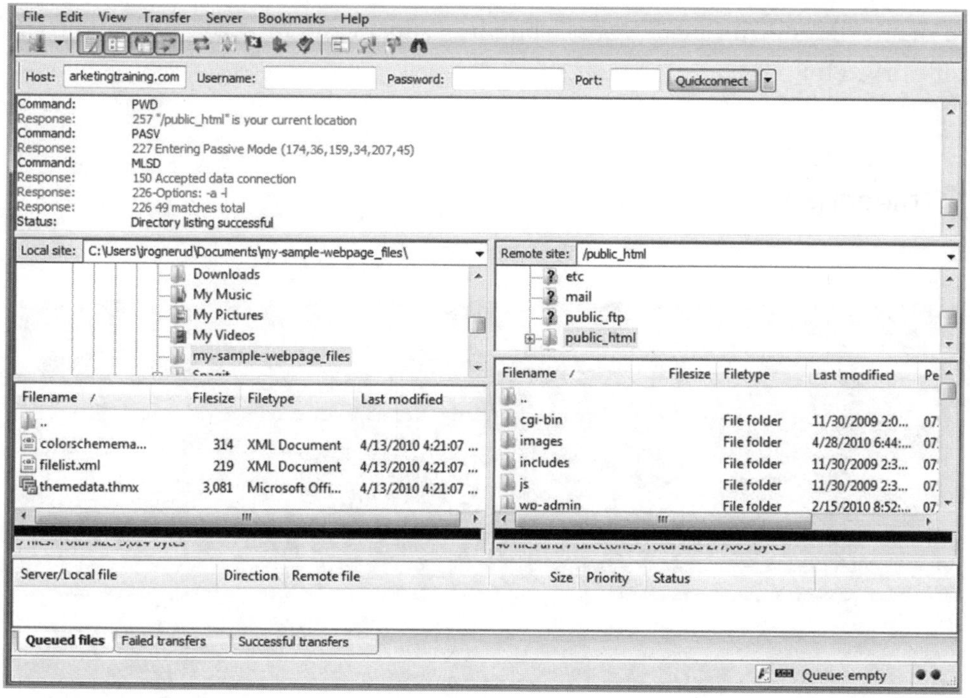

FIGURE 3–20. Screenshot of FileZilla, a free FTP solution.

The Web Hosting Companies

I have used a number of companies, including Netfirms, 1and1, Yahoo!, Bluehost, Verio (previously best.com), Yahoo! Webhosting, and GoDaddy as web hosting providers. If you are using WordPress and want high performance hosting and support, you should consider WPengine.com or WebSynthesis.com.

GoDaddy is $4.49 (small business selection, for one year), which is attractive for many startup companies. With the multiple options—from plain hosting service, shopping carts, and blogs—it's a powerfully simple system. It does try to sell you everything. Know what you need upfront, and stay within budget. GoDaddy's "upsell" system is amazing—you want fries with that?

Yahoo! has its Small Business Web Hosting solutions at http://smallbusiness. yahoo.com/webhosting. You don't have to worry about using FTP programs, setting up your domain name information, or even designing your website because it has templates that can take care of all that for you. Everything comes together in a nice package with Yahoo!, and I sometimes recommend it to my newbie friends. If they are serious, I tell them to install and develop a blog with a reputable hosting company, customize their themes, and get a professional, personal design.

Technology advancements can even provide website design directly in a web browser. Companies like Moonfruit have come out and created some pretty compelling offers. I liked the way Moonfruit made website building super easy. Yes, even my mom tried it, and it worked for her.

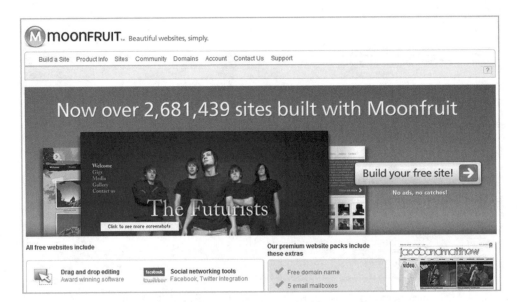

FIGURE 3–21. Moonfruit screenshot.

Dealing with Error Pages

Unfortunately, good web page design shouldn't end with only one version of a website. You'll want to update your site periodically with new information to encourage a steady stream of visitors. In doing so you might find that you might have to rearrange files, change their names, or remove them completely from your website. This is not without consequence, because if you don't update the URLs associated with these files, your visitors will see the dreaded 404 "File Not Found" error page. To address this problem, you could use a 301 redirect or a customized 404 error page. This section talks about both these options.

301 Redirects. A 301 "Moved Permanently" redirect is a process that does what its namesake indicates: it redirects old URLs to a new URL. It isn't the only redirect process out there; there are also 302 "Temporarily Moved" redirects, along with HTML meta tag or JavaScript redirects, but these tend not to do well with search engines. In fact, many sites, including high-profile sites, have encountered problems with being indexed in Google when they used these redirects—problems so major that the sites actually got penalized, meaning their listings were completely removed. Don't believe the search engines ever take action? In 2006, Google delisted BMW Germany as part of its anti-spam efforts, so it is possible to be penalized. Use this as a lesson for your own website. If you're going to do redirects, only use a 301. Major brands get special treatment from Google (like it or not), and so consequently BMW was back in the index within 24 hours.

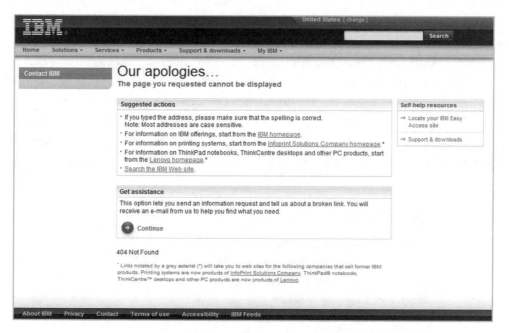

FIGURE 3–22. IBM error page—404 Page Not Found.

INSIDER TIP

Use 404 error pages to upsell services and drive people to sign up on your site. You can even place AdSense ads if you are trying to monetize. Every site is different. IBM 404 error pages will not have AdSense.

To initiate a 301 redirect you have several methods to choose from. The easiest way is to do it through your web hosting company, as some provide special 301 redirect software. Another relatively easy method is to manipulate your .htaccess file. This file contains instructions for several things, such as error management, security concerns, and specifications for redirection. To obtain a .htaccess file, download it from the root directory where your web pages are held on your web host's server. If you don't have this file, you can create a new one using Notepad or another text editor. You must save it with the extension .htaccess. In either case, you should include the following line of code (example only):

Redirect 301 /old/oldsite.html http://www.yoursite.com/newurl.html

The "Redirect 301" portion of the code tells the browser or search engine that the upcoming link, "oldsite.html," should be redirected to the new link, http://www. yoursite.com/newurl.html." When listing the original URL, omit the "http://www" or the code won't work. If this doesn't result in a successful 301 redirect, try using Apache's mod_rewrite module.

When you've completed the necessary steps to initiate a 301 redirect, test the new link to be sure everything works as intended. If you are involved in any link exchanges (discussed later in this book), make sure you contact the webmasters to let them know your site has been updated. Granted, most of the 301 redirect methods discussed here should automatically transport a visitor to the updated URL even if the original one is entered in, but cover all your bases anyway. These

INSIDER TIP

As a rule, and especially if you have good ranking on certain pages, don't touch or update those existing pages using 301 redirect. Adding quality, keyword-rich pages is of great search and user benefit.

301 redirects will be of great help when you transfer to a new server. While not 100 percent foolproof, it does a great job.

In terms of search engines, if you use a 301 redirect, you are very likely to retain your original rankings, even though you should expect them to change. It may take a while for the new URL to get indexed and seen, but once it does you'll have the same advantages as you did with your old URL.

Customized 404 Error Pages. Some webmasters prefer to use a customized 404 error page instead of the 301 redirects for their missing URLs. Customized 404 error pages are more creative and engaging than the standard "File Not Found" message. Some can be designed in such a way that visitors barely know they're on an error page. This is especially the case for customized 404 pages that use the same layout as the rest of the website. Other customized 404 error pages have a humorous design to entertain the visitor.

Then there are those who try to use the 404 error page as an opportunity to advertise affiliate websites they're promoting. Customized 404 error pages are only limited by your imagination and creativity. See the member section for examples of 404 pages.

To create a customized 404 error page, you design it as you would any other web page, using the website creation software mentioned earlier in this book. Once you've completed this step, there are three ways to get your website integrated with your customized 404 error pages:

1. Use the 404 customization option offered by your hosting company,
2. Use Apache or other server software, or
3. Use your .htaccess file.

If your hosting company offers 404 customization, use this method over the others since it will integrate more easily with your website. If you're trying to integrate a customized 404 error page with Apache, you'll have to insert the following code into your httpd.conf file (which you will have to obtain from your web host if you're using a hosting company):

ErrorDocument 404 /yourcustomized404-404.shtml

You would use a similar, yet different coding structure if integrating a customized error page through your .htaccess file. The code for that is:

ErrorDocument 404 /404-yourcustomized404-page.html

For the specific codes of other server software, you would have to look for them through Google or by consulting their help or troubleshooting documentation.

ELEMENTS FOR WEBSITE SUCCESS

With your website complete and uploaded onto your web host's server, you now need to do some "webmaster editing" to make sure that your site is in working order and that it's structured in such a way that it incorporates the principles of good SEO optimization. In this section, you learn about the elements to be reviewed and/or set up when your website is done. These elements include website structure, website title, and website description.

Website Structure

If a website structure contains complicated hierarchies, it won't index well with search engines. This is why you should stick with the most basic website structure, which is known as the flat or linear structure. With a flat structure, you have a homepage that introduces your topic, then links to various subtopics, which could be listed on the left side of the screen. These subtopics should always be visible; the only thing that should update is the right side of the screen. This would show the current subtopic selected (or the homepage).

When designing your subtopic web pages, you need to ensure they aren't too far away from your homepage. A best practice is to only take a maximum of two clicks to get from your subtopic page to your homepage. Make sure to not create deep nesting of pages that are hard to get to. Users and search engines will feel the pain, and so will you. Don't make your website complicated by including subtopics of subtopics. At most, you can add another subtopic link on the left side of the general subtopic screen, or include more detailed information on the specific page of a subtopic. In essence, make your subtopic link pane a clear, keyword-related link for each of your web pages. To get a visual of what this means, take a look at Figure 3–23. Keep in mind, this is a pretty "skinny" site for content, but I'll use it for display.

CLUE TO COLORS

Many webmasters choose web colors based on the content. For example, health sites may have lighter, soothing colors while exercise sites are bold and bright. You can test user engagement with your web analytics and tools like CrazyEgg. com and ClickTale.com.

FIGURE 3–23. Yourdomain.com screenshot (now redirects to 1and1.com as an affiliate).

The subtopic links are on the left side of the screen. When you click on them, the right side of the screen updates with the pertinent information. In the screenshot, the subtopic "Cheap Web Hosting" was selected, so the right pane updates with a list of advertising links related to this subtopic. If you click on one of these links, you don't get a change in the subtopics listed on the left panel; instead, you're taken to the advertiser's website.

Now, don't think that a flat structure alone is enough to ensure that your website has been designed with the highest capacity possible. Get some human opinions on how your website is structured. Let people you know online or offline go through the site and note their experiences with it. Ask them to give their general opinion of your site structure: Are there enough or too many subtopics? Does the site look too busy with extra ads? If your site is laden with Flash animations or videos that take longer to load, ask if the wait time is acceptable. And don't forget to get opinions on general things related to the design of your site, such as layout, color scheme, and font usage.

After getting a good human opinion, get a computerized analysis of how well your site structure will perform. You can do this with software known as A1 Website Analyzer (microsystools.com/products/website-analyzer/).

Website Analyzer does what a human eye can't do. It uses a series of formulas to determine the value of the web pages in your site structure. The program will return a "link power" score to tell you about the effectiveness of the website setup. The program also tests for broken links as well as providing response times for 404 error pages. Use A1 Website Analyzer to see if the images used on your website are too big, and have it perform a special test to see if your site can handle increased bandwidth. The data from this analysis are exported to an XML or CSV format.

The cost for A1 Analyzer is only $69. This price includes the software and upgrades for one year. To obtain the software, you can either pay the fee upfront, or download the program and try it out before making a purchase. If you do the latter, you're given a 30-day evaluation period. During this evaluation period you are allowed to try out a full version of A1 Analyzer.

ONLINE RESOURCE

Remember to review the membership area for additional software and tools: www.jonrognerud.com/optimizationbook.

Website: The Page Title

The website title appears on the left side at the top of the browser window. Titles not only let your visitors know what your site is about, they are also one of the elements used by search engines to determine what search terms to place your site under. To give your website a title, you must use the title tag within the <head> portion of the HTML code of whatever web page you want a title for. For example, take a look at the following coding:

```
<head>
<title>Web Page Title Goes Here</title>
</head>
```

This simple piece of code is all you need to create your website title. Based on this code, what would appear in the browser window is "Web Page Title Goes Here." Of course, you will replace this with your own website title. It's the starting point for the title/keyword(s) for your page.

W3Schools.com is a great resource you should use to test the immediate output of your results. See the screenshot of the TITLE tag example in Figure 3–24.

How do you create a title for your website? Well, as you did with your domain name, you want to include relevant keywords, which you find from the keyword research. If your company name includes a relevant keyword you can include this toward the end of your title. For example, the title "Buy Cheap Computers from Computers-R-Us" lists the keyword "computer" twice and is likely preferred for smarter retrieval by search

HTML <title> Tag

w3schools.com

Example

A simple HTML document, with the minimum of required tags:

```
<html>
<head>
<title>Title of the document</title>
</head>

<body>
The content of the document......
</body>

</html>
```

Try it yourself »

Definition and Usage

The <title> tag defines the title of the document.

The title element is required in all HTML/XHTML documents.

The title element:

- defines a title in the browser toolbar
- provides a title for the page when it is added to favorites
- displays a title for the page in search-engine results

FIGURE 3–24. W3schools.

engines. However, the title "Buy Computers from Electronics Depot" may not do well. This is because it contains two unrelated keywords: "computers" and "electronics," and unless you are a strong brand, the competitive nature of the keyword computers is not a good strategy for your page/site The search engine robot would get confused because it wouldn't know whether to index the site according to computers or electronics. In this situation, leave the company name out or find a keyword that would match it. In this instance it could be "electronics." The revised title would be "Buy Cheap Electronics from Electronics Depot."

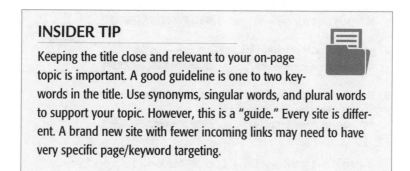

INSIDER TIP

Keeping the title close and relevant to your on-page topic is important. A good guideline is one to two keywords in the title. Use synonyms, singular words, and plural words to support your topic. However, this is a "guide." Every site is different. A brand new site with fewer incoming links may need to have very specific page/keyword targeting.

When creating your title, make it brief: that is, no more than 65 characters. A longer title won't increase your chances of getting ranked higher in search engines, since most search engine bots read only the first 65 characters. The rest of the title would get truncated, something that wouldn't look attractive, depending on how your title is worded. Also, don't get lazy thinking that if you put "Home Page" as your title the search engine will show whatever title appears on your homepage as your website title. Not only will it not do this, but you will suffer two consequences. First, the title won't look good to visitors, as they will see Home Page as a title for web pages that don't relate to the homepage. Second, the search engine bot will index your site as "home page," which won't get you anywhere with search engine listings. It only takes a few minutes to think of a suitable title for your web page; go on and use this time to think of appropriate titles. It could make a world of difference when it's time for your site to get indexed. You also want your title to be descriptive so that when users bookmark your site, it's easy to remember and access. A combination of keyword research and click-through analysis will be important. I've seen small changes in the title improve engagement (clicks), which is a very powerful and important option. And, as you can see from the recent study from Moz.com, the TITLE tag is a highly valued factor for search engines. And, as you can see, the incoming text link with a keyword rich anchor text holds an ever better value for search engines, and specifically Google. You'll learn more about this in the link building section.

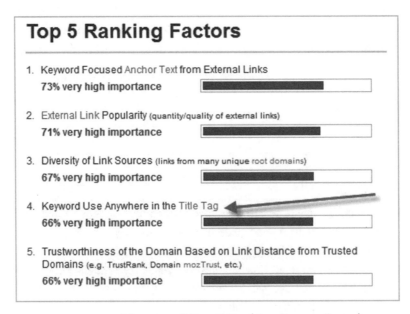

FIGURE 3–25. Moz.com "Top 5 Ranking Factors" study.

Website: Page Description

The meta description of your website neither appears in the browser like the website title, nor is it shown on your website, once your visitor gets there. Where it appears is in the listings of the search engine results.

A keyword-rich description tag doesn't help your ranking. With my own testing, I have not found it to impact rankings but it certainly helps click-through rates. Either way, you want to have your description keyword-optimized for your visitors' benefit, so they can get a clear view of what your website is all about. A strong call to action with a phone number in the description is a smart tactic to get users to act. I have people calling me direct from organic listings, without ever visiting my page.

To incorporate a description from your website, as with the title, you use HTML tags. There's a difference from the type of tag you used for title, though. The difference is there's no specific description tag; instead it's a property for what's known as a meta tag. What is a meta tag? A meta tag is a type of HTML coding that provides descriptive information about your website. Search engine bots read meta tags to determine where to place websites. The next chapter delves into meta tags, but for now the meta tag code you need for a website description is:

```
<head>
<title>Web Page Title With Keywords Go Here</title>
```

FIGURE 3–26. Jon Rognerud search results—TITLE+DESCRIPTION tags text.

```
<meta name="description" content="Your website page description with
keywords also here">
</head>
```

The code that has been bolded is the necessary meta tag. This description should be placed on every page on your site. Note: For larger systems, a CMS can be programmed to auto-populate some of this information. Some pages will be more important than others. Google will also pull what it thinks is most relevant, and it's not always static. The element that lets the search engine know the description is the name property. As you'll learn later, the name property can be set to a variety of elements, but when it's set to "description," the search engine is able to read the description of the website. In our example, the description is "Your website description," which would be posted in search engine listings.

However, sometimes search engines treat this differently. Yahoo! will sometimes skip this description, and read directly from text on the page. If you are listed in ODP (DMOZ) or Yahoo!, special tags override descriptions from those directories. Google calls these "snippets" (Figure 3–27).

```
<meta name="robots" content="noodp">   (Google)

<meta name="robots" content="noydir">   (Yahoo!)
```

FIGURE 3–27. NOODP NOYODIR tag examples.

In terms of how to write a description, make it more original than your title. Also, while you do want to incorporate keywords, don't make your description simply a glorified list of keywords. Remember, real people are going to see your description through the search engine listings. If it's not written appropriately, visitors may think the site is not relevant or, even worse, think it's a spam ad. Make sure your description is well written, with appropriate sentence structure and grammar, and keep it short. While there is no consensus on what is considered too long for search engines, most webmasters tend to make their descriptions about 15 words long or approximately 160 characters, using one or two sentences.

Sage Lewis put together a study about Google, Yahoo!, and Bing at sagerock.com/blog/title-tag-meta-description-length/ if you want to read more.

WANT MORE ROGNERUD ADVICE?

I've been working online since the mid-1990s, and have architected, written, and launched many websites since then, both as an independent consultant with smaller businesses as well as a contractor and employee at larger corporations.

I've seen the good, bad, and the (really) ugly when it comes to creating, organizing, and managing web and marketing projects online. Chances are, I've seen EXACTLY what you are going through, or trying to do now. I can probably help you get set off in the right direction.

When you're ready, hop on over to www.jonrognerud.com and click on "Products and Services."

Your satisfaction is important to me, and guaranteed. So, you risk very little by checking it out at least.

For the buyer of this book:
Visit www.jonrognerud.com and click on products and
services now. See how I can help you.

Chapter 4

How to Perform Competitive Research

Competitive research and analysis is important for any business, whether online or offline. In this section, you'll learn the process and tools we use to analyze marketplaces and to find out more about your competitors.

You should use these techniques for your own business, and you'll get more insights to your marketplace and competitors that can and will give you a bigger edge. You should not take this lightly, and make sure you spend enough time to get a clearer picture. It will save you money in the long run and help build your business faster.

Additional tools and tips are available in the Resources section, and also online in the membership area at www.jonrognerud.com/optimizationbook.

LEARN TO ANALYZE THE MARKET

Marian called my office to ask for SEO help for her website. She had an information products website. She was a speaker, and had hoped to take her knowledge and turn it into passive income so that she could cut down on her travel schedule.

She had spent thousands of dollars on her site and several internet marketing campaigns, but had failed to sell more than a few books. "Jon, help! This internet venture is bleeding me dry. What am I doing wrong?" I grabbed a notepad and pen and started to ask some questions. "Tell me more about your target market, Marian."

"Well, they are internet users."

I asked the question in a different way. "Can you describe your ideal customer? What problems are they trying to solve? How do they decide to buy from you? Are they male or female? What age range do they belong to? What do they do for a living? What are their incomes? Are they college graduates or have no college at all? And, what separates you from your competitors (Unique Selling Proposition, or USP)? Why should I buy from you vs. any other competitive option? (Including doing nothing at all?)"

Marian was stumped. We talked for 30 minutes, and she could not provide a single viable detail about her target market. Marian is a highly intelligent woman who had enjoyed years of success in the corporate world. Yet, even she made the mistake that so many make online: She lacked a marketing plan. (When I showed her Quantcast.com, she started to get the picture. You should, too. But be forewarned: A tool is just a tool. You need to dive deep into the psyche of your market. You'll learn more about this later.)

Website marketing is really no different than marketing for other media such as television, radio, or magazines. While you don't need a marketing degree to successfully promote your website, understanding the basics of market analysis will get you a lot farther than competitors who don't have this knowledge. What should you know about

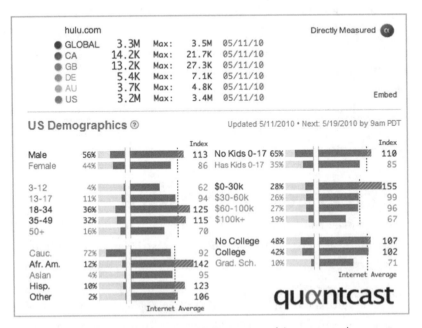

FIGURE 4–1. Quantcast US Demographics screenshot.

the basics of market analysis? A market analysis should include: market size, market growth rate, market profitability, industry cost structure, distribution channels, market trends, and key success factors. This section discusses each of these elements in detail.

Market Size

Market size refers to the size of your potential customer base. In the case of internet marketing, a basic keyword analyzer can give you some idea of what people are looking for, at least on the internet. However, it isn't a cure-all, because you have to deal with the element of competition (which is covered in upcoming sections). This is not to say that website marketing isn't worthwhile, but you may have to use other keywords for marketing purposes. Therefore, you need to know if what you're promoting has a large enough market even when lesser keywords are used. This is why you should also consider offline means of determining your market size. You can find data through the government (Census Bureau, Small Business Administration), industry trade associations, and professional organizations. Even customer surveys. You can also visit your local library's reference section for a wealth of industry data and statistics.

Market Growth Rate

A large market size is nice, but if your market isn't going to grow over time, you won't be able to rely on it for future sales. Conversely, if you find that your market size is initially small, but will grow over time, you may still want to consider using that market outlet.

To determine your market growth rate, first think about any products or services that relate to what you're trying to promote. What keywords are associated with these companies? This is not for the purpose of using those particular keywords, but rather to get a view of how well similar businesses have fared.

Another approach you could take is conduct surveys (try SurveyMonkey.com) asking X number of people if they would be interested in your product or service, and what problems they are facing in their business. These surveys don't have to be elaborate. In fact, you could start by asking friends or family. Begin by getting the opinions of at least ten people. You could ask more questions on Yahoo! Answers, specific niche groups (Google Groups), and Epinions.com. There are other advantages to soliciting feedback from your "potential market." The feedback could uncover potential gaps or flaws. It could also lead you to think of avenues that you would not have pursued. If you look at eBay, Amazon, and Shopping.com—you'll find top sellers of products that may help you. Google Trends and Google Ad Planner can also provide really good insight. Note: numbers are guides, should not be construed as actual, and will vary from tool to tool.

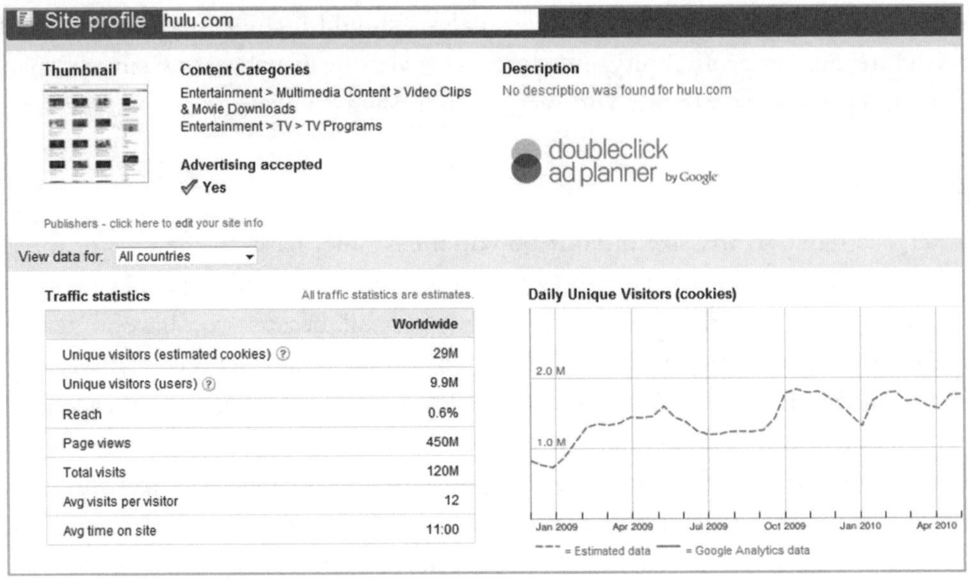

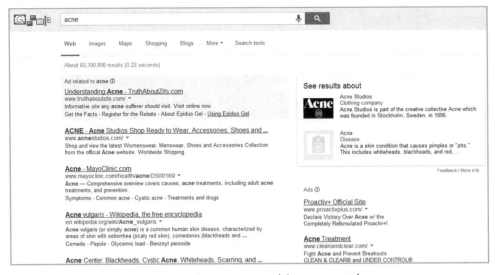

FIGURE 4–2. Google Ad Planner—Hulu Site Profile.

If the results of your surveys are positive, consider pursuing your business idea as it exists. If only a small group is interested in your project, you have an advantage and a disadvantage. The advantage is that with a smaller number of people interested, you have a niche market you could exploit. The disadvantage, however, is that depending on the size of the niche, you may not get as many sales or leads. If you pursue a niche

FIGURE 4–3. Acne—competitiveness results.

market, go for one you can dominate. A current trend in business is to "go small," which simply means slicing your market into segments and rather than trying to dominate a broad slice, dominating a niche. If you do choose a broad, or "popular," market, research the gaps in that market and compete by fulfilling a need that is unmet. For example, in your industry is service a common facet that is lacking? If so, make service one of your core competencies and compete by leveraging that.

If you include the keyword phrase you are targeting as a "phrase" or even "exact" match into Google, you'll see a more narrow view into the number of searches and ads applicable (see Figure 4–4). It's a guide that can help you to see how competitive it is. Here, you can see that *acne* by itself is too broad a keyword for targeting but contains a massive number of pages containing that word (as expected). You'll also recognize highly trusted domains to be listed, as well as our friend Mr. Wikipedia.

However, if you break this down further and use a long-tail keyword, placing it in brackets (quotes), you'll see a more reasonable number. You also see that it contains ads and that people are paying, which assumes that it's a profitable niche (see Figure 4–4).

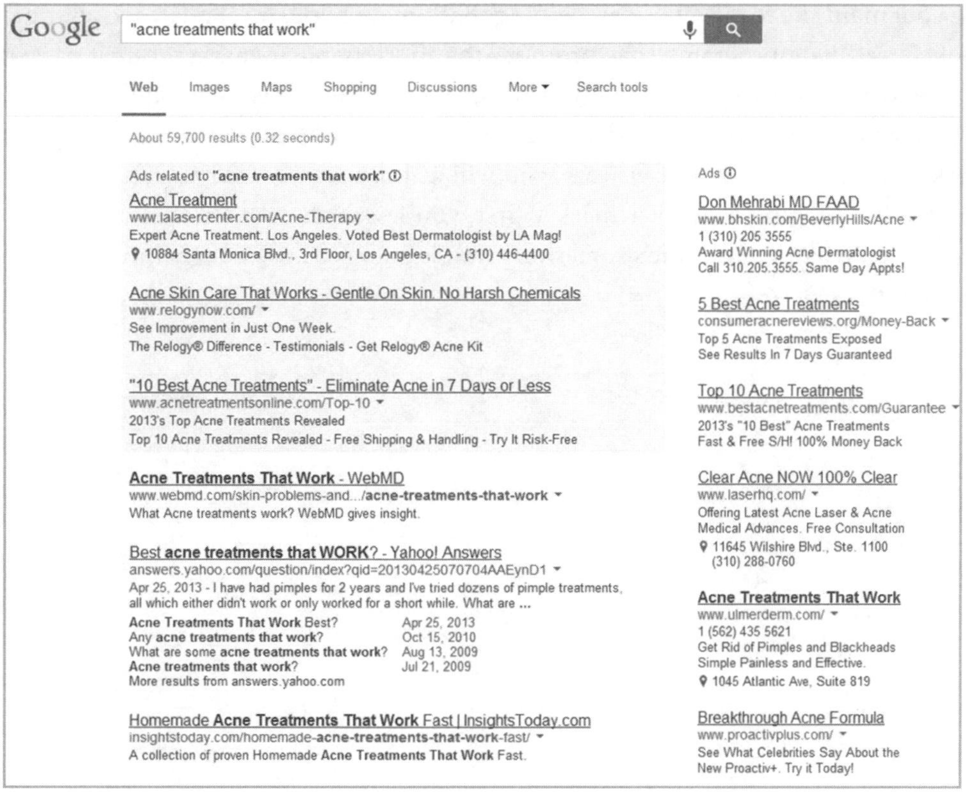

FIGURE 4–4. "Acne" search—broken down.

FOCUS GROUPS

Need an opinion? Create your own focus group to gain information on your market. Invite a group of people from your target demographic to your office or other quiet gathering place, and collect your necessary data. People are often willing to participate for something as simple as a paid lunch! These are sometimes referred to as "masterminds."

To validate this even further, you can get guidance numbers from the Google keywords tool. You can see that it has reasonable traffic and an advertiser and figure the click cost is "high." Here, I show the phrase match option in results, but I'll normally check phrases and end up using the exact matches for my campaigns. Review the arrows below for more detail, and test this yourself.

Whether you choose a niche market or a larger market, all of these principles apply. Use your main site to talk about something that's more popular yet relates to your niche. Look for affiliate programs that promote the more popular market, but leave you a chance to make some money. You can advertise your business as a separate subtopic link or as a separate website altogether. What happens is that by promoting a more popular market you get a number of visitors who will at least get exposed to your business. If you concentrate on the weaker market first, you lessen the chance that you'll get any visitors at all, particularly if it's something that is going to have a higher market growth rate over time.

Keyword Planner — Add ideas to your plan	Your product or service: acne treatments that work					

Targeting
- United States
- All languages
- Google
- Negative keywords

Customize your search
- Keyword filters
  - Avg. monthly searches ≥ 0
  - Suggested bid ≥ $0.00
  - Ad impr. share ≥ 0%
- Keyword options
  - Show broadly related ideas
  - Hide keywords in my account
  - Hide keywords in my plan
- Include/Exclude

Search terms	Avg. monthly searches	Competition	Suggested bid	Ad impr. share	Add to plan
acne treatments that work	720	High	$3.48	0%	»

1 - 1 of 1 keywords

Keyword (by relevance)	Avg. monthly searches	Competition	Suggested bid	Ad impr. share	Add to plan
acne treatment that works	260	High	$3.77	0%	»
acne treatments that work fast	70	High	$3.49	0%	»
best acne treatment	14,800	High	$2.79	0%	»
acne treatment	33,100	High	$3.27	0%	»
acne treatments	2,400	High	$3.73	0%	»
natural acne treatment	5,400	High	$3.96	0%	»

FIGURE 4–5. Google Keyword Planner screenshot for "acne treatments that work."

> ### INSIDER TIP
>
> An affiliate program is like a reseller or revenue-sharing program. I split money with you, depending on what and how much you sell. A broker house, such as Click-Bank.com for digital products, is a great place to begin. It even takes care of the monetary transactions for both parties. Commission Junction (cj.com) is also popular, but is slanted more toward physical goods. See the Resources section at the end of the book for even more sites.

Market Profitability

Market profitability determines how prosperous a market can make a business. Harvard business professor Michael Porter is famous for his Five Forces of Competitive Position Model. The model provides a simple perspective for assessing and analyzing competitive strength and position. Porter's five forces that drive competition are:

1. Existing competitive rivalry between suppliers
2. Threat of new market entrants
3. Bargaining power of buyers
4. Power of suppliers
5. Threat of substitute products (including technology change)

How to Compare Market Profitability

Use Porter's model to analyze each element and assess how each will affect your market profitability. If you're new to business and marketing principles, do a little research and learn how to assess yourself and your competitors. In the internet marketing arena, a quick and easy way to analyze the competitive landscape is to use the keyword analyzer.

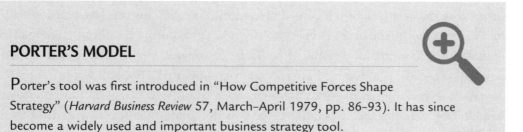

PORTER'S MODEL

Porter's tool was first introduced in "How Competitive Forces Shape Strategy" (*Harvard Business Review* 57, March–April 1979, pp. 86–93). It has since become a widely used and important business strategy tool.

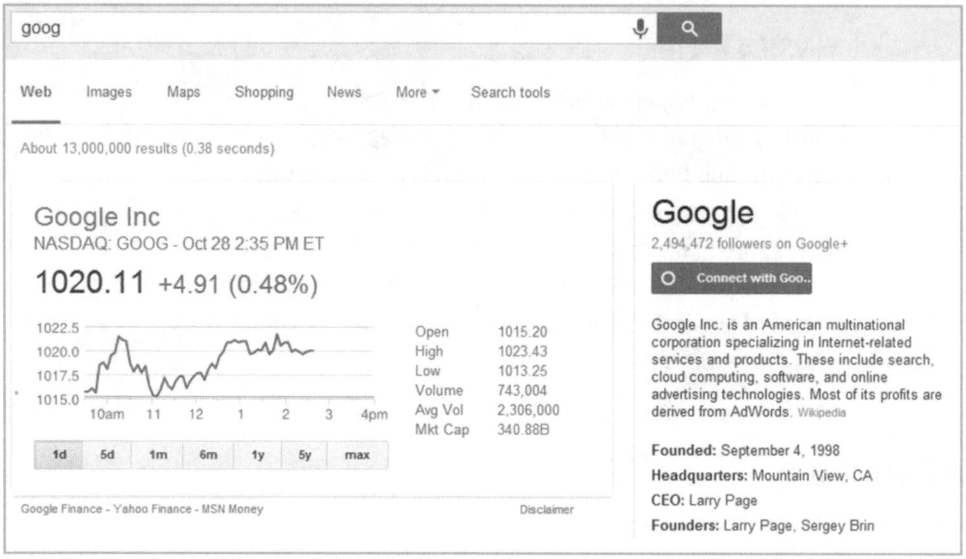

FIGURE 4–6. Google stock ticker search.

Highlight one of the terms that pops up. Enter the term into Google or another popular search engine. Take a look at the sponsored listings (these appear at the top of the search engine results) and the pay-per-click ads (these usually appear on the right side of the screen). Note the companies that pop up, and do a detailed search on them. Wikipedia is a good resource because it can tell you all kinds of basic financial information about a company. You can find out more using ticker symbols, and Google will present the OneBox for that symbol.

For extensive business information, Hoovers.com and InfoUsa.com are two of the best sources of comprehensive company data. Some of its information is free, but a paid subscription will give you access to tremendous amounts of key data. Dun and Bradstreet (dnb.com) and Yahoo! Finance are also great sources of company data. Salesforce.com has Data.com and provides lots of company details.

Of most importance is the revenue information: If it has gone up, there will be a little up arrow next to it; if it's gone down, a down arrow. This can give you some idea of whether your own market is going to be successful, but be careful. If a company is making huge amounts of revenue, it could be considered a rival market with barriers to entry, especially if it doesn't have too many competitors. IBM and Apple are perfect examples. If you wanted to try to manufacture a whole new brand of computers, you wouldn't be very successful because these two dominate that scene, with IBM being the leader. Most of the software and peripherals made are created for either of these computers. Obviously, potential customers wouldn't want to buy a computer that they couldn't even use because they wouldn't be able to find software or peripherals designed for the new computer.

Expanding on the IBM/Apple example, however, if you were able to come up with a new computer that was significantly cheaper than IBM or Apple machines provide your own brand of software customers could buy, many might consider making the switch. So, if a market does have barriers to entry, it doesn't necessarily mean the market is closed to you. You may just need to develop different tactics to get your products or services sold. There are companies that provide simpler computers to developing countries, for example, and the Toshiba laptop Viamo, which is specifically designed for medical purposes. Serve unique, different, and useful products to niche markets, and you can win.

INSIDER TIP

Make it easy for your audience to see your unique sales or value proposition. In a different marketplace, millions were made on the slogan: "Fresh, hot pizza delivered to your door in under 30 minutes—or it's free" (Domino's). It began with a strong promise; it was specific, and contained a guarantee. Can you do something similar for your business? What small change could you make today? I suggest a strong offer coupled with an incredible guarantee.

Industry Cost Structure

Cost is one of the most important elements when it comes to marketing. Naturally, most consumers want to get the best value for their dollar, but don't get trapped into thinking that lower means better. If you price a product or service significantly below the industry cost structure, consumers might become suspicious. They may think you're charging less because your product or service is not as legitimate or valuable as a more established one. Consequently, they may buy at the higher price from a different company.

This is why you will definitely want to check out your competitors' pricing before determining the prices for your products or services. The best way to do this is to use online comparison sites. Most, such as Google Products, show the prices that products or services are going for, but others such as ConsumerSearch.com show this and also provide consumer reviews. The downside to sites like ConsumerSearch is that they tend to be limited in what they show, which is why you want to use more than one of these portals.

Once you get abreast of your competitors' pricing structure, you should set your prices accordingly. As a newcomer to the industry, you don't want to price too high,

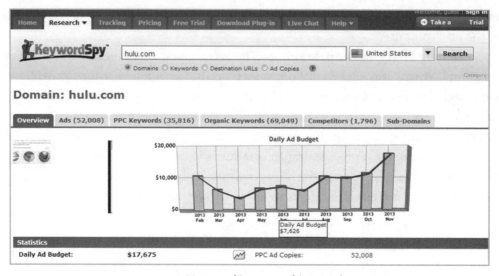

FIGURE 4–7. KeywordSpy—tracking Hulu.com.

unless you're offering something spectacularly better than your competitors. On the other hand, you don't want to price too low. You'll want to price mid-range. Many established businesses such as Amazon or Walmart price only a few dollars less than their competitors, yet when they do their promotions, instead of saying such-and-such item is a couple dollars lower, they'll say they're offering a 50 percent discount, or something of that nature. You may want to try that approach for your own business. However, Amazon and Walmart have built-in cost efficiencies that let them price lower; take care that you run the numbers and understand your costs so you that don't price below your margins.

Since keywords form the core of search engine marketing, you'd be wise to reveal what your competitors are using. Tools like Spyfu.com and KeywordSpy.com are good places to start.

Keep in mind that what you are really selling to customers is "value." While it's important to understand competitive pricing and to price accordingly, customers pay for the value you offer. Your pricing is not only the result of competitive models but should factor in your cost structure. You may have a lower cost to deliver a product or service and, as such, can price a little lower than your competitors. Be careful, however, when engaging in a price war, for in these wars there are no winners. An old sales adage says that if you win customers on price, you lose them on price. What this means is that when price is the key element in deciding to buy, customers will buy from someone else if they have a lower price. The airline industry is a good example of ongoing price wars. It's far better to create value and sell to deeper needs than price alone.

Distribution Channels

In terms of distribution channels, how are you marketing your product or service? Are you using an online distribution channel or a brick-and-mortar one? Are you using both? If online, how will your service be delivered? For example, a bookseller might use self-publishing portals and affiliates as distribution channels. You may think that how you sell your product or service wouldn't matter in an age when millions of Americans and people overseas have access to the internet. However, this does not necessarily mean that they'll be comfortable buying over the internet from you. A lot of consumers feel uncomfortable buying from new ecommerce sites, especially if their business is exclusively online. They may worry that the site is not legitimate, and they are risking their money. Granted, this may not be as much of a concern if you're selling cheap products, but for merchandise or services that are higher priced, your company might get bypassed for a more established company with a track record.

While you can control for many of these factors, remember that they call it "building a business" for a reason. Very few businesses skyrocket from $0 to $10 million overnight! You get customers by applying sound business and marketing principles. Customers are taking a risk when buying from you (as they are with every business), but there are ways to minimize that risk for the customer. Money-back guarantees are a classic way to minimize risk. You are assuring customers that they won't lose their money by offering them a guarantee. We live in an age of skepticism. Folks have been burned too many times. The irresistible offer works, but don't make it so grand that nobody will believe it. That can end up working against you. Marketing guru Dan Kennedy's book *The Ultimate Marketing Plan* (Adams Media, 2006) talks about this, and gives you more tips you can use.

ONLINE RESOURCE

Read more about conversion and landing page techniques available online at www.jonrognerud.com/optimizationbook.

Another way to minimize risk and establish trust is to offer "proof." Testimonials are a wonderful way to give proof of your value. As you obtain customers, ask if they would be willing to provide a testimonial. You could offer an incentive for them to do this, such as a free item or a discount on their next purchase. If they are web marketers, you could offer to promote their website on yours in exchange for their testimonial. When collecting your testimonials, if your customers will let you try to include their email addresses so potential customers will have a way to contact them. Anybody can make up

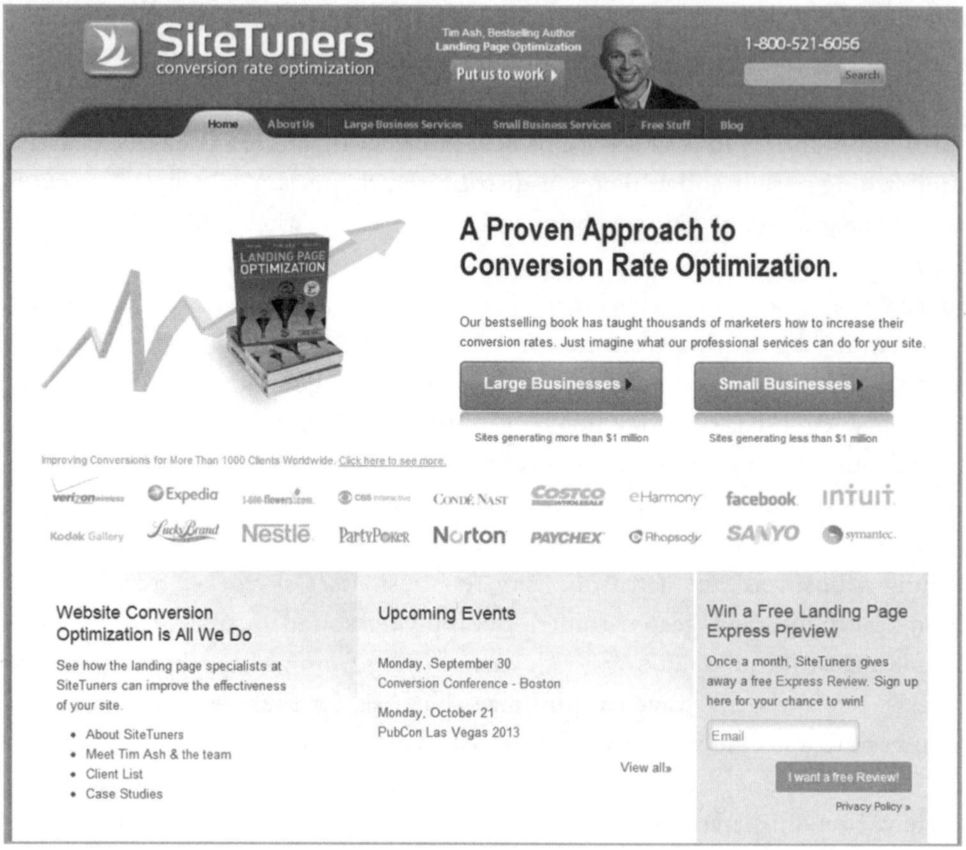

FIGURE 4–8. SiteTuners' homepage.

a testimonial, but if you provide an email address, many visitors feel the testimonial is more concrete, because they have someone they can contact.

Tim Ash, founder of SiteTuners.com in San Diego, uses his own site to test various elements on the page, and includes a large list of testimonial logos and a link. These items don't take over the look of the page. He told me they have been tested, and have worked well in the background, as "faded" items.

Another thing you can do is join the Better Business Bureau. This costs a few hundred dollars, but the investment is well worth it. A lot of people trust the Better Business Bureau; in fact, if a business is not established, it's the first resource that I go to for determining whether they're legitimate. Of course, you have to make sure that your business does right by its customers because the Better Business Bureau will report you. Then again, you should be doing that anyway. Besides, businesses that aren't members of the Better Business Bureau also receive bad reports, which is one of the reasons people love the company so much. Once you join the Better Business Bureau, you are able to post its logo on your site. This logo alone will significantly improve consumer confidence in your business. This is particularly the case if you are trying to sell in an industry where the distribution channels have traditionally been through brick-and-mortar enterprises.

Market Trends

Market trends refer to how a market is changing. Market trends include customers, competitors, and the industry as a whole. Being able to determine a future trend and positioning yourself to take advantage of it is a competitive advantage. It's important to understand not only what customers want today but also what will they want tomorrow. Are there unmet needs in the industry? What are your competitors doing? Are they shifting strategies?

Here again the survey is a useful tool. However, instead of surveying outsiders, you survey those who have bought from you. Current customers are one of the most valuable and underused resources of any business. Current customers can help you improve your business and develop products and services that have a market (rather than creating something and hoping there's a market for it), and they're an excellent source of revenue (upsells and referrals).

If your business is new and you don't have a customer base, you'll want to conduct surveys on the basis of how customers' needs were met from businesses similar to yours. Again, Yahoo! Answers can be useful for this purpose. If you're carrying out a survey of your own customers, you can do so from their email (assuming they are on your email list) or from a special survey area on your site. (You don't need to have surveys visible from your homepage if you don't want to.) You'll want to offer an incentive for the survey, though many companies seem to have success even when they don't offer incentives. If your resources are low, consider trying to get surveys for free, but you'll have to send it to a larger number of people if you don't offer an incentive.

LIFETIME VALUE

When calculating your marketing ROI, don't forget the lifetime value of each customer. The lifetime value is how much that customer will spend with you over time, rather than on a one-time sale. For example, if a customer will buy from you an average of four times spending $2,000 total and you spent $10 to obtain him as a customer, your "profit" per customer is $1,990.

ONLINE RESOURCE

A free tool (paid services means more features) that you can use to easily create surveys is Survey Monkey.com.

Key Success Factors

What are key success factors? In short, they are all the elements you must have to be successful. For example, commonly accepted key success factors include brand or name recognition, access to unique resources, customer loyalty, financial resources, and access to distribution channels. This section goes through each of these recommended key success factors.

Brand/Name Recognition. When you're starting out, you won't have the advantage of a big name, unless you're successful enough to merge with an already established company. So, to build up your reputation, do good business. Make sure you respond to your customers' orders promptly. If you can't, set up an autoresponder and/or hire a person to deal with orders. (You'll want to do the latter if your business becomes extremely prosperous.) Offer rebates if the customer is dissatisfied with your product or service. Most of all, keep up a friendly persona. Generally, as the adage goes, the customer is always right. This is not always an easy rule to live by, but it's important that a beginning business try as much as it can to observe it.

The more you do good business and the more you promote yourself, the more you will get a name going in internet markets. The speed of information today can help or harm you. If you deliver terrible service, a blogger can write about his or her experience and within hours your name and reputation can be decimated throughout cyberspace.

It's easy to track this via Google Alerts, or for instant updates check search on Twitter. SocialMention.com is another free tool, as is Mention.net. (Radian6.com and ScoutLabs.com [now Lithium Social Web at lithium.com] are powerful tools in this arena, but quite costly.) Trackur.com from expert marketer Andy Beal is your best, low-cost solution for this. You get a free trial to start.

Problems inevitably occur, but be responsive and fix them so that you build a solid foundation of integrity for your company. Of course, with the prevalence of the internet today, a name in internet markets almost guarantees a name in offline markets, although this is not always the case. Specialized services that cater to small niches may only find their fame through search engine placement.

Access to Unique Resources. Do you have direct access to a specific market, particularly one that would be interested in the products or services you have to offer? For example,

FIGURE 4–9. Trackur reputation management monitoring.

if you sell children's products and you're active at your child's school, the teachers and the parents of the other children could be a perfect base to whom you could market. Your personal connection with this market gives you an advantage as someone serving that market. You have access that another marketer would have to obtain through email marketing, direct mail, or even search engine marketing. Additionally, if your customers like your products, they could use word-of-mouth to market your products further to their family and friends. Don't underestimate the personal element when it comes to marketing.

Customer Loyalty. If you do well by your customers, more often than not they'll do well by you. Recurring customers not only ensure a steady stream of income, they can

---

INSIDER TIP

Don't get caught having somebody build traffic to your site if you don't have unique and compelling content with a simple "1–2–3" click purchase opportunity. You're wasting your money. Think of traffic in terms of conversion. Checkpoint: If you were a potential customer, would you buy from your own site? If not, what would you change?

---

also do your marketing for you through word-of-mouth and/or testimonials. Existing customers give you unique reach to your target market—other people like them. Too often businesses fail to develop long-term relationships with their customers. Even if you're in a business where repeat sales are years apart, e.g., real estate or automotive, your current customers can be a good source of referrals. Treat them well and not only will they buy from you again, they'll tell others to buy from you, too.

Financial Resources. To start your business, you're going to need money. However, depending on what you do, you may not need much money. For example, a virtual service such as word processing wouldn't require much in startup costs. All you really need is a computer and a printer. Even printing costs could be reduced if you email documents to your clients. As long as you can get your website indexed high in search engines, you could make money without having to invest much.

INSIDER TIP

If you start a Google AdWords campaign, it will cost you $5. You can go to eBay and search for "AdWords coupons." You could buy one for $20 instead and receive a $100 voucher you can use to test your keywords, ads, and pages! That's $80 more to do some testing with. Ultimately, if you cannot afford to buy a customer, you don't have a business.

On the other hand, if you're running a business that requires inventory, you may need to invest thousands up front. If you can't sell the inventory, you would incur a financial loss, which could force you to shut down your business. This is why you need to carefully examine your market before you open your internet doors. If it looks like you're going to make a profit, you can consider getting a business loan so you don't have to risk all your own money. If you're trying to sell a smaller amount of inventory (say, less than $5,000), consider getting a credit card. Credit cards are easier to get than business loans, and the monthly payment even at $5,000 would probably still be affordable.

Access to Distribution Channels. Don't limit your advertising to search engines, even if you get a first-place ranking. Other advertising mediums include direct mail, radio, magazines, and, when you really get money, television. Google AdWords, for example, is available for print, radio, video, and mobile. If you're low on funds, you can use the cheap, old-fashioned method of flier distribution. Make sure to get permission before you distribute your fliers, so you don't get in legal trouble. (I placed a promo business card in an office elevator once, and somebody took the time to leave me a message to stop—in a not-so-friendly way. I did.) The best marketing strategy employs more than one medium. Today, you should consider online and offline strategies (i.e., postcards). Some tips to start a direct-mail campaign can be found on http://www.jonrognerud. com/how-to-kick-start-direct-mail-marketing/.

Again, this is why it is vitally important to develop a comprehensive marketing plan for your business that maximizes your opportunities. A simple (but not easy-to-complete) SWOT analysis is a great start. Google it, and download a template to fill out, or head over to the book membership area (www.jonrognerud.com/optimizationbook) to download a sample.

INSIDER TIP

One of the top product lines to get into are information products. They have the lowest overhead and the biggest ROI. There are internet marketers making millions every year selling their own and affiliate market products—no inventory! Go to ClickBank.com to start. Consider adding a product for your own company. You are now in the educational-centric, info-based marketing business!

What Happens When You Don't Use Market Analysis

Remember our story of the pizzeria in Chapter 1? While failure to market ultimately led to the demise of the business, the owners made a crucial mistake before opening—they didn't conduct a market analysis. The business was family-run. The family was Italian and loved cooking, and had become legendary for its unique homemade pizza creations. The father and sons had worked in restaurants, so were familiar with the industry. It had been a long-held family dream to own a pizzeria. When the space became available, they decided that the timing was right.

The location was heavily trafficked, and they believed that the other businesses were a perfect complement—no competitors. On the surface it seemed like an ideal location, but deeper digging would have turned up a contrary opinion. The location was conducive to the other businesses.

The surf shop was close to the beach and had convenient free parking. The dry cleaners was a long-established business that offered delivery and pickup service.

However, people on their way to or coming back from the beach weren't stopping for pizza. Those in the mood for a slice of pizza would grab one while at the beach. People leaving the beach weren't stopping as they were likely eager to get home and get cleaned up from a day at the beach. Just a few blocks down, another busy strip mall offered space for lease. This location was close to nearby businesses and had other food businesses that would have complemented the pizzeria.

What can you learn from this story? Basically, do your homework before you start your business so you can save yourself a lot of time and money. While many business owners have failed, only to find success later, you'll reach your goal much faster with a little advance research. A market analysis is not a guarantee of success. Many factors contribute to success. However, you owe it yourself to be armed with as much information as possible to ensure that your business model is viable. Of course, even the best market analysis can't offer a 100 percent guarantee—you'll never get that in the world of marketing. But if you do it right, you can get perhaps an 80 percent guarantee that your business will be successful. This is a lot better than doing nothing, which would give you a guarantee of 0 percent.

WEBSITE ANALYSIS

Periodically, you should perform a detailed analysis of your site to see if it's still optimized for search engines. To do this you need a software program. Some of the hosting companies may have companion products (GoDaddy TrafficBlazer) or you could use a free site analysis program. A good free site analysis program can be found at Websitegrader.com.

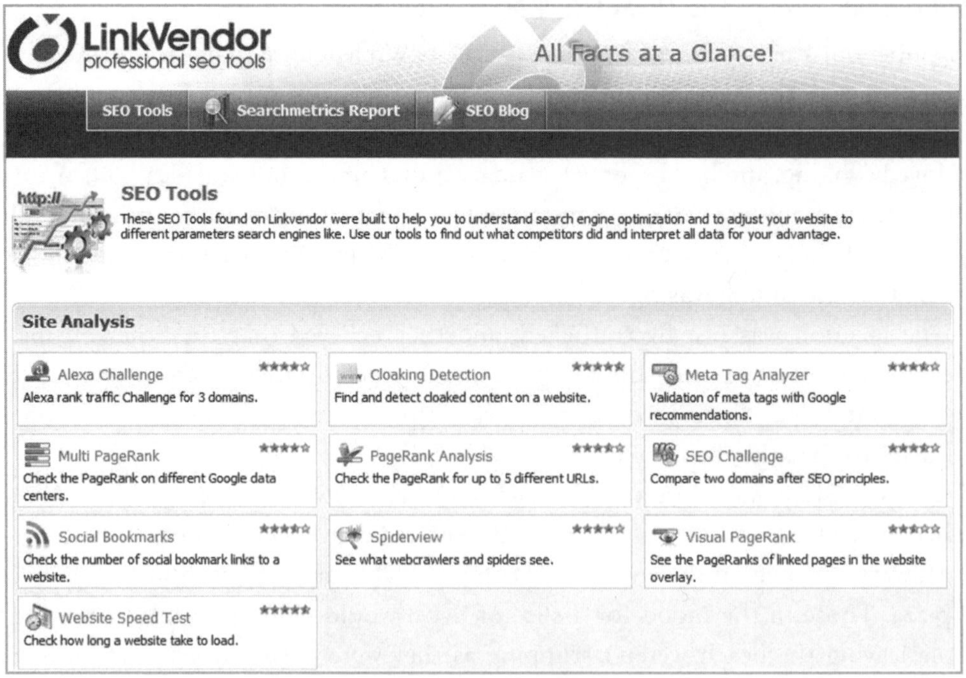

FIGURE 4–10. LinkVendor tool set.

LinkVendor.com is another web-based program that offers so much you almost don't need a paid site analysis program, although a paid program in some instances might be faster than LinkVendor. LinkVendor services are provided via SearchMetrics.

Paid programs may provide even more features, deeper insights, automatic reports, downloadable templates, better integration with all your online marketing efforts, and more.

You can try power tools from Raven for free (30 days) that help you track every aspect of your search marketing campaign, even social media. Raven has keyword and competitive research tools; link, contact, and blog managers; a social media monitor; SERP trackers (ranking); and even a custom Firefox plugin as a toolbar. Pricing starts at $19 a month. Visit RavenTools.com.

What do most site analysis programs check for? Use LinkVendor.com as a model; a good site analysis program should check for link value, link popularity, domain popularity, IP domains, page rank, SEO comparisons against other sites, your site's SERP (Search Engine Results Page), outbound links, keyword density, cloaked links, how your site is being spidered by search engine bots, and how fast your site is operating. The following paragraphs describe each of these factors to give you a better understanding of how effective your site really is.

Here is a list of free tools you can use for social media tracking and monitoring:

- Google Alerts
- Bloglines.com (now local)
- Search.twitter.com (use advanced search)

FIGURE 4–11. Raven Internet Marketing Tools.

- Mention.net
- Keotag.com
- Netvibes.com
- Topsy.com
- Datasift.com (Twitter Firehose and more)
- Socialmention.com

Some paid tools are:

- Trackur.com (fast, easy, good place to start)
- Sysomos.com
- SalesForce Marketing Cloud, formerly Radian6, (expensive, but the most all-inclusive)
- For tech-minded folks: Write your own app or service. Use Datasift.com and its APIs to access the history and social media (big) data

I have found that most pro SEOs use a pool of tools. There is simply no one tool to do it all. In fact, as you become more proficient, you may pull back from some of these paid tools and only use two or three. You have become the master and certainly don't need a (paid or otherwise) tool to reveal your keyword density. Consider building your own if you want exact requirements for clients (assuming you're a search service company, for example).

ONLINE RESOURCE

See other tools in the bookmark section of www.jonrognerud.com/optimizationbook. An advanced tool like OpenSiteExplorer is used by top SEO firms and marketers to analyze link profiles, a key SEO component.

Link/Advertising Value

Internet marketing should not end with search optimization. It's a multichannel, multifaceted approach. Establishing partnerships are important online and off. Search engine ranking, as one measure, is not affected by linking to established high-trafficked sites. But you do provide value to the user, so I recommend it. Do this through a link exchange, in which you advertise a webmaster's link on your site in exchange for its advertising your link on its site. Otherwise, you should consider purchasing advertising space from another website. However, big caveat here: Do not do this as a regular exercise. A good value exchange is based on trust and equal interest and understanding of trust.

TRADE RULES

Keep in mind that while buying and selling links is not recommended by the search engines (Google in particular), you may buy and sell advertising space. Google recommends using a special tag (rel=nofollow) on the hyperlink to not unfairly inflate or pass PageRank.

The old reciprocal link exchanges have been overused. Other options exist for visibility and traffic. The best resource you can use for finding link space for sale is through self-service portals such as AdBrite.com (now sitescout.com). Also, when you search for blogs (blogsearch.google.com), you'll often see an empty 125-by-125 box with "Advertise here." Simply contact the webmaster and negotiate a price. Demand detailed traffic reports, and make sure it's relevant to your business. Negotiate terms. Do not just accept what they say.

Before you buy advertising space, however, make sure what you're buying will earn you enough profit. This is where determining link value comes into play. If you're using LinkVendor.com as your site analysis program, all you have to do is enter the URL of the website you want to advertise on, along with the currency in which you would like to see the value. If the resulting link value is high yet the price advertised is low, go ahead and purchase advertising space from that website. If the link value is low and the price is high, leave it alone. If the link value and price match, you can make the call. But remember: this is only a tool. Speaking directly to the webmaster or owner will have the biggest impact and will help with a go/no-go on an advertising ROI for you.

The link value tool can also be handy for determining what you should charge for advertising space once your site is popular enough for you to offer this option.

Link Popularity

Link popularity refers to how many web pages link to your site. If you're using the link popularity tool on LinkVendor.com, the tool will show how many links are linked to

ONLINE RESOURCE

See the Bookmarks section on www.jonrognerud.com/optimizationbook for other power tools. The list is updated there.

Backlinks						
	Google G	MSN	Yahoo Y?	Ask	Yahoo!Directory Y?	DMOZ
Links	27	-	708	163	0	0
Sites	66	89	26	11	-	-

FIGURE 4–12. Backlinks analysis chart.

your site on the basis of the most popular search engines: Google, Bing, Yahoo!, Ask, and Alexa. It will also list what is being used in your meta tags, your keywords as listed by Alexa, and your Alexa traffic rank. Alexa is a popular site that helps you determine the traffic of a particular website. However, I don't use one specific site metric over another, and never use them as facts, only guides.

Domain Popularity

There's a lot of controversy concerning link popularity, due to link farms and link spam. In response to this problem, Google checks domain popularity, which is how many sites link to your direct top-level domain name, rather than a specific page within your site. The thought behind domain popularity is that if your top-level URL (rather than a specific page), is linked to the webmaster's interests in advertising your site are more genuine. However, the rules change often, so make sure to visit Google's Webmaster Blog and Guidelines often.

LinkVendor.com's domain popularity tool returns detailed information regarding your domain popularity. This information includes the number of sites yours serves as a backlink on, your page rank (discussed later in this book), and a number determining the effectiveness of your link, otherwise known as link strength. Next, the website returns a detailed list of all the sites that link to your domain name. The site tells you the exact URLs of the websites, the websites' IP addresses, and the page rank of each site. And even better, you can choose to view your results by listing the URL first, the page rank first, or the IP address first.

The downside to this tool is that it can take a long time to list your results, especially if your site is established. The site even tells you that it can take up to 15 minutes to return results. Unfortunately, there is no way around this. What makes it worthwhile is that it does return a lot of helpful information at no extra cost to you.

The LinkVendor tool provides a lot of detail. You have some other options, as well. One new service is the Moz Open Site Explorer (see Figure 4–13), where you can compare URLs against each other. This paid service is growing in popularity. Go to the member access for more information: www.jonrognerud.com/optimizationbook.

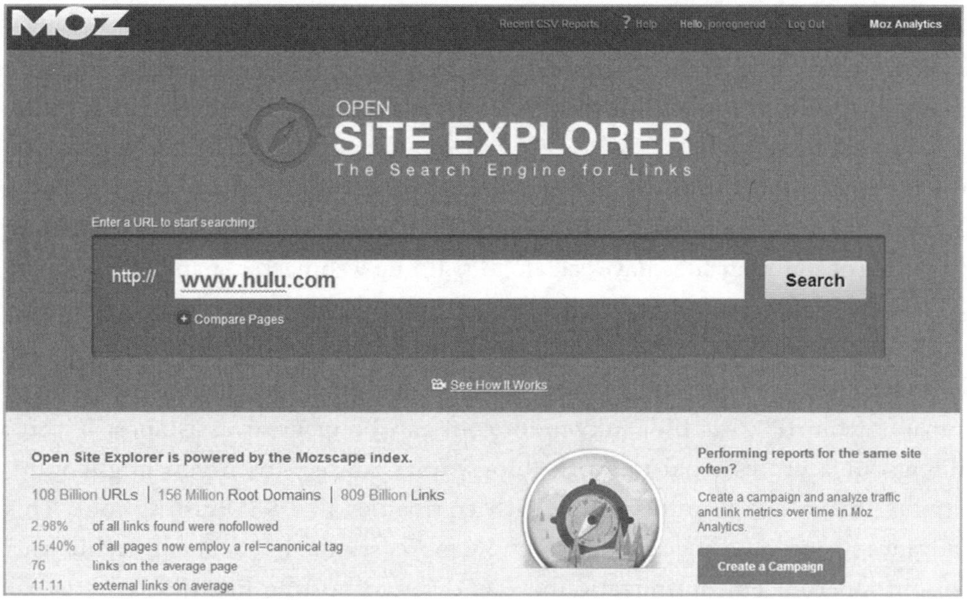

FIGURE 4–13. Open Site Explorer Link Data Checker.

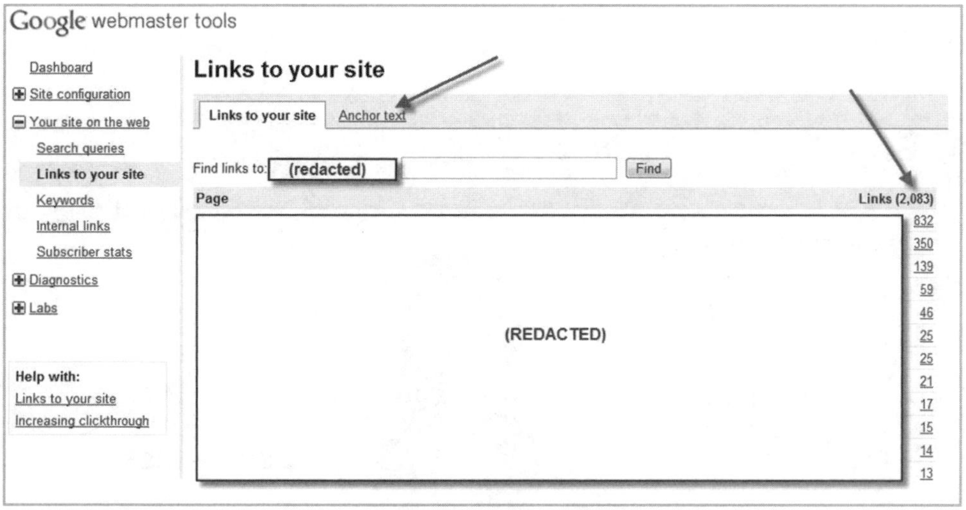

FIGURE 4–14. Google Webmaster Tools.

Do not forget to locate all the data that Google Webmaster provides (see Figure 4–14). It's free, and provides excellent data. It is a must for a serious webmaster today. (Sign up for free at google.com/webmasters.)

IP Domains

The IP domains tool (called "Domains from IP" on LinkVendor.com) shows the domains that link to your IP address. Knowing which sites also share your IP address can help you investigate if there are questionable websites that could potentially harm the reputation of your IP address. Google has stated that this should not be a primary concern of a webmaster. However, my findings have seen that across multiple industries, top-ranking sites have "clean" IPs. If one webmaster spams, then everyone on the same IP address is negatively affected, even if they didn't participate. This is why it's best to get web hosts that use separate IP addresses for each of their clients. Yet, if you can't find one and/or you need the affordability of virtual hosting, the "Domains from IP" tool on LinkVendor.com can be of great assistance. If you are building out a professional network (blogs, for example), then you might want to try (more expensive) account setups with companies like SEOhosting.com. This is an advanced topic, and if you want to know more, see me in the membership area at www.jonrognerud.com/optimizationbook. Advanced hosting like the example below is not required, but is provided as an additional resource. But remember: unnatural and obvious "footprints" on the web can easily be spotted by Google. Any changes may not affect you immediately, but over time you may see less-and-less traffic coming in to your website(s), all due to your trying to game the system.

FIGURE 4–15. SEO Hosting.

PageRank

Your page rank is extremely important when it comes to search optimization. Page rank is calculated by a complex formula that takes into account 200-plus signals, which include the incoming links and their value. At the heart of Google's search engine algorithm is PageRank™. As the name implies, it's a system for ranking web pages. In Google's own words (google.com/technology), "PageRank relies on the uniquely democratic nature of the web by using its vast link structure as an indicator of an individual page's value." In essence, Google interprets a link from page A to page B as a vote by page A for page B. But Google looks at considerably more than the volume of votes, or links, a page receives; for example, it also analyzes the page that casts the vote. Votes cast by pages that are themselves "important" weigh more heavily and help to make other pages "important." Using these and other factors, Google provides its views on the page's relative importance. The simplest way of explanation: Who was the most popular girl or boy in high school? Those people received a "vote" from the other students, and they were always in focus.

Of course, important pages mean nothing to you if they don't match your query. So Google combines PageRank with sophisticated text-matching techniques to find pages that are both important and relevant to your search. Google goes far beyond the number of times a term appears on a page and examines dozens of aspects of the page's content (and the content of the pages linking to it) to determine if it's a good match for your query.

The resulting number ranges from 0 to 10, with 0 being the least relevant to 10 being the most relevant. You can determine your PageRank by typing it in Google's toolbar (if you have this installed in your browser), or you can use LinkVendor.com. Unlike Google's toolbar, LinkVendor.com will tell you if the page rank value returned is accurate. There is also a Google toolbar value (green bar) and the page's true value, the PageRank. Do not place much focus on the green bar. In my mind, Google should remove it. I cannot tell you how many times I tell my clients to focus on other, more important issues. Traffic and conversion, for example!

SEO Comparisons Against Other Sites

LinkVendor.com puts a little fun in site analysis through its "SEO Challenge" tool. This makes SEO comparisons against other sites. You enter the sites you want to compare, and LinkVendor identifies the "winner" and the "loser." The "winner" shows the winning domain name along with a graphic of a crown and a number showing how effectively optimized it is. The "losing" domain name will show the domain name, a trash can graphic, and the same number. Aside from the comedic relief this tool offers, it can actually be a great way to see how your competitors fare when it comes to search engine marketing. If the competing site ranks high, you might want to look at it to see why it's doing better than yours and implement those strategies. You may even want to email the webmaster to see if he or she would be willing to sell advertising space or do a link exchange. (Be careful with this last option, as mentioned earlier. Think about partnerships that make sense and help the users first!)

SERP (Search Engine Results Page)

SERP shows you results from your queries, and you can find out how high your site is in search engine results according to a particular keyword. Wikipedia defines SERP as "the listing of web pages returned by a search engine in response to a keyword query. The results normally include a list of web pages with titles, a link to the page, and a short description showing where the keywords have matched content within the page. A SERP may refer to a single page of links returned, or to the set of all links returned for a search query" (en.wikipedia.org/wiki/SERP). With LinkVendor.com's SERP tool, you enter the URL you want analyzed, the keywords that pertain to it, and the search engines you want to see results for (which are Google, Bing, and Yahoo!). By selecting the appropriate extension, you can also see SERP data for foreign versions of these search engines. For example, if you wanted to see how your site fares in the French version of Google.com, you would select .fr as your extension.

FIGURE 4–16. Google in French.

Outbound Links

Outbound links are links on your site or page that would send your visitors to a completely different site or page. Balancing outbound links is not hard. Ask yourself: What would be a useful link to my reader? How can I provide more information, and send some "link love" across to the other domain? However, it's a fact that overuse is not helpful, and mass listings of links can be associated with spammy sites. One recommendation is no more than 100 links per page. I have found that if I can serve my user and track what I am doing, those results speak better to an outbound link strategy. Don't just pick a number, test it. Every website and marketplace is different. Brands have a different treatment, as you know. Remember: too many outbound links take visitors away from your site, something that you don't want, unless you are trying to coerce the visitor to click on your advertiser, AdSense, or affiliate links (which calls for that strategy). Don't create links for the sake of link building, as this not only diminishes the value to your potential customers but can also get you into trouble with search engines. We also know that PageRank, a measure of authority/trust on the internet and in Google's eyes, gets less valued as more links on a page dilutes each link. Don't over-analyze this. Think about what your users would want first. Helpful links to more information and resources most always win. A highly valuable website on the internet is Wikipedia. Any article there provides many quality outbound links. It's a strong resource, shows authority, and is helpful.

Keyword Density

You learned about keyword density earlier in this book, but as a refresher, keyword density is the percentage of times a keyword appears in your website content. Some of the keyword tools that you learned about earlier, while very useful, lack an element that LinkVendor.com has—namely, the ability to show you your exact SERP. LinkVendor.com's keyword density tool shows you the keyword density of each keyword found on your site. It also provides a graphic of the top search engines, including Google, Bing, Yahoo!, and Ask. If you click on this graphic, you are directed to your exact SERP. Please note: as a tool, this is good, and an example of how many of them work. Don't spend too much time on the density analysis. Focus more on content, structure, and links. Keyword density is "old school." Because this is a sore topic for many, send me a note at contact@jonrognerud.com, and I'll be happy to answer questions about this.

Cloaked Links

Cloaked links are links that are "hidden" from the view of the site visitor. This could be because they are linked through a banner, a button, or text. Cloaked links are a popular approach used by many affiliate marketers to hide unattractive and intimidating affiliate links that, for the visitor, are hard to remember or even undesirable to click on (because some people may be less likely to click on an affiliate link when they see it as an ad).

When designing your website, you might have so many cloaked links that you lose track of them. This is where LinkVendor's cloaked link tool comes in handy. Once you enter the URL, you are shown which links are cloaked. The site shows you graphical versions of these links rather than giving you the specific link itself. There are several plugins for the WordPress platform. Search for "cloaked links" or "affiliate links" in the search area for plugins.

Search Engine Spidering Tool

Search engine spiders, also known as bots, scour the web looking for websites to include in search engine listings. While keywords are important, spiders determine listings by the number of incoming, quality, and relevant links related to a site (incoming links refers to how many websites link to you). Outbound links are helpful to users, but

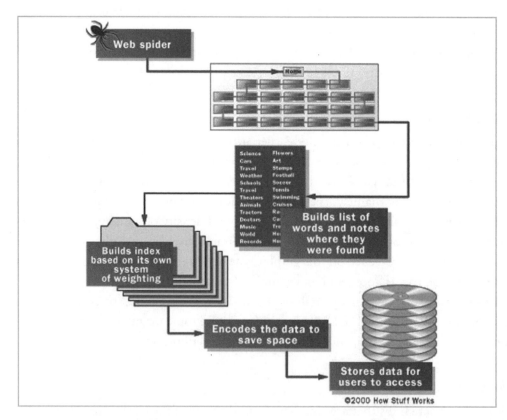

FIGURE 4–17. Spidering and indexing for a Search Engine.

do not impact search engines rankings directly. Google shows relevant pages within seconds, and it is done in real-time. Spidering is done ahead of time.

LinkVendor's spiderview shows you everything you need to know about how search engine spiders are crawling and then indexing your site. When you enter your URL, LinkVendor returns meta tag information that's been spidered, text from your website that's been spidered, outbound links, incoming links, and images links. You have options to select to show source code, no-follow links, and more.

Site Speed

Site speed is a very important element when it comes to internet marketing. Generally, visitors will only wait up to three to five seconds for a web page to load, though modem users might be more patient, waiting up to 30 to 60 seconds. Website visitors might be more understanding if they know the site is complex, which is particularly the case for gaming sites or sites with video. But there is a limit to their patience. If you're unable to get your site delivered within that window of a few seconds, you can pretty much guarantee that you'll lose a great deal of traffic and lowered return visitors. Google made an announcement about speed of sites and ranking, which you can read more about on googlewebmastercentral.blog spot.com/2010/04/using-site-speed-in-web-search-ranking.html.

There are several plugins for the Firefox browser (ySlow at https://addons.mozilla. org/en-US/firefox/addon/yslow/), and a internet bandwidth speed tester tool for Chrome (at www.speedtest.net). Try both of them, see which one you prefer. LinkVendor's "Speedtester" tool lets you know how fast your site runs for all types of connections including dial-up, ISDN, UMTS, DSL, T1, and T2. The Speedtester tool also returns the percentage of HTML coding you have in relation to the percentage of actual content. Remember site speed is measured both in speed of loading a page from a server, and the speed/access point to the internet. You may have fast access to the internet, but the website and pages may be poorly optimized. Google recently introduced a new tool (PageSpeed Insights) that you can try here: https://developers.google.com/speed/pagespeed/insights/.

ONLINE RESOURCE

Webmasters should try the websiteoptimization.com/ services/analyze/ tool and see how their site performance can be improved with the many good recommendations it provides. It's free.

Miscellaneous Tools

Site analysis programs may include additional tools that could be of assistance, yet don't relate directly to site analysis. In the case of LinkVendor, this tool would be its handy "URL Rewrite." If you remember earlier in this book when error pages were discussed, you read about 301 redirects and ways to initiate them. One of these methods is using the Apache rewrite module. If you need the exact coding to determine how to initiate a 301 redirect for your webpage, you can use LinkVendor's URL Rewrite. You enter your URL and in return you receive a customized Apache rewrite code you can use in your .htaccess file. These will show a directory- or comma-based pathing structure, but be careful with dynamic session id's. You may want to contact a technical person if you are not sure what you are doing. Send me a note, if unsure, at contact@jonrognerud.com. Note: if you are using WordPress, many plugins exist to handle these issues for you automatically. Simply install the plugin, configure it, and configure the commands.

KEYWORDS YOUR COMPETITORS USE

It's important when analyzing keywords that you know which keywords your competitors use and if you're in the proper league to either continue to use them or try for keywords that are still popular yet not used as often. Some paid keyword analyzers can tell you which competitors use which keywords, but this is often limited to what is used for AdSense campaigns. AdSense ads are different than regular search engine listings. A good way to determine what keywords your competitors are using is to use keyword research tools to extract keywords from their pages, and then copy and paste your selected keyword into a search engine such as Yahoo! or Google to see where they show up.

An easy way to find out target keywords for your competitors is to see what Google thinks they are. You should load up the new interface to Google Keyword External tool. (Now being rolled out, and updated to look/act like the version supplied within Google AdWords.) The new keyword tool allows you to select languages, local search targets, and more. In the example below, I used "dog training supplies." Type that keyword phrase into Google and pull back the top five organic listings to start. I started with jjdog.com. You can expand this later to also include paid listings and their landing pages, and to perform deeper, targeted scans.

Steps to discover these keywords from competitor domains:

1. Access the keyword tool https://adwords.google.com/select/KeywordToolExternal. (Please read the updated information as the new Keyword Planner has replaced the old Keyword Tool. It's now part of Google Adwords, and you need to log in first.)
2. Input your competitor website, in this case "jjdog.com."

DON'T FORGET GOOGLE

Obviously, when researching keywords, you always want to include Google because it dominates the search market. Also, consider using Google Trends and Ubersuggest.org. And, with Bing serving results for Yahoo!, try their Ad Intelligence Keyword Plugin for Excel.

3. Review the listings, and scroll down to view all and the collection of keywords including ad group ideas.

You would pick the keywords that have (exact) search counts, and that closely match your site as a starting formula. A combination of head and long-tail keywords should be included in your tracking sheet (Excel). As you enter some of these keywords into Google, you'll see varying results for paid results. These will help you understand how "commerce viable" a keyword is. The more ads, the more you can consider it to be a moneymaker. Don't think that no ads displayed is a loser, but I would normally be very suspicious. You can further input top keywords into Spyfu.com and Keywordspy.com

Search terms		Avg. monthly searches [?]	Competition [?]	Suggested bid [?]
seo		90,500	High	$9.23

1 - 1

Keyword (by relevance)		Avg. monthly searches [?]	Competition [?]	Suggested bid [?]
what is seo		8,100	Medium	$4.64
seo companies		4,400	High	$28.00
local seo		4,400	High	$12.11
seo company		12,100	High	$21.77
seo pricing		480	High	$8.93
seo optimization		2,400	High	$18.72

FIGURE 4–18. Google Keyword Planner.

to discover more detail, including potential paid campaigns and their resulting landing pages. It will give you a good, broad view of your competitor's use of keywords, pages, and overall strategy.

For each of the top five sites, select out keywords that seem reasonable, match your market, and have search volume and then take a look at the results that come up. Don't worry as much about the sponsored listings, as these spots are out of your league if you have limited funds. Expand the research, and focus on the first ten direct listings of the search engine results. Ask yourself: Do these listings relate to the keyword at hand?

When I typed in the keyword phrase *dog training supplies*, I revealed dog accessories, products, local businesses, and interesting dog accessories on the first page of the Google results (see Figure 4–19).

As you learned earlier in this book, having the exact keyword phrase in your title helps you rank better with search engines. Additionally, you can check on the number of

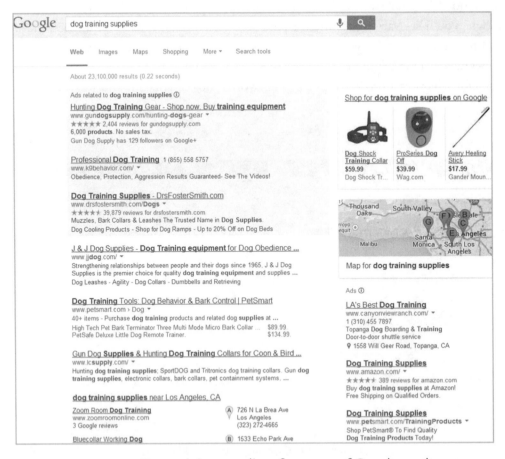

FIGURE 4–19. Dog training supplies—first page of Google results.

inbound links of these sites. Use LinkVendor to do this. If you have a Google webmaster account (you must), your incoming links will be revealed there. Note: The old Yahoo! SiteExplorer was retired in 2012 and now redirects you to Bing Webmaster Tools. We're using OpensiteExplorer.org (from moz.com) instead and can see that it reveals a large link count back to the domain jjdog.com. However, quality links back to you is of higher priority, rather than simply hunting down links. I've seen and worked on sites that outrank others simply by working on the quality rather than the quantity. The search engine will return how many inbound links the website has. Make sure to select the "Except from this domain"—we want to show only external links, not links within the site.

Now, what do you do with all this information, particularly if the number is high? Even if the number of inbound links is in the thousands, you don't necessarily have to discount a keyword. In order for inbound links to be useful for search engines, they must relate to the keywords used throughout your website. For example, if you're looking to rank well for refinancing loans yet your inbound links are for subprime mortgage loans, you'll get a good search engine ranking for subprime mortgage loans rather than what you originally wanted, which was refinancing loans. A solid information architecture with keyword research to build out your pages will help avoid this problem. You will make sure that you target pages across your site, not just your homepage.

You'll get some legitimate traffic, since some subprime loans are also refinancing loans, but the traffic wouldn't be as good (relevant) as if you had inbound links that related directly to refinancing loans. If this is what is happening with your competitor's keywords, you can take advantage of it by creating a site with the appropriate inbound links.

Note: With Google's Penguin updates, it's more important than ever to focus on quality of links. If you find that your rankings and traffic have been dropping sharply, you may have been penalized. If you received a notice inside your Google Webmaster Tools area, you have some work to do. Visit the member access area at

---

ONLINE RESOURCE

I use ahrefs.com and opensiteexplorer.org—powerful SEO tools for checking backlinks. Visit the membership site at www.jonrognerud.com/optimizationbook for more information and downloads.

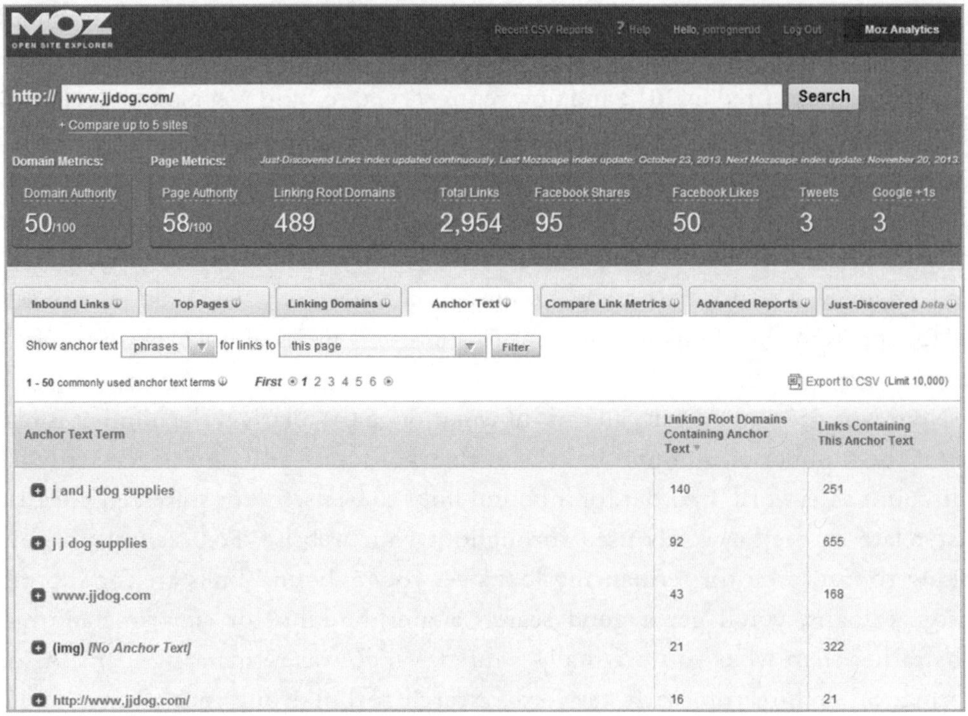

FIGURE 4–20. Open Site Explorer—anchor text tracking.

www.jonrognerud.com/optimizationbook to see an example of disavowing links and more.

How can you determine if a competitor's inbound links relate to the keywords used on its site? OpensiteExplorer.org will show your competitors' anchor text and a lot more around domain authority, diversity of linking domains (important), and total links (see Figure 4–20).

A powerful tool that you can try on a 30-day free trial is Market Samurai (Figure 4–21). It provides a complete, integrated system for all online marketing efforts, and it's a killer tool. The link analysis can show you all incoming links sorted by PageRank or by anchor text use, and can easily be exported. Find out who they are, and submit for a link. You may be surprised to find out that top listings (first page) of Google have low PageRank values but extremely targeted page and anchor text matches. This is a big secret to success. Contact me for how to use this product. I have prepared some simple videos for your use at contact@jonrognerud.com.

You can effectively compete even if a site has a smaller number of legitimate inbound links. The key is to ensure that your links directly relate to the keywords used on your site; if your competitors do not, you may be rewarded with top placement.

FIGURE 4–21. Market Samurai.

Chapter 5

How to Find Your Gold: Step-by-Step Guide to Keyword Research

Bob found that the "real estate market" was extremely competitive based on number of websites returned from initial top-level keyword research, and he wasn't sure how to get the best results for his client. He had a list of keywords from the client but wasn't sure how to choose the best ones on which to compete.

 Bob was familiar with the basics of keywords. To learn more, he decided to use a real estate client as a test case. Bob talked to the client about her website traffic and told her that he wanted to use the company as a case study for improving results. The client happily agreed.

Bob typed "real estate" in the search engine and—no surprise—he got millions of results. He searched for his client's name and was surprised when it wasn't in the top results. He was wondering if she had excluded the website from search by mistake or oversight. He played around with different combinations and took notes on what he found.

Unsure of how to proceed, Bob turned to online webmaster forums for help. A few people pointed Bob in the direction of software programs that would help make keyword selection easier. Bob signed up with Wordtracker.com and KeywordDiscovery.com, but there was still more work to do. He had also learned about the updated tools at Google, and bookmarked them as well (Google Keyword Planner and Google Trends).

Earlier in this book you were introduced to the concept of keywords. You were taught how to use keyword research tools to decide how to write your content. We discussed keyword competition and learned how to determine highly competitive keywords. Now, it's time to delve deeper into every aspect of keyword research.

Begin your keyword research by creating a seed list. You can use Wordtracker or other keyword tools (see Tools for Analyzing Keywords in this chapter) to find the most popular terms in your seed list and reject those that have low volumes. There are many options available if you need help creating your seed list.

A few suggestions are listed below.

- Mail, print ads, direct mail, catalogs, and anything that has ad copy related to your site
- Online trend tools such as Digg (digg.com), Zeitgeist (Google), Topsy.com, Reddit.com, google.com/trends, and also Google/trends/topcharts
- News articles—Yahoo!, Google News, specific niche news directories and sites
- Competition—extract keywords using techniques described above
- News.google.com
- Review hottest bookmarks using sites such as Digg and Del.icio.us
- Topix.net—aggregates in local areas
- Techmeme
- YouTube
- Amazon—best sellers (great for drilling down into niches)
- Shopping.com—best/top sellers
- eBay marketplace research services, eBay pulse
- Reviews.ebay.com
- Yahoo! Answers
- Google and Yahoo! groups
- Review directories such as dir.yahoo.com, dmoz.org, and business.com

The "allin" commands can help in your analysis. For example, in the search box you would type allintitle: "dog training supplies" (intitle alone will do the same, when using quotes around the search phrase). This tells the search engine to find all sites with dog training supplies (in that order) in the title. When I type this into Google, it returned 6,370 results. (Please note: only use this number as a guide, it is not reliable, and it has been misused by too many marketers who think they know.) Most searchers don't know these commands, but they are good techniques for you to know when researching. Consider adding the http://www.wordstream.com/keywords tool to your arsenal.

When researching keywords, you want to dig deeper into the "long tail." The long tail represents the multitude of search terms beyond the top ten or 20 that visitors use to find your site. For example, your keyword may be *chocolate*, which drives traffic, but many more visitors combined find you by using "chocolate gifts," "corporate chocolate gifts" and "dark chocolate gifts." While "chocolate gifts," "corporate chocolate gifts," and "dark chocolate gifts" do not individually pull as much traffic as *chocolate*, collectively, they pull far more traffic and will yield a better conversion for you. Think of the long tail as starting with what's popular but continuing to follow that trail to the end. Search marketers are discovering that the long tail is responsible for the bulk of traffic—completely opposite of what was previously believed. However, it's still important to have a balanced focus on both traffic and conversion. Consider what's most important to your business.

Broaden your search to related terms, and dig deep again. Organize and prioritize what you find. Many people give scant attention to developing a really great seed list. If

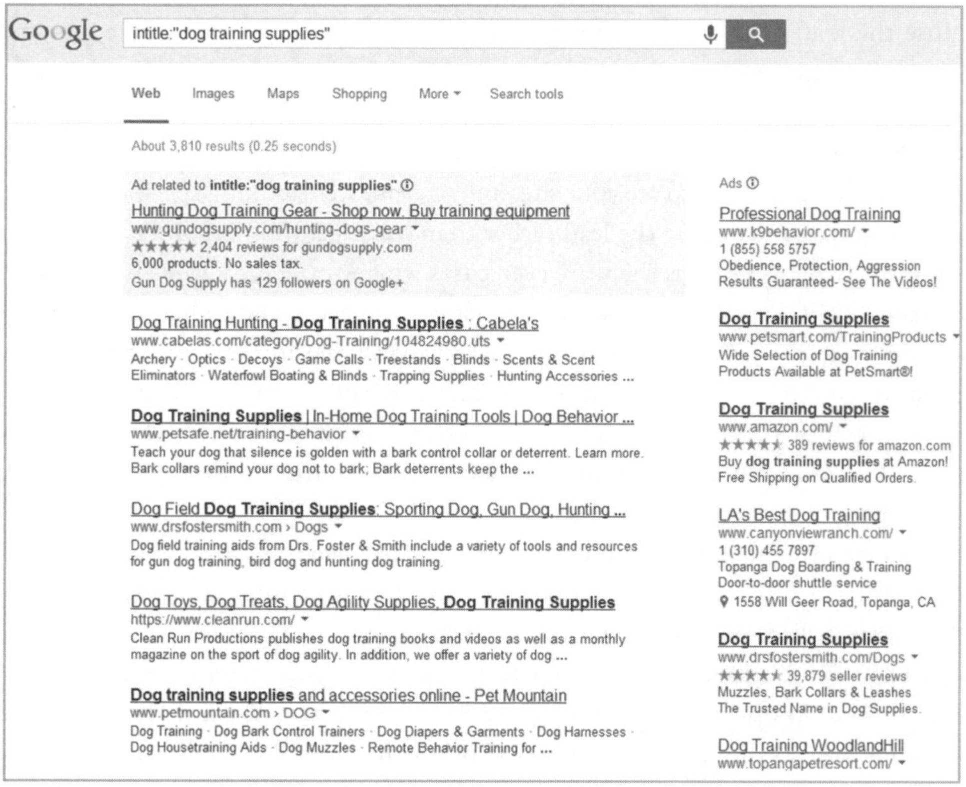

FIGURE 5–1. Allintitle/Intitle for "dog training supplies."

you only do the obvious, you'll end up with obvious results—just like everyone else. To get outstanding results from your keyword research, you've got to apply creativity and hard work to the first step, generating your keyword seed list. You may want to prioritize into buckets and use the tabs at the bottom of Excel to organize them. Remember, if you fail here, you fail in search engine optimization. Keywords help drive content initiatives, traffic, layout, targeted visitors, and conversions!

GENERAL FACTS ABOUT KEYWORDS

Keywords typically range from two to five words, though there are popular one-word keywords. Keywords may also be referred to as search phrases, keyword phrases, or query phrases. Regardless of what you call them, it's important that the keywords you choose are relevant to your site's goal, theme, and subject matter. Don't optimize for generic keywords (even if they relate to your site) just because those keywords might have more traffic. For example, "real estate" is a generic keyword that gets a lot of traffic. However, if you're a real estate agent in Sterling Heights, Michigan, a better keyword phrase might be "real estate agent sterling heights michigan." With generic keywords, you might get some visitors initially, but they won't convert to sales or leads because the traffic you get is not really interested in your website. Someone typing "real estate" may have been looking for real estate loans, real estate schools, or even information on foreclosures.

When you choose the right keyword combination for your website, you attract visitors who actually want to see your site—in fact, they were looking specifically for it. In essence, you're prequalifying the lead rather than casting a wide net and throwing back most of the fish! Sometimes there are even cases where you might want to optimize for a less competitive keyword because the few visitors you get would be highly interested in what you have to offer (especially if there aren't many websites offering that particular product or service). This niche marketing tactic might generate only a few hundred visitors, but if they convert, it's many times better than the thousands of irrelevant hits you could get from a popular, yet unrelated, keyword. Traffic is meaningless if no one is buying what you have to offer. Got it?

Additionally, there are certain types of keywords that are a potential gold mine because they're often ignored by many webmasters and internet marketers. These include misspelled keywords, keyword phrases that use Boolean operators, and advanced search options. If you're new to the internet, you may not be familiar with the term Boolean operators, but they really aren't a big deal. Basically, they're special commands you use in a search engine to bring up more specific results. The most popular Boolean operators for search engines include AND, OR, NOT, and " " (double quotes). Learning how these operators work is not hard. And they tell the search

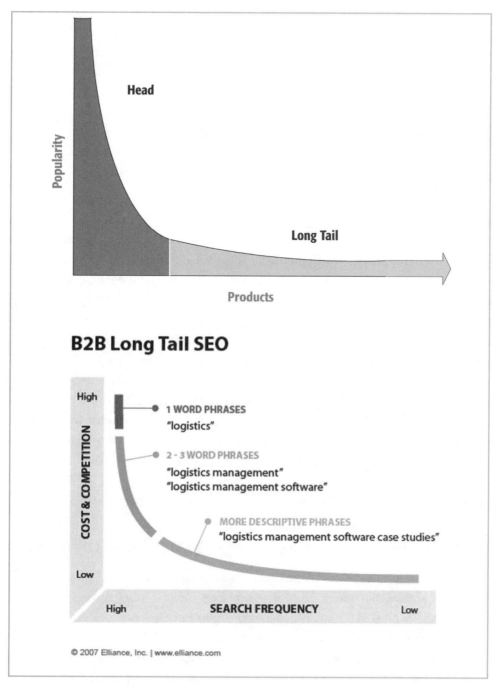

FIGURE 5–2. The long tail for B2B term logistics.

engine to look for two sets of keywords (Google, however, uses an automatic Boolean AND, a default). For example, the keyword phrase "necklaces AND earrings," would

INSIDER TIP

Because most search engines index documents, you can place misspellings inside PDF, DOC, and XLS documents, and they will be picked up. Don't exclude this strategy, especially considering the poor spelling tactics from visitors abroad! Of course, the competitive landscape will determine relevancy and position results. Google applies a "Did you mean" spelling check (very good at it)—and it's likely that your listing would be lost, so test it first.

return results that would include these two words somewhere in a website. They can be shown individually or simultaneously. If you used "necklaces OR earrings," the search engine would return websites that contained listings of earrings or necklaces. They would be shown separately. NOT excludes certain keywords from search engine listings. Still using "necklaces and earrings" as the example keyword, if you said "necklaces NOT earrings," the search engine would return only websites containing the term "necklaces" in their content. Finally the quotation marks "" specify that everything within them must be found on pages, and is returned bold-faced in search engine results. For example, typing "necklaces and earrings" would return search listing results that show these terms exactly as listed. It is important to note that "" allows for more specific results than AND, since AND may or may not return results that show necklaces and earrings together.

SOUR GRAPES

Don't think misspelled words are limited to search engine placement. eBay users use the eBay search function to find items of interest. eBay insiders have noted that if you search for misspelled auctions, you can often find deals on merchandise that has few to no bids due to the misspelled word. I read a story about a man who sold a rare type of wine. He misspelled the name of the wine, allowing the winning bidder to buy it for only a few hundred dollars. The winning bidder turned around and sold the wine for over $300,000! Undoubtedly, if he sold it on eBay, he checked the spelling first! But, as with anything online, you must make sure to operate ethically, and don't get involved in possible scams, which this story feels like to me.

> **INSIDER TIP**
>
> Remember, if you are using the Meta Keyword tag extensively, you are giving away your keyword secrets to your competition if they read your source code (and they do). Focus on content and solutions instead.

So, how would you optimize for misspelled words and keywords with Boolean phrases? Wouldn't this look a little odd in legitimate content? You would be 100 percent correct in this assumption, which is why you would try not to use these throughout your content. The exception could be if a misspelled word is very common and wouldn't look wrong to website visitors. An older tactic was to put these in the keyword property of your meta tags. I have seen (interesting) uses of adding misspelled keywords on a page as a way to offer (deliberately) a way to search by these keywords, not prominently placed on the page, but still with the potential to impact search results.

Wait a second . . . Keyword property of meta tags? This is not as relevant anymore. Google doesn't use the keyword tag. Basically, the keyword meta tag was used to tell search engines what keywords you want your site to be indexed by. The syntax of the meta tag keyword property is listed below:

<meta name="keywords" content="enter, your, keywords, here">

In the case of keywords and misspelled words, you place them where you see the "enter, your, keywords, here." These should be included with your regular keywords.

For search engines these days, don't put too much emphasis on the keyword meta tag, as it's largely ignored. I include it here as reference.

TOOLS FOR ANALYZING KEYWORDS

Earlier you were introduced to keyword tools and instructed to jump to this section for more detail on paid keyword analyzers. Yahoo!'s Search Marketing tools are powerful, but you need an advertising account, and log in. This used to be the old Overture tool—RIP.

GoodKeywords is another freeware tool that's great for beginners and experts alike. It can be downloaded from goodkeywords.com (see Figure 5-5). Once you start getting some sales, consider investing in a paid keyword analyzer.

Google has a free keyword tool (https://adwords.google.com/ko/**KeywordPlanner**/Home) that also shows you advertiser competition, the current month's search volume, and the average search volume.

The tool is helpful not only for PPC campaigns, but for creating your keyword seed list.

FIGURE 5–3. Yahoo!—Search Marketing – Now BingAds.com.

Don't forget to use Google's regular search. As you have seen, a new three-column display (the infamous "May Update" in 2010) allows more power searches—from real time streams, to videos, blogs, images, news, and more. The Wonder Wheel is a great way to see relevant keywords and possible pages you can create. We now see Google Instant as well, with developing impacts on both organic and paid search.

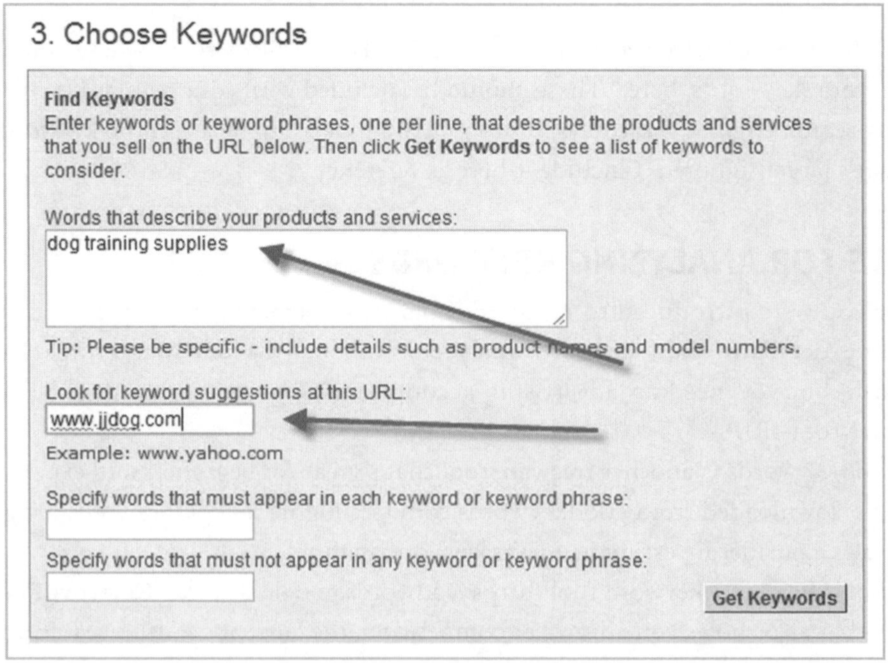

FIGURE 5–4. Yahoo! Keyword research dog training supplies input.

FIGURE 5–5. Good Keywords Freeware keyword tool.

FIGURE 5–6. Google standard search—related search options.

The most popular paid keyword tools are Keyword Discovery and Wordtracker. The nice thing about these tools is that you don't have to download anything, as it's all available online. The keyword tools identify all the variations of your search phrase, including synonyms and misspellings commonly searched for by those seeking similar sites. They also tell you how many hits a keyword has received (Figures 5-7 and 5-8 on page 146-147, respectively).

INSIDER TIP

If you are doing research on competitive keywords, type them into Google. Copy that resulting URL directly into the Google keyword tool using the landing page option. Google will effectively spider the search links, and retrieve (tons of) keywords from that search URL. Lots of great keywords in less than a minute, and the relationships/groups are already created for you.

With Keyword Discovery and Wordtracker, you get a thorough analysis of your keywords. With Overture's keyword analyzer tool you only get a list of each instance of a keyword and how many people have searched it. In the long run, you'll find that the paid keyword analyzers offer a lot more assistance in your internet marketing campaign than the free ones.

Expect to pay about $50 a month each for Keyword Discovery and Wordtracker. Both, at the time of this writing, have free trials. Use the free trial to evaluate both

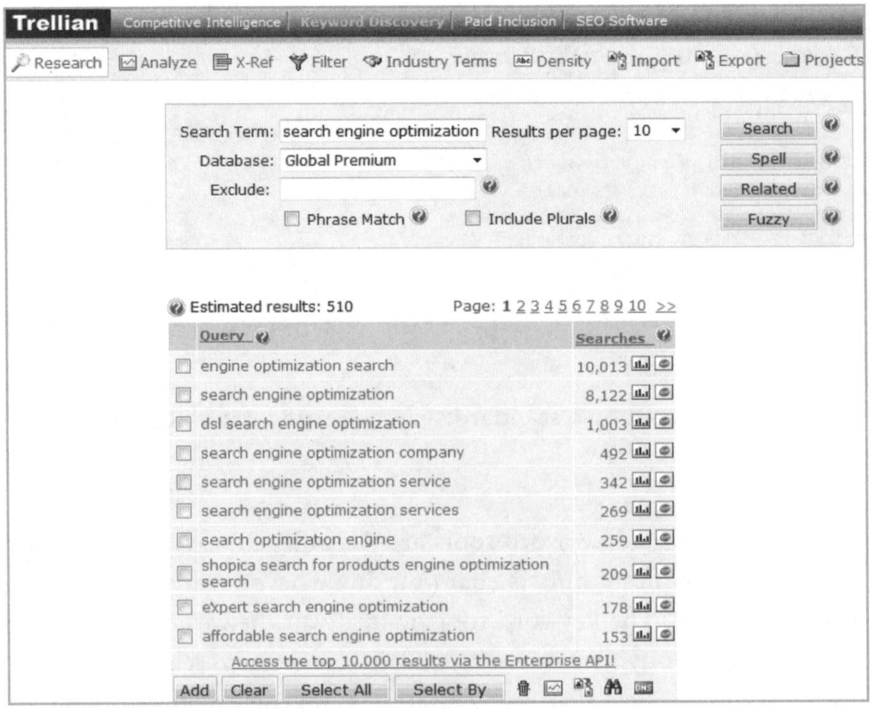

FIGURE 5–7. Keyword discovery.

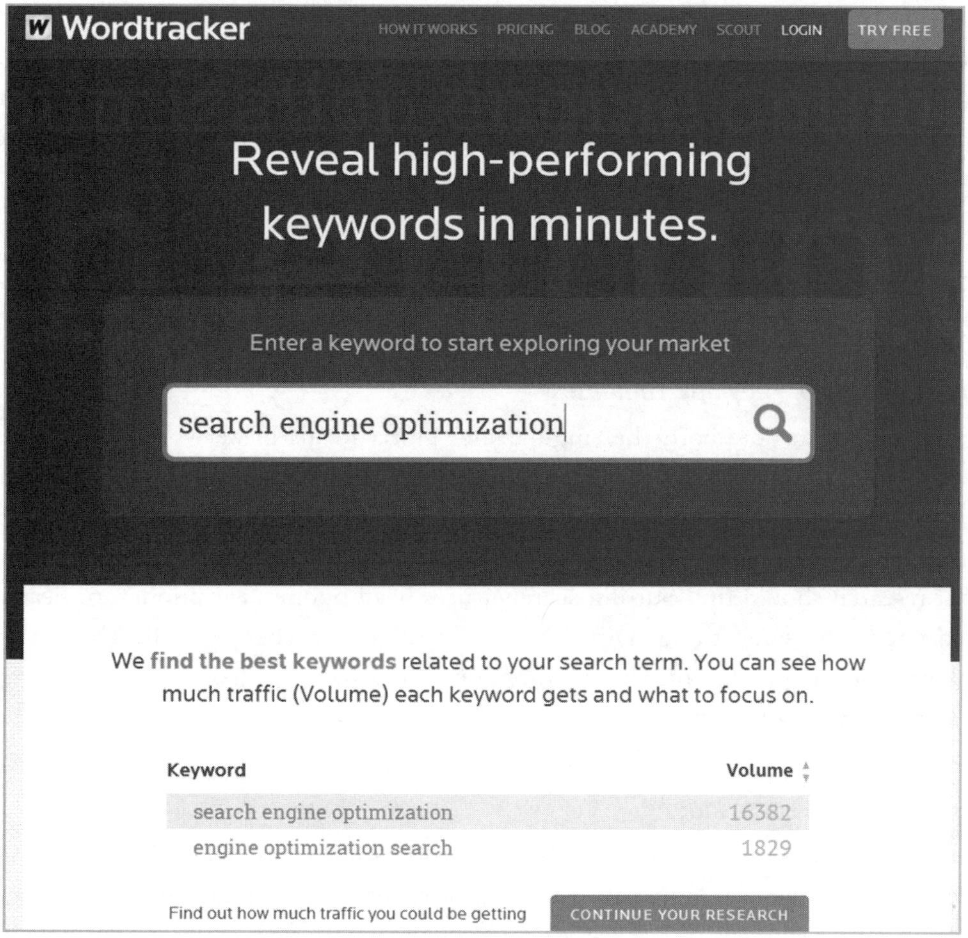

FIGURE 5–8. Wordtracker.

and pick the tool that best meets your needs. If your budget can afford it, subscribe to both.

What's the best way to use Keyword Discovery, Wordtracker, or a free keyword tool? The first step is to think like your customer. Enter phrases that your potential customers may use. Ask others in your office as well as friends to do this. For example, if you're a web designer, your customers may enter *websites, good web design, fast web design,* or *professional website.* Don't worry about proper grammar or spelling because, as you already know, misspellings are common among search engine users. Improper grammar is also common. Additionally, avoid searching industry jargon, unless your target audience would use the jargon in its web searches. For example, people new to internet marketing wouldn't know anything about SEO optimization. So, if they're searching for a book related to SEO, they may instead enter "search engine marketing." More advanced marketers would be acquainted with the term and enter it properly. If you're really stuck on what you should promote in terms of jargon, be on the safe side and try for both, though in terms of search engines the more you can optimize for just one keyword the better. It's important to keep the relationship of the keyword(s) from search to the resulting page.

In the next section we cover a few pointers that will help you manage your keyword research.

You Say Tomato, They Say Tomatoes

It's important to note both the singular and plural forms of keyword phrases. Even though they are essentially the same, sometimes one form might bring more hits than another. Keep in mind, this goes for the correct form of a keyword along with misspellings. For example, job seekers may search for *resumes* more often than *resume*. Your research should find out if a searcher uses head phones, ear phones, or headsets to describe the same thing. Different locales affect searches as well. Think about internationalization. In the United Kingdom, SEO fully spelled out is *search engine optimisation* (with an "s," not "z").

Keyword Effectiveness Index

The Keyword Effectiveness Index (KEI), provided in some tools, determines a keyword's value by calculating its popularity along with the number of competing websites. A higher KEI means that a keyword may have less competition and would be a strategic pick for you. Wordtracker defines the KEI in this way: "The KEI compares the count result (number of times a keyword has appeared in our data) with the number of competing web pages to pinpoint exactly which keywords are most effective for your campaign."

Wordtracker computes the formula for you, but it breaks down the phrase to P, which denotes the popularity of the keyword, and C, the competitiveness. There are other formulas created by search marketers, such as $KEI = (P^2/C)$, i.e., KEI is the square of the popularity of the keyword and divided by its competitiveness.

There is no need to be overly concerned with the formula. KEI helps you find easy-to-optimize secondary and tertiary phrases. If you find keywords with high KEI, by all means use them. Keywords with a low KEI may also be useful if they have a high search value. Competitive research is important, and reviewing the KEI number as an approach should ultimately only be used as a reference, not relied upon as the final word. A good rule of thumb is: research, analyze, apply, and test/validate. Repeat.

ONLINE RESOURCE

To get a view into cost per keyword and traffic estimations, see Google's own free tool at AdWord's Keyword Planner. (See Figure 5–9.)

Export and Sort

Another important productivity feature with Keyword Discovery and Wordtracker is their ability to export files into Excel format. With Excel you can sort your data in a variety of ways. You can also create charts and graphs for it, so you can get a clear visual picture of keyword performance. Then there is an option offered by Keyword Discovery and Wordtracker to store your keyword data online, but for many people this feature isn't as useful as storing the data offline.

Some keywords are so competitive that the only way you can take advantage of them is through a pay-per-click campaign, especially if you have a large budget and are short on time. SEO is a long-term commitment, as you have come to see. The other side to this is that pay-per-clicks are expensive. Some can be as low as 5 cents or as high as $112.13 (The keyword "mesothelioma" at the time of this writing).

While $112.13 per click is out of most people's budgets, even a keyword that's one cent per click can get expensive if a person gets thousands of clicks across multiple keywords and has not monitored the campaign. If you decide to do a pay-per-click

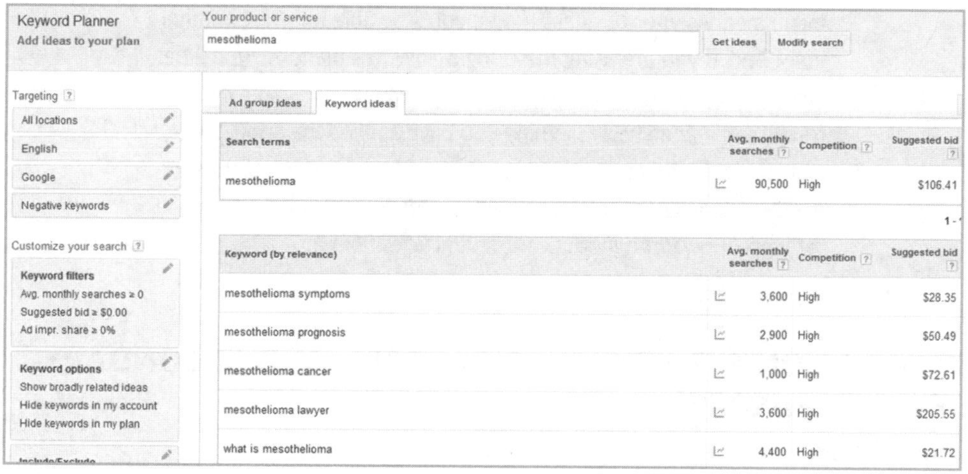

FIGURE 5–9. Google Keyword Planner with Traffic Estimates and Costs Per Click.

campaign, stick with the least expensive keywords, track for conversion, and pay close attention to your sales rate. A starting number could be a sale per 500 clicks. (This would cost you $5 if the price was one cent per click). If you aren't getting conversions, add more targeted keywords, test the ads, positions, landing pages, and study analytics and interactions on why your site isn't bringing in sales. To look at this in another way, if you had 100 clicks and 1 percent of the people took the desired action (conversion), your lead result would be one. Move the clicks and the conversion rate up, and you're heading in the right direction. I continue to see a lot of wasted dollars. Business owners understand these concepts, but you'd be amazed to learn how many don't know their conversion rate or what the intended user actions are on the page(s). We talk more about pay-per-click campaigns in Chapter 10.

 Bob was ready to begin optimizing his first site. Before testing his skills on clients, he offered to optimize his neighbor's site free of charge. He would track the results and use the site as a test case. Bob knew that he needed a keyword analyzer tool but was unsure which one to use. Using Google, he found Wordtracker, Keyword Discovery, and Google keyword tool. He checked all three sites and decided to use the Google keyword tool (GKT). The program appeared to be as effective as KeywordDiscovery or Wordtracker, and it was free.

INSIDER TIP

If you can't afford a top-of-the-line keyword tool, then it's better to stick with the free programs we've mentioned. As your business grows, you'll be able to invest in other tools. And, if you are using the Google AdWords platform, you'll be able to leverage the tools fully, including capturing valuable data from Google Analytics, assuming you have applied the appropriate analytics script to your website pages. Visit google.com/analytics to get started, and see the Member Access for a short video on how to set it up (www.jonrognerud.com/optimizationbook).

OPTIMIZATION STRATEGY FOR PRIMARY AND SECONDARY KEYWORD PHRASES

Primary Keyword Phrases

Your primary keyword phrase is a little like your elevator pitch for the internet. It's a single keyword phrase that aptly represents what your website and business offer. The

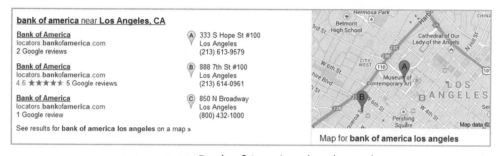

FIGURE 5–10. Bank of America—local search.

primary keyword phrase is the main phrase that appears throughout your website as the overarching topic, or theme. Because primary keyword phrases tend to be more generic than secondary keyword phrases (discussed in the next section), they are more competitive and harder (take longer) to optimize.

When determining your primary keyword phrases, be sure to include variations. For example, if you wanted to use home loan as a primary keyword phrase, you might use *bank of america home loan* or *bank of america real estate home loans* as more specific variations. With new search engine updates to local search, and personalized search, your local region searches would show up automatically. We also look at explicit searches, as well as implicit searches. For example, some will add a "local modifier" (explicit) to our search phrase above. Other will not (implicit), since Google will use the origin of the search to determine local research. Either way, consider both. Optimizing for keywords with local modifiers is a smart, viable strategy, and in some cases might be easier than the standard results.

By using variations of your primary keyword phrase, you prevent the likelihood of using a keyword that's overly broad and not specific enough. Your keyword research and competitive analysis will help narrow this down. Running a short PPC campaign to reveal more significance on possible ROI and impressions (how many times your ad is shown during a period) can be a smart approach. You can then take your findings and push them into SEO campaigns.

Secondary Keyword Phrases

Secondary keyword phrases are like primary keyword phrases. The difference is that a secondary keyword phrase is not searched on as frequently as your primary; but it may allow you to look at more opportunities for ranking and traffic. Still using the *home loan* phrase as an example, a secondary keyword phrase could be *mortgage loan*. TIP: Type this term into Google and see related searches at the bottom of the results page for more ideas.

TREND FINDER

You can review search trends using the Google Trends tool found at google.com/trends.

More Suggestions for Choosing Keywords

Generally, the more specific your primary and secondary keyword phrases with related content, the better chance you'll have of ranking high. Think about using keyword combinations that most webmasters ignore, such as three-, four-, or even five-word phrases. Mine your web analytics for more, and keep building content. You could also include a geographical (city, region, town) reference for your keywords to make them even more specific. For example, instead of trying to optimize for *real estate*, try for *maryland real estate* and *maryland real estate agents*. You might specifically look for agents within a company, say *century 21 real estate agents*.

Soovle is a visual search engine. From one screen you get access to data from Wordtracker, Google, Yahoo, Bing, and Trend Data (see Figure 5–11). You type in a keyword, and you get search results on one side of the page and keyword clouds on the other. You hover over a word and it brings up all other related words.

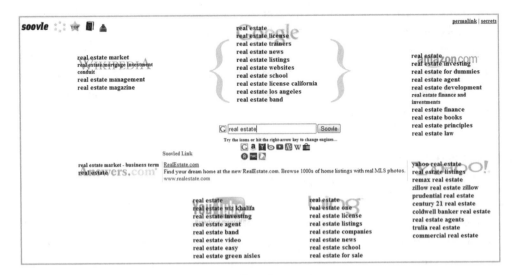

FIGURE 5–11. Soovle—real estate.

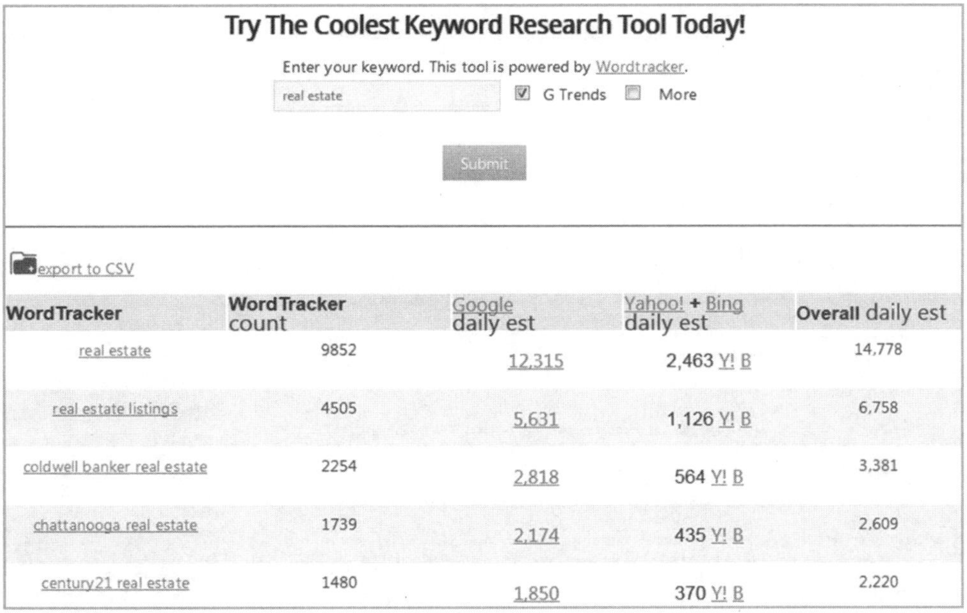

Try The Coolest Keyword Research Tool Today!

Enter your keyword. This tool is powered by Wordtracker.

real estate ☑ G Trends ☐ More

Submit

export to CSV

WordTracker	WordTracker count	Google daily est	Yahoo! + Bing daily est	Overall daily est
real estate	9852	12,315	2,463 Y! B	14,778
real estate listings	4505	5,631	1,126 Y! B	6,758
coldwell banker real estate	2254	2,818	564 Y! B	3,381
chattanooga real estate	1739	2,174	435 Y! B	2,609
century21 real estate	1480	1,850	370 Y! B	2,220

FIGURE 5–12. Aaron Wall—Keyword Tool.

Aaron Wall's SEO book (tools.seobook.com/general/keyword/) is a great keyword tool as it pulls in search volumes from Google, Yahoo!, and Bing (see Figure 5-12). From one screen you can link to Wordtracker, Keyword Discovery, Google Trends, Yahoo!, and AdWords. Think of it as a one-stop shopping tool for keyword research. It was free for the longest time, but a subscription is required now.

Spyfu (spyfu.com) lets you download competitive keywords, rankings, and PPC data. You type in the domain name and receive a list of results. The tool is free but offers advanced analytics for a subscription fee.

Another competitive keyword tool is SEMRush.com. You receive some results for free. You have the option to buy the full results for your search term for a flat fee or subscribe for full access.

An additional keyword tool to help you is Bing (https://secure.bingads.microsoft. com/), which you also need an account for.

A powerful solution (get your account set up first) is to download the Advertising Intelligence plugin for Excel (see Figure 5-13). It's a "must-have" tool for your keyword research, and with Bing serving results and growing in search market share, you'll get better and better data (http://advertise.bingads.microsoft.com/en-us/bing-ads-intelligence).

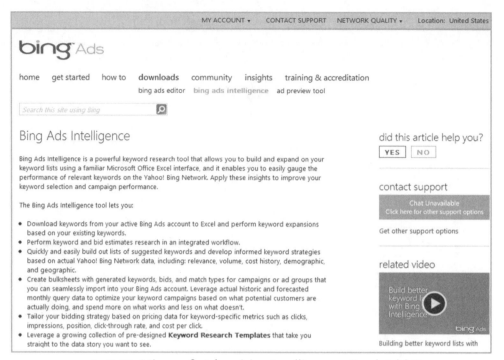

FIGURE 5–13. Microsoft Advertising Intelligence—Excel Add On.

KEYWORD OPTIMIZATION STRATEGY

There is much discussion about this in the SEO community. How many keywords should I optimize my page for? Your keyword research and competitive research (keywords, links, social graph) will tell you. And, if you are a brand new site, your strategy will be different than that of a long-time, trusted site. If you are a brand, you can do pretty much what you want!

It's a good idea to optimize each of your web pages for no more than three keyword phrases per page, which would include your primary keyword phrase, your secondary keyword phrase, and variations on them. Can you optimize a page for five keywords? Sure you can, but a well-organized, easily navigable site is a better choice in my mind. Keep in mind, you must think about your users first, search engines second. Send me a note at contact@jonrognerud.com if you want to discuss your particular circumstance. Targeted keyword pages must have your primary keyword phrase and your best secondary keyword phrase. Of particular concern is your homepage, which needs to put extra emphasis on your primary keyword phrase. This is because search engines are more likely to give your homepage a higher ranking than the other pages on your site (and external links tend to be drawn to the homepage most of the time).

Your goal, however, is to build out an architecture and quality content that attracts users, links, and overall activity across your whole site. Links should not just come to your homepage, but naturally spread out across pages (and domains, in a wider network). Your architecture will be such that all links to other pages fall naturally, and will include keywords as anchor text, both externally and internally. Think about Wikipedia. It has content and (keyword) links distributed across the whole site in a user- and search-friendly way. That should be your goal as well.

Chapter 6

Optimizing the Social Web: The Psychology of Your Audience

nderstanding your audience—your customer—is not only very important in marketing, but it will help you to think strategically about how to change your web pages, headlines, emails, ads, links, and overall messages to target it directly. You'll be able to narrow your focus ("niching down") and answer this question: "Who are you talking to?" Big advertisers spend huge amounts of money on research to find out about a market and its buyers. You must do the same, even though your time and budget may be smaller. Yes, it is that important.

A top search engine ranking is a waste if the messages you convey don't convert to sales. Pay special attention to the Needs Hierarchy. This is the secret formula for all human needs, and you can speak to it via your online (and offline) marketing materials. You'll see that this will open up the conversions WITH them. Gone will be the days of just blasting irrelevant messages AT them.

KNOW YOUR AUDIENCE

 Bob did not do much research on his market before starting. He had now been coaching for two years and assumed that his online business would be the same as his offline business. In his coaching business he had successfully worked with both men and women of various ages. He had started in his local geographic area and through referrals and speaking engagements had obtained clients across the state.

The online coaching was a way for him to cut down on traveling and to be able to develop a secondary income from selling informational products. Bob often met with clients face to face for the first one or two sessions and then continued coaching by phone.

The print graphics practice had been successful, and Bob wanted to build up his telephone and webinar style coaching business, which would allow him to get more done in fewer hours. He also believed that he could eventually make use of purely virtual web coaching sessions and even group webinars.

The problem was that Bob's success offline was not immediately transferred to the web. Bob had failed to assess his online competition and his target market. In fact he had not clearly identified his target market, so his site and its message were ineffective and resulted in capturing very little targeted business. He had spent much time in the offline world. (Note: Real life success coach Anthony Robbins only recently started using the online opportunities and admits he was slow to the game. He hired some of the best expert online marketers and has grown very fast as a result of this.

In Chapter 1 I discussed how important it is to have a marketing plan. A key part of this plan is to know your market. While this book doesn't go into depth on how to write a marketing plan, it is important to at least identify basic information about your market. Too many people ignore this key step in internet marketing campaigns, but you need this information. Knowing your market will help you determine what keywords to choose as well as the direction to take to update your website.

I also talked about building out a SWOT document. It will make you think. Don't make it a 15-minute exercise. And don't be afraid to face your own demons during this exercise. It's not always pretty, and if you have partners to work with, make sure everybody is on the same page (or pain bodies will come and hunt you down!).

How do you obtain general information about your audience? What should this information consist of? This section answers those questions by explaining the process of analyzing the psychographics and demographics of your audience, along with the best ways to acquire this data. You should reference some of the tools I talked about—Quantcast, Google Ad Planner, and ComScore. Run some tests in Facebook, which has incredible targeting opportunities (see Figure 6–2). Visit the member's area at www.jonrognerud.com/optimizationbook for more specific tactics on Facebook ad campaigns.

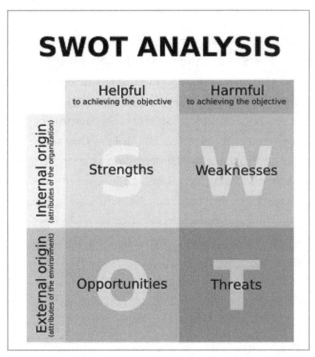

FIGURE 6–1. SWOT Analysis. (*Source*: businessteacher.org.uk/wp-content/swot-analysis-image.png)

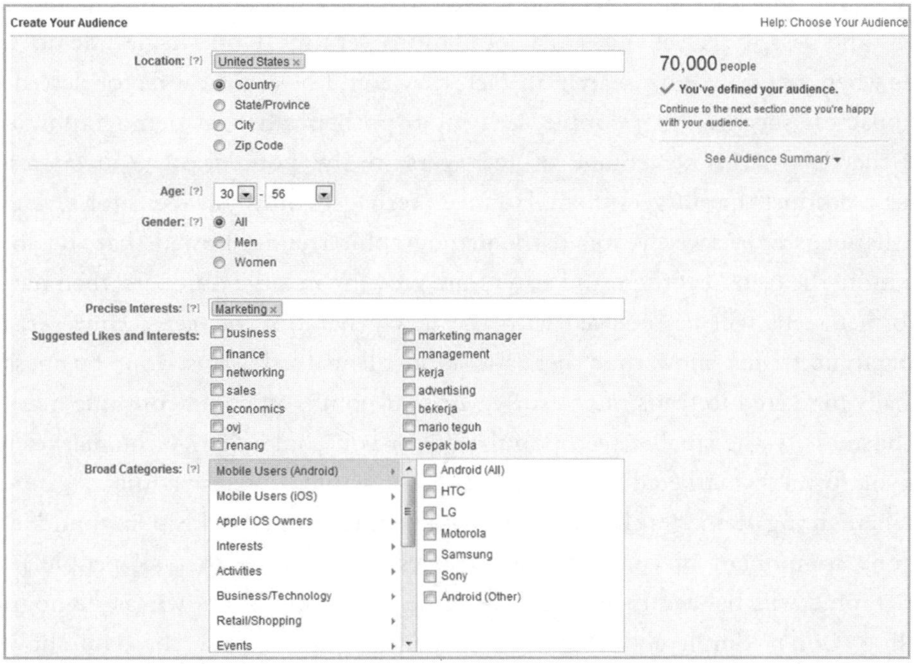

FIGURE 6–2. Facebook demographics targeting test.

Psychographic Analysis

A psychographic analysis is an investigation of consumer behavior. It is also called a lifestyle analysis or AIO (Activities, Interests, Opinions) because it relies on a number of statements about a person's activities, interests, and opinions. In essence, you are determining consumer interest, what they like, and how they live.

A psychographic analysis provides you with information beyond who will buy, or buys, your product or service. It gives you the drivers that make them want to buy it. There are a number of approaches to segment your market. The Values and Lifestyles (VALS) approach developed at Stanford Research Institute International is widely used. Some examples of psychographic information you can research include consumer spending patterns, level of brand consciousness (for your service/product, are consumers brand conscious?), what influences their buying behavior, and what promotional efforts they respond to most often.

When we discuss landing pages and conversions, we talk more about intent, wants, and needs, and how they can be used to leverage content and positioning.

Demographic Analysis

Demographics refers to the physical characteristics of your audience. These characteristics include location, age, marital status, occupation, educational level, disabilities, race, income level, and even an individual's mode of transportation. Demographic trends identify and describe the changes in a population over time. Don't neglect demographic trends when you do your research. In fact, they could be a critical factor determining your business success. For example, let's say hypothetically that demographic trends show there's a large percentage of teenagers in the population. You successfully market a product that targets them. However, teenagers only stay teens for seven years. What happens after seven years? If the demographic trends showed that the younger generation, the teens' brothers and sisters, are growing in large numbers, then naturally the former teens will be replaced with the new generation of teens. However, if the demographic trends show that there's a standstill in birth rates, your business that originally marketed to teens might suffer. At that point you could continue marketing your business to the smaller teen population, or you could change the market to the teens you formerly marketed to, who at this point would be young adults.

When doing demographic marketing, it's important to keep in mind this is only one component of your analysis. You cannot assume that all people in that demographic will behave in exactly the same way. This is known as demographic profiling. Don't completely avoid certain markets just because the data show they might not be interested or eligible. If the data look negative on the surface, see if there is a potential for market growth among that demographic. Video games are a perfect example. When they started out, they were marketed to children and teens. Little emphasis was given to creating games for adults. Things changed as technology improved, especially when the Playstation came out. Now, if the marketing executives responsible for marketing the Playstation console and games had gone with the previous demographic trends, they wouldn't have made much of an attempt to market to an older audience, that is, individuals ages 18 to 90. They didn't, and slowly but surely more and more games for adults were created. Now, it's easy to find video games that are geared to an adult market.

The same principle could be applied to games targeted at women. While that market is still underdeveloped, it's come a long way since video games first came out. There are now more games like The Sims and Dreamfall that try to create an entertaining experience for both genders. Previously, women were so ignored in the video game industry that it was a source of controversy when a gaming company braved the market and produced a game with a prominent female character.

How to Find Out the Psychographics and Demographics of Your Market

To determine the psychographics and demographics of your market, there are a variety of sources and methods you can use, including surveys and specialized marketing software. The American Marketing Association (www.marketingpower.com) offers a number of free and low-cost marketing tools. To access the tools, you will need to sign up for a free subscription, but you'll be able to read case studies, research, look up terms and definitions, and more.

Hitwise (hitwise.com) offers competitive intelligence products and services for online marketing, online advertising, and search marketing. You can obtain in-depth demographic and industry insight. Hitwise is a paid service.

Nielsen//NetRatings (www.nielsen-online.com/intlpage.html) offers some free data and rankings and also has a number of paid products and solutions for internet marketing and online advertising.

We've already learned about creating surveys for your audience. We won't go into much more detail in this section except to add that there are survey networks you can join if you have the cash. Be careful, though. Many of these networks claim to offer money to respondents in exchange for their participation in a survey, but many of them tend to avoid payment. So, if you do decide to use a survey network, research it before you start doing business. Survey networks that don't pay tend to be talked about a lot in message board forums, so an easy way to determine if a survey network is a scam is to enter its name in a search engine along with the term "scam."

The other method to discuss is using software to size up your market. You can obtain demographics info from Quantcast.com. The software is free; it lets you track your site in its vast database and will create more detail for you by applying a simple script to your page. You can also buy information products or customized lists based on your data sets from InfoUSA.com, an aggregator of business listings across the United States.

You can obtain keyword competitiveness data from SEMRush.com or SpyFu.com.

THINK LIKE YOUR AUDIENCE

What separates the average internet marketer from the highly successful one? It's not necessarily marketing skill in itself. You could have the highest search engine rankings in the world, yet if your copy doesn't touch your visitors' emotional impulses in some way, you won't get sales. Compare that with internet marketers who may not have as high a search engine ranking, but get more conversions because they relate to the consumer better. This section explains how you can relate to your customer better by analyzing the basics in marketing psychology, which would include Maslow's Hierarchy of Needs along with the general thought processes of various marketing groups.

Maslow's Hierarchy of Needs

Maslow's hierarchy of needs (en.wikipedia.org/wiki/Maslow's_hierarchy_of_needs) is a basic psychological theory that businesses often use to evaluate their marketing tactics. Usually displayed in pyramid format, the theory explains that humans are driven by five levels of needs: physiological, safety, love/belonging, esteem, and self-actualization (see Figure 6–3).

In the same manner, Bruce Clay and his team looked at how to use this model to infer a SEO hierarchy of needs (flickr.com/photos/bruceclay/3875105591/) of a typical online website optimization program as illustrated in Figure 6–4. If thinking in this way, you should be well on your way to building a solid online presence. Start at the bottom, and work your way up.

Physiological. Physiological needs, which are at the base of the pyramid, include all the physical needs that must be met for healthy functioning. These include eating, drinking, sex/reproduction, sleep, and eliminating wastes. Grocery stores and fertility clinics are examples of businesses that fulfill physiological needs.

In developed countries creating a business based on physiological needs alone won't guarantee success, simply because there are so many of them already. Businesspeople must give their businesses a unique spin to compete with other enterprises selling

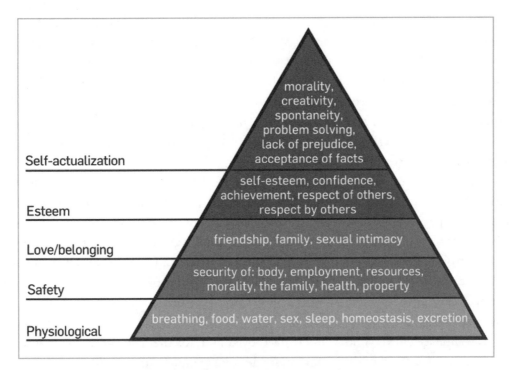

FIGURE 6–3. Maslow's Hierarchy of Needs.

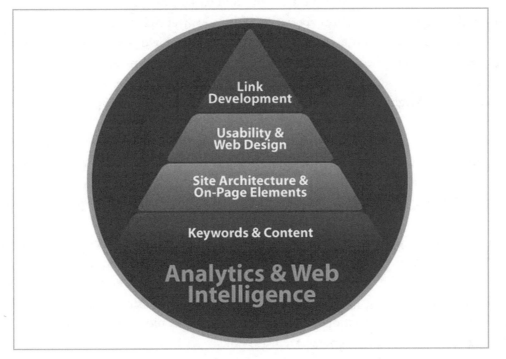

FIGURE 6–4. SEO Hierarchy of Needs. (From BruceClay.com)

products that meet physiological needs. For example, online grocery stores are a limited market. I live in Southern California, where Vons and Albertsons are among the grocery stores that deliver. However, in other areas, even where online delivery exists, the online stores either have limited inventory or don't deliver to certain areas. The need for fast and quick groceries without having to travel to a grocery store is attractive both in the product being provided and the marketing "hook," which would be the online aspect. Of course, a newcomer in that business would have to provide a larger inventory along with making their service available nationwide.

Safety. People cannot be happy if they don't feel safe. So products that ensure the safety of individuals and their families tend to get noticed. Self-protection products such as pepper spray (where legal) and personal alarms are two examples. Products or services that protect the home or the possessions in it, such as a product that prevents a door from opening, are another example. Competition isn't eliminated, as you still need to do your research, but remember that a lot of people are willing to make the necessary investment if they feel they're going to protect their lives, families, or possessions.

Love/Belonging. Everyone wants to feel loved and accepted, so products or services that promote this level of the hierarchy are definitely important. Dating sites are a good example of services that meet the love/belonging need. Social networking sites such as MySpace and Facebook also meet this need. A variant of the love/belonging need is promotion of products that are expected to indirectly meet that need. For example, some weight-loss products show a woman as being more dateable or even marriageable after she has lost weight. The products in and of themselves do not meet the love/belonging need, but by promoting how much more beautiful and attractive a woman is to men after she loses weight, companies promoting diet products give the impression that their products are the "solution" to finding romance.

Esteem. Services or products that meet a person's esteem needs give them a sense of accomplishment and respect, both from others and for themselves. An example of an enterprise that meets esteem needs is colleges.

Self-Actualization. Self-actualization can be defined as the process of people meeting their goals. Because this is at the highest level of Maslow's hierarchy of needs, it can be hard to define exactly what types of products or services meet self-actualization goals because they differ from person to person. Some markets, such as home businesses, are successful because they meet generalized self-actualization goals—in this case, the dream of being rich and financially sufficient. Others work on the basis of niche markets. The plus side with self-actualization is that it's a market that could be met through products that are low-cost and easy to make, such as books.

THE BASIC MARKETING GROUPS

This section goes into detail about the basic marketing categories your audience will fall into. These categories are age, gender, race/nationality, socioeconomic status, familial status, business-to-business (B2B), health/disability, religion, and occupational status.

Age

The average person lives 80 years, with each period of his or her life offering a different set of interests than before. This section will talk more about these periods and the products and services people are interested in during each period.

Baby/Toddler (ages 0 to 2). At this stage of life, people are incapable of verbally expressing what they are interested in, yet marketers still take advantage of this demographic. Why? Because while babies and toddlers can't say what they want or need, their parents can. So if you're promoting a product or service geared to babies and toddlers, you should consider yourself to be marketing to the parents. Sure, babies can give cues if they like a certain toy, food, or television show, and parents respond to that. But you need to market your product or service to the parent first before thinking about how the baby will respond to it, though some may consider these things as interrelated.

To get ideas of the types of products geared toward those in babyhood, take a trip through Babies "R" Us or look at the commercials on BabyfirstTV or the PBS Kids Sprout channel.

You can use the internet to search baby products. Use the keyword analysis techniques you learned about earlier to determine which baby products sell the best. You can go right to the source. No, not the babies, but the parents who buy for them. There are a number of blogs and forums for parents. Find out what parents are discussing. You'll discover products they're recommending (or not recommending) as well as unmet needs. Don't be afraid to ask questions, as this could be a potential marketplace for you.

Child (ages 3 to 12). My own kids are in this age group. How fun it is! Send me a note at contact@jonrognerud.com if you are a parent, would love to share stories on how you balance online marketing, being an entrepreneur and business owner, and managing your time effectively. If you look at most of the commercials that come on during kids' shows, you'll discover what, to a marketer's mind, interests kids. This would basically be toys, sweet foods, and, to a lesser extent, clothes. One neglected market is education, though with games like V-Smile (a special video game system that only plays educational video games) this is changing. Other aspects that are neglected—at least on TV commercials—are products relating to sports and other outdoor activities, and books.

One major disadvantage with this market is the inability of children to buy their own merchandise. They aren't in as bad a position as babies or toddlers, as they can at least verbalize to their parents what they want. However, ultimately the parent is the one who has the final say on whether or not the product gets bought. So, if you're selling a product or service related to the children's market, make an effort to impress the parents. For food, you could emphasize health benefits. For toys, you could emphasize educational benefits. But remember, there are some toys that only a child would see value in; a parent would buy it because their kid wanted it. Marketing a child's love for a product could be the "hook" that gets a parent to buy, even if the product offers no other benefit.

Teenager (ages 13 to 19). The teenage market is interesting because some teenagers have access to funds through part-time jobs or allowances and they have autonomy to spend it as they choose. Other teenagers may have money but not autonomy; that is, their parents have veto power over books, games, music, etc. Still others may have neither. However, you don't have to worry as much about marketing to their parents, because teens are developing adult interests.

Some things teens are thinking about include dating, education (especially in terms of going to college), friendships/popularity, making money, video games, and buying a car. There are also overlooked niche markets, such as teenage mothers. Generally, they would have the above-mentioned interests, along with the interests an adult would have when it comes to getting things for their young children. Additionally, teenage mothers may be thinking about how to get a decent job without a high school diploma.

Young Adult (ages 18 to 25). Young adults can be difficult to market to because they usually don't have much money. They're at a point in their lives where they're trying to be independent and maybe they can't rely on their parents for money (although some reports indicate more than 50 percent live at home). For this reason marketers don't hesitate to promote credit cards to this demographic, and their campaigns tend to be successful.

Yet, young adults are complex. Most are trying to find ways to get established. This age group is particularly influenced by their peers. Music, clothing, technology, gaming, cell phones, and ringtones are all products of interest to this market. This demographic, along with teens and tweens, tends to be brand conscious. Influential peer groups include young Hollywood, so products or services approved by rappers, professional athletes, and celebutantes have an almost built-in guarantee of success.

Young Money magazine is a good place to find out what interests the upwardly mobile in this demographic. Its readers tend to be college grads on a fast track to the executive suite.

Adult (ages 25 to 40). Around age 25, many adults have established a good foundation. Most are no longer students and are a few years into their careers. They have their own cars and addresses (although many return to live with parents). Some are married or thinking of marriage. So, what would they be thinking about as they progress through their adult years? Buying houses is a very big thing to them, along with settling down. If they have already done these things, then their concerns would focus on products or services that could be of value to their families. They are also concerned with improving their financial security, whether it's by getting better jobs, starting their own businesses, and/or improving their credit scores. Some adults are interested in continuing their education to get a master's or even a Ph.D. degree.

Middle Age (ages 40 to 60). Middle-aged individuals have basically accomplished all of the things that adults and young adults are still striving to attain. They have their education, career, house, and family. In fact, when it comes to family, the middle-aged are at the point where their kids are about to move out of the house and start their own lives. For houses, they might be on their second or third house by now. So, what else is there to think about in one's life?

One of the biggest things middle-aged people think about can be summed up in one word: *retirement*. Even if they have good jobs, without a suitable retirement package they might be forced to continue working even if they don't want to. So, making money and securing good retirement plans are of interest to many middle-aged people.

Some additional concerns could be for their children, especially when it comes to their teens' college education. They think a lot about their health, so supplements might sell well with them. They are thinking about their weight and sexual health (women focus on how their bodies are changing through menopause, while men may focus on impotence). Both genders will be thinking about how to address hair loss and graying hair.

The Elderly (ages 60+). If elderly people are mobile and have money, they are thinking about how they can pass their time. This age group loves going on cruises and visiting resorts. They also like spending money on their grandchildren. They probably don't think much about buying additional homes, yet they may want to make investments to remodel their current homes. Or, they may decide to sell their houses and move into assisted-living communities.

This is the best scenario with an older person. Scenarios that are not as good are those where the elderly person has to go into a nursing home because of medical problems. Depending on their mental faculties, they might take an interest in which nursing home they go to; otherwise their children may have to make this decision.

Elderly people also think about death. Granted, it's a grim thought, but it's a market that tends to purchase grave sites and insurance policies. They are also thinking about how to set up their wills.

Gender

Things have changed when it comes to men and women, at least in the United States. You can't be sexist and assume that a woman is going to buy a vacuum cleaner just because she's at home. Yet, even with the progress that has occurred when it comes to equality between the sexes, there remain some significant psychological differences between men and women—differences that impact their spending habits.

Women. Most online marketing campaigns market things such as clothes, perfume, jewelry, romance novels, weight-loss products, and household supplies to women. While these do seem to do well, some may interpret the perpetual marketing of these types of things as having sexist overtones. However, as with every demographic, don't limit yourself to broad-based assumptions. Women's interests expand beyond these categories. A lot of women work, so products or services that relate to career advancement would be of interest. There are also niche markets among women that a marketer would have traditionally promoted among men. These include sports equipment and video games. Finally, women are often key or primary decision makers for products and services for the whole family. This means that women may make the buying decisions even about products designed for men. Incidentally, women are the most active and engaging group in social media, overall. Why do you think that is?

Men. Many of the products marketed to men are sports equipment, grilling, clothes, knives, razors, guns, video games, and, to a lesser extent, cologne. Dieting, a market traditionally geared more toward women, has always been a niche market for men. There is a niche that is virtually untouched—men who are at home during the day. This could be due to working at night or being work-at-home husbands. Either way, it is assumed that some of the types of things that would interest women in terms of cleaning and cooking products wouldn't interest men, though with the growing niche of men at home, that is changing.

Race/Nationality

Marketing by race or nationality is controversial if you're not of the same race as the group of people to which you are marketing. So generally, try to avoid doing this unless you are promoting an enterprise that, due to being clearly geared for a particular race or nationality, wouldn't cause offense if promoted by an outsider. For example, let's say you created a website talking about colleges, with historically black colleges being one of the subtopics. If you advertise this web page on a "black" website (such as a message board), you would still be marketing in an ethical manner.

More questionable marketing tactics would be pushing certain products or services based on a stereotype of a race or nationality. An example could be a discounted assumption that the majority of Asians are into education; hence, promoting SAT prep books or software to a mostly Asian audience might not be appropriate. A better marketing approach would be to say that people aged 15 to 18 are interested in SAT prep books or software, since the SAT is the key for getting into college.

It's important to note, however, that if you are the same race or nationality as the people you are marketing to, you might be able to think of a lot of niche markets, since you are directly involved in the culture. You can think about needs that are being met for other communities, but not your own. You can also market on a more personal/human level. Your visitors will be more attentive to what you have to say if they feel that you are sympathetic to their interests.

Socioeconomic Status

Socioeconomic status refers to what financial class a person belongs to. The main classes include poor, lower middle class, middle class, upper middle class, and rich.

Poor and Lower Middle Class. Poorer people are concerned with finding ways to survive. Since they have limited funds, they don't have money for vacations, investments, or home ownership. However, most do want to find a way out of their situation, if possible. Promoting free government services, especially those that provide employment and/or educational assistance, works well with this demographic. Also, think about promoting resources where they can obtain free health care.

Keep in mind that poorer individuals may not have enough money to afford to surf the internet at home. This means that they have to access it through libraries or college campuses. They may not feel safe making purchases in these environments, since the computers are public. Thus, you may want to consider promoting informational sites. Or, you will want to make sure that they feel comfortable buying on a public computer. Always use SSL (secure sockets layer) for transactions dealing with personal or financial information. Let your visitors know this when they visit your site.

Middle Class and Upper Middle Class. This group is in an interesting position when it comes to their access to financial resources. They are far from poor (although many have said the economy is erasing the middle class), but they do not have the disposable income that the rich do. Yet, through credit cards and bank loans, they tend to be able to take advantage of the same types of things that rich people do. Middle- and upper-middle-class people go on vacations, buy boats, send their kids to private schools, and buy nice homes and cars. However, many are doing so while getting into a mountain of debt. For this reason, think about promoting refinancing, mortgages, and credit repair with this demographic. Business opportunities are also of interest to the middle and upper middle class, since they still want to make enough money to get to the "next level." And unlike poor people, they have enough money to try out a business opportunity.

Middle- and upper-middle-class people are interested in discounted services and merchandise. Most do not have to pinch pennies as much as a poorer person, but they still want to get the most for their money.

This market also prizes education, both for themselves and their children. Some middle- and upper-middle-class people may be able to pay for their education themselves, though knowledge of loans, scholarships, and free government programs is of interest.

The Rich. Rich people have enough income that they can generally buy whatever they want. In terms of what they buy, they are more interested in the names and labels associated with their merchandise. Extremely rich people will also buy things that people with less money would never dream of, such as islands. The rich are also concerned about education, but for them it would be Ivy League and private schools.

Rich people are also interested in how to make money. While they won't be interested in the so-called "business opportunities" that are advertised on the internet, they are interested in investments.

Familial Status

Familial status can be broken down into singles, married with no kids, married with kids, and empty-nesters.

Singles. Singles are categorized as those who are unmarried or not in a committed relationship. They can live by themselves or have kids. If they have kids, then some of their buying interests would be similar to those of married people with kids.

What are singles interested in when it comes to buying? Matchmaking services are popular with this market, but remember in this day and time many singles don't feel the need to rush into marriage. Other things that interest them could be in the self-actualization area. They may also be interested in social events that would bring them new acquaintances.

In terms of housing, the singles market may not be as interested in purchasing a home, but, on the other hand, many are. Singles with kids will probably feel differently, so don't hesitate to promote mortgage loans with this market.

Married with No Kids. Couples with no kids can either be in the process of having kids or have decided that they don't want kids at all. If a couple is trying to have kids, they will be interested in buying a home for their upcoming family, along with purchasing baby products. If they don't want to have kids, then they could have some of the same interests as single people. In terms of home ownership, it could be either/or for couples who decide not to have kids. They see a benefit to home ownership, and since they're already married, they don't have to deal with the legal issues of ownership that a single person faces when becoming part of a couple. However, a childless couple may not feel as pressed to buy a home as a couple that plans to have children.

Married with Kids. Couples with kids are not in the position to be as interested in social events, going out, or partying as couples without kids or singles. They are interested in daycare/babysitting, products related to their kids' education, and other things related to kids or family. They are interested in acquiring mortgages, and, if they already have one, they might want to refinance.

Empty-Nesters. Empty-nesters are couples or singles whose kids have grown up and moved out of the house. Age-wise they can be as young as 35 (if they had their kids in their teens), but most are middle-aged or elderly. Figuring out how to handle their children's college expenses is a prominent issue with this age group. Older empty-nesters are interested in their retirement plans. Younger, single empty-nesters might be interested in dating at this stage, since their kids are no longer a concern. Both groups may also take more of an interest in social events and vacationing.

B2B

Business owners are interested in products or services that will either help sustain their business or increase marketability or productivity. Examples of products required for the general functioning of a business include office supplies, desks, computer equipment, and industry-specific products (such as a steam cleaner for a carpet cleaning business). Website design is an example of a service that could increase marketability for a business, while an electronic envelope stuffer could increase productivity.

Health/Disability

A lot of marketing potential is available when advertising to this market, but you have to make sure you hit a niche market rather than something general. For example, if you ran an AdSense site for progeria (a condition that causes children to age prematurely), you might get more clicks than if you ran an AdSense site for high blood pressure. While high blood pressure would offer more in terms of general searches, the competition would be so fierce that you wouldn't be able to rank high anyway. Progeria offers much less competition, so visitors would be more likely to go on and click through to your site.

Religion

Religion opens up many doors for niche markets. Examples could be Christian movies, books, video games, or clothing. There are many more niches, including those with no direct tie-in to the religion itself, but to their interests—for example, family-oriented movies or games.

Occupational Status

For certain types of jobs, people may need to purchase supplies that are not available where they work. For example, teachers often purchase art supplies, paper, and other materials for their classrooms with their own money. There are also industries where a person may have to take a test to get licensed for his occupation. In this case people would be interested in buying training materials, which can be in the form of books or computer software.

MARKETING

The marketing terms and categories may be a lot to take in at one time. However, it's a key ingredient in your success. The discipline of marketing is important because it uncovers whom we should target, why, and how we should reach them. For example, many marketers believed that making things pink was a good tactic for marketing to women. Make it pink and pretty and women will come. Wrong! Some women hate pink, and most want clear-cut solutions to their problems. Many are making buying decisions for the whole house, so presenting them with enough information to make those decisions is a good strategy. Your market should drive your messaging and not the other way around. This is no less important in search marketing. Take the time to understand, identify, and properly target the right audience and you'll get a tremendous return on the time invested in doing so. And don't forget to use and think about this framework and approach for targeting when you do your research on Amazon, eBay, ClickBank, Commission Junction, Google (search, paid, content), and related tools talked about in earlier chapters.

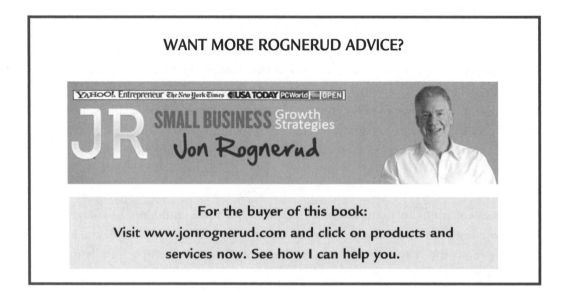

Chapter 7

Why Ethics Matter Online and What You Can Do Now

Bob began writing articles about coaching topics to boost his visibility online. He loved writing and felt that he was providing good information that would boost his other marketing efforts. He started posting to three or four sites initially but then found software that would post to hundreds of sites at once. He tested carefully and tried to provide useful content. He found that mass posting was not a great option, but started to focus on quality article and blog sites.

Bob had also learned the value of keyword descriptions and tags. He found popular and related keywords and sprinkled them naturally in all of his articles and posts. He did the same thing for his website, and focused on very high quality for readers and linkers. A woman named Nina, who was also an SEO expert, found Bob's site when searching for keywords Bob used. An issue is that Bob's content had little to do with the keywords used, and there was a lot of repetition on the homepage and interior pages.

Normally, Nina would have been irritated and continued her search but she had a feeling that Bob's intentions had been good. Nina read through his actual content and thought Bob had a lot to offer. She emailed him and they connected by phone the next day. Bob was shocked when after exchanging greetings, Nina said, "Did you know that you were practicing some forms of spammy SEO?"

Throughout this book you have learned how to design your website, how to look for the right keywords, and how to consider the psychology of your audience when writing your content and/or choosing your keywords. We've also touched on several search engine and web optimization principles. Now, it's time to roll up our sleeves and discover the ins and outs of search engine optimization.

In this chapter you learn basic search optimization guidelines, along with the more specific guidelines of Google search engine optimization. Why Google? Well, because Google consistently leads all others in search engine traffic and dominates the marketplace with approximately 65 percent (http://www.comscore.com/Insights/Press_Releases/2013/6/comScore_Releases_May_2013_U.S._Search_Engine_Rankings).

It makes sense to optimize for the greatest amount of traffic and have your efforts rewarded across the board.

DISCOVER REAL SEO ETHICS AND WEBMASTER GUIDELINES

A discussion of search engine optimization would not be complete without addressing what happens when good SEO goes bad. As with other things, many of the practices that are frowned on were once legitimate. However, when good practices are overused or used for bad purposes, it penalizes everyone.

SEO, like every other discipline, has legitimate, industry-accepted practices and those that strive to "trick" the system. Industry insiders refer to unethical or unfair practices as black hat SEO.

The terms white hat and black hat were actually taken from old cowboy movies (commonly called Westerns). In these movies the good guy always wore a white hat and the bad guy always wore a black hat. So the sheriff of the town would ride in with a white hat to fight off the robbers who wore black hats. For ages in Western history black has often been associated with darkness, shadows, and evil, and white has stood as a symbol of goodness and purity.

In the cyber world black hat was first used in reference to hacking, but the basic principles are the same when it comes to search engine optimization.

However, there's debate about what is "unfair or unethical." A common thread to what is black hat is "unfair manipulation." Some would argue that SEO in and of itself is a manipulative tactic. After all, the purpose of SEO is to manipulate the search engines into ranking your site higher, right? Wrong! SEO and SEM (search engine marketing) are equivalent to creating advertising messages for television, magazines, or other formats. You strive to gain the attention of your target audience—the audience that needs and desires what you sell. You aren't trying to twist their arm and falsely manipulate them into buying your product or service.

This false assumption about sales and marketing is why so many fail at the practices. If you believe that selling is mind manipulation, you may trick a few people into buying your goods and services, but you won't create long-term, sustainable relationships. My goal with this book is to share with you good, sound practices and the underlying principles that will not only help you earn money today but also well into the future. I believe good business is based on relationships, and a foundation built on deceit and trickery does not support that goal.

What is considered black hat SEO varies. Clearly, hacking somebody's website is beyond ethical, and nobody should do this! Sometimes black hat is designated by search engine guidelines. The practice itself may not be unethical but simply scowled on by the search engine. There are black hat practices that intentionally set out to harm the competition. These tactics are widely embraced as wrong. Black hat sometimes involves property rights (stealing content from others). The biggest debates about black hat are practices so designated because they result in "unnatural rankings." It's important to understand the many facets of SEO so that you'll know what not to do. Some practices that may appear harmless can get you in trouble with search engines. I believe that if you aren't hurting someone, you're following the best rule. For example, a mother searches for a baby stroller but is instead taken to an adult site. That could be considered "hurting" another person. Don't do that.

In the example below, the users are led to believe they'll receive an informational article from a .EDU (educational) institution, but they are taken directly to a shopping site. It uses a temporary redirect (302) and masks the link.

Webmasters who use white hat SEO techniques are as concerned about their visitors' experience on their website as they are with ranking high on search engines. Thus they concentrate on creating content that both their visitors and search engines are hungry for, forming legitimate relationships with other websites for link building and proper use of meta tags. You have already learned how to create appropriate SEO-optimized content along with how to use meta tags. You were introduced to link-building concepts, but only the basics. Before we can delve more deeply into what you need to do to embark on a successful link-building campaign, we have to lay a foundation of the rules.

WHAT YOU SHOULD NOT DO: BLACK HAT SEO

So let's talk about black hat SEO. Black hat SEO optimization has no consideration for website visitors. Its only goal is to get ranked high in search engines. Black hat SEO optimization techniques are considered "spamdexing."

Spamdexing (content spam, link spam, and cloaking are examples) is a practice that tries to manipulate the search engines' indexing to produce higher ranking results. An

MAKE IT YOURS!

One tip to try to "make it yours" is to interlink to other articles and posts on your own site, and brand it in resources boxes and elsewhere. But realize that many syndicated networks remove links in the middle of the content/article, and allow "resource box" (bottom) links only.

example of spamdexing is keyword stuffing. In keyword stuffing you stuff competitive keywords on a page on your site simply to manipulate search engines rather than deliver useful content to the user. The content may not even make sense. It's simply a trick to manipulate the engines to rank you higher. You can also "overstuff" the page's meta tags.

Duplicate Content. As Google defines it, duplicate content means you have the exact text on a different page in the same site. It's not a problem here and there, unless it grows and is unchecked. Then you will (intentionally or not) be caught in "content filtering," or the "slow ranking death." This also applies to sister sites, or sites to which you are linked, and where content is re-used (scraped) without your approval. Duplicate content doesn't mean that every single word on all of your pages must be unique, but if you use a tool like Copyscape.com, it should not have any red flags. Black hat duplication is copying and pasting the same paragraphs from one page to another. This practice can, and most likely will, drop your site's rankings, and possibly exclude content from the main index. Syndicated content (distribution of pages/content via syndicated networks) with correct original attribution is not treated as duplicate content per se, so if you carry a news feed on your homepage that may also be found on 1,000 other websites, the search engines won't drop your ranking for it. However, you should track and watch this as part of your ongoing SEO work.

Note: Syndicated content is highly contested in terms of how much it can affect your site in the rankings and a much-discussed topic in search forums and at search conferences. Suggestions about "freshness" of data and origins are still being offered.

Link farming is the process of exchanging reciprocal links with websites to increase search engine optimization. The idea behind link farming is to increase the number of sites that link to yours, because search engines such as Google rank sites according to, among other things, the quality and quantity of sites that link to yours. In theory, the more sites that link to yours, the higher your ranking in the search engine results will be, because more links indicate a higher level of popularity among internet users.

However, search engines such as Google consider link farming as a form of spam and have implemented procedures to banish sites that participate in link farming, so link farming has garnered negative connotations across the internet.

The difference between good link building and bad link building is how it's done. Link spamming is another type of link farming in which you use software to generate lots of links over a short time. Google in particular looks unfavorably at lots of links over a short time, not built naturally, and with varying anchor text changes. In fact, Google refrains from the use of the term "reciprocal link exchanges" in its documentation. If you have a relationship with a few related marketplace website owners—and that truly offers good value—you should not worry about exchanging a few links. Don't make it a regular practice, however.

There are many service providers who promise to help you boost your link popularity by automatically entering you in link exchange programs they operate. The programs often link your page with websites that have nothing to do with your content. Users should be aware of the repercussions of this action. The major search engines penalize sites that participate in link farming, thereby negating their intended effect. A link farm is a web page that's nothing more than a page of links to other sites.

As I said earlier, some practices are black hat because the search engine frowns on them. For this reason it's important to read the webmaster guidelines provided by the search engines. Google, in particular, may punish you by banishing your site to the still-existing supplemental index (fondly known as Google Hell), and you may not even understand why or how you got there! That's why you must understand the good and bad so you'll know what not to do.

I'll refer to the SI (supplemental index) below. Terminology has changed over the last few years. Here's a quick check example to see if you are in SI. If you input your domain with site:yourdomainhere.com and page through the results, you'll be able to see it, if showing: "In order to show you the most relevant results, we have omitted some

INSIDER TIP

Good, unique titles and internal link structure using keywords, deep linking, and unique content for every page will help you stay clear of content filtering and likely prevent it from happening. If you must include text on your page because a requirement from an organization (often found in the real estate field for example)—add the text as an image (gif/jpg) to the page so search engines will not filter you for duplicate content.

entries very similar to the [n] already displayed. If you like, you can <repeat the search with the omitted results included>."

Google's supplemental index is like the digital basement. You're still listed on Google but not in the more visible core index. Relegation to the supplemental index can significantly impact your revenues. A few things that can relegate you to the basement are duplicate content, a lack of links to other quality sites (yes, confusing, you can't have too little or too many) and pages internally, and pages with only a few words and pictures and little content.

Office politics have made their way to cyberspace as well. Black hat sabotage is unfortunately alive and well in search engine marketing. Using black hat SEO, a competitor can harm your site rankings. In a practice sometimes called Google bowling, someone else frames your site for link spamming. They generate automated links to bad neighborhoods and make it appear that you're guilty of link spamming. Google then drops your search rankings.

One of the most famous examples of link spamming was a "miserable failure." Thousands of links using "miserable failure" in the anchor text pointed to whitehouse. gov, President George Bush.

When asked about negative SEO, Matt Cutts, a senior software engineer for Google, offered this comment: "Piling links onto a competitor's site to reduce its search rank isn't impossible, but it's extremely difficult. We try to be mindful of when a technique can be abused and make our algorithm robust against it. I won't go out on a limb and say it's impossible. But Google bowling is much more inviting as an idea than it is in practice" ("The Saboteurs of Search," Andy Greenberg, Forbes.com, October 2007).

What Is Content Spamming?

Content spamming involves tricking a search engine into thinking a website has relevant, keyword-rich content when it really doesn't. Some of these methods create website copy that not only is irrelevant but cumbersome for the website visitor to read. Others show nothing to the visitor, but are still considered black hat. The specific types of content spamming are outlined below.

Keyword Stuffing. Keyword stuffing comes in four categories: content keyword stuffing, image keyword stuffing, meta tag keyword stuffing, and invisible text keyword stuffing.

Content Keyword Stuffing. Remember when you learned earlier that your content might (used as a guide) have a keyword density of no more than two to five percent? When it has a keyword density that's higher, not only does its ridiculousness negatively affect your credibility in the eyes of your visitors, it's also flagged for spam. It's more appropriate to look at keyword density for black hat, perhaps. As mentioned earlier, don't overthink the keyword density for your normal writing and content. Natural copy and thinking about your users work best.

Don't confuse legitimate SEO writing with keyword stuffing. More than likely, even if you're an average SEO writer, you won't do keyword stuffing. Writers who do keyword stuffing do it on purpose and know that their content looks crazy. They don't care about their visitors; they just want to rank high in the search engines and hope that the visitor will concentrate more on the banner or link ads than the content. An example of keyword-stuffed content could be as follows:

> Cheap Laptops offers the best in cheap laptops. The cheap laptops available from CheapLaptops.com are as low as $300! Not only that, but the cheap laptops from CheapLaptops.com make the cost even cheaper with its free shipping, available for a limited time. Also, the cheap laptops are not cheap when it comes to the brands available. With CheapLaptops.com, you can buy Sony, Gateway, Dell, Toshiba, Acer, HP, and more. Just because CheapLaptops.com offers cheap laptops doesn't mean that you'll have to settle for generic brands. Indeed, you won't be able to find cheap laptops anywhere else but from CheapLaptops.com. So come on down and get your cheap laptop today from CheapLaptops.com. You'll be happy once your brand new cheap laptop from CheapLaptops.com comes in the mail. On top of that with CheapLaptops.com you don't have to pay shipping for your cheap laptop. Try getting that from Amazon, eBay or other sites selling cheap laptops. I guarantee you won't be able to find free shipping on cheap laptops at any place other than Cheap Laptops.com.

See how insane that is? And can you guess the keyword density for that awful content? With as many times as "cheap laptops" appears, you would think the keyword density would be crazy, like 20 percent. But it was only 8 percent, not much higher than what you can legitimately do, which is 5 percent. Don't worry. More than likely you won't produce such trash because you're not trying to. For comparison purposes, below is an example of appropriate SEO writing that adheres to the guidelines you learned earlier in this book.

> If you're looking for a good deal on laptops, look no further than CheapLaptops.com. With CheapLaptops.com, you can buy laptops for as low as $300. Some of the brands that are available include: Sony, Gateway, Dell, Toshiba, Acer, HP, and more. Additionally, as an added bonus, the site is offering free

shipping for a limited period of time. So, if you're looking to save money on your next laptop purchase, consider visiting CheapLaptops.com. There's even a free gift waiting for you—act today!

This copy is significantly easier to read, and more important, won't get flagged as spam. In the long run, you'll want to stick with this type of copy. The first one may get you a high ranking for a short time, but once search engines catch up to the spam technique, your site will get banned.

It should be noted that there's an even more blatant variant of content keyword stuffing. This form may have legitimate content in the areas of the website that are most likely to be visited, (such as at the top or, more commonly, toward the middle of the page), but at the bottom is garbage. It's usually not even in the form of content, but rather a bunch of keywords.

Image Keyword Stuffing. While Google and other search engines can't read images or text that might be on them, they do read what is in the "alt" attribute (often incorrectly referred to as an image alt tag), which offers a description of what an image is. It's not used much anymore. The proper way to use the alt attribute is shown below:

```
<IMG src="yourimage.gif" alt= "short description of your image, possible
related keyword"/>
```

The IMG is the tag that tells the browser an image is about to be shown. The "src" attribute is where you enter in the name of your image along with its extension. Then there's the "alt" that spammers love to exploit. The normal use of the alt tag is to place a one-word description of your image. It can be a keyword if the keyword relates to the image. If it doesn't relate, then you should say what it is. For example, if "yourimage. gif" was a picture of a purse, the alt tag should say "purse." But the following is what a keyword stuffer would do:

```
<IMG src="purse.gif" alt= "coach purse, designer purse, chanel purse, whole-
sale purse, louis vuitton purse, gucci purse, prada purse, dooney bourke
purse, replica purse, vera bradley purse, purse party, handbag purse, coin
purse, discount coach purse, baby phat purse, juicy couture purse, coin
purse, knockoff purse, dog purse, purse forum, photo purse"/>
```

They fill the "alt" tag with keywords unrelated to the image. The hope is that by doing this the image gets indexed in the image results of Google or other search engines offering an image-based search. When images are displayed in these listings, the website that contains them is also displayed. Of course, the keyword stuffer won't get this result, and if they do, it's temporary. This tactic, being not as "bad" as other ones, may not get the site totally banned, but it certainly will get the website a lower ranking.

> ### ONLINE RESOURCE
>
> The alt attribute was developed for 508 accessibility reasons. Get more tips at webaim.org/standards/508/checklist.

Meta Tag Keyword Stuffing. From your newly acquired knowledge of meta tags, can you guess where a keyword stuffer would do their dirty work? Yes, in the title tag. Keyword stuffing the title tag can cause lots of keywords to show up in the title browser and make the site look unprofessional. Another black hat technique is to spam the keyword and description attribute. It's not uncommon to stuff so many keywords into these attributes that the HTML code is pages long.

Invisible Text Keyword Stuffing. Invisible text is the practice of putting lists of keywords in white text on a white background. This practice is to get more spiders to crawl the site. The webmaster makes the text the same color as the background, so it's invisible to the visitor. For example, if the background is white, he would make the invisible text white. Regular content would appear in a table or image, so that it's still visible. The hope is that the search engine will index a site that, to the naked eye, looks legitimate. Quick tip for Windows users: Try Ctrl-A (select all) on the page, to see if anything is hiding on the page.

Gateway or Doorway Pages. Gateway or doorway pages are small web pages that contain a small amount of content and link to a legitimate web page. They used to be considered a white hat SEO tactic, until people started using them strictly for the purpose of tricking spiders to index the site higher.

Scraper Sites. Scraper sites, also called Made for AdSense sites, are created from programs called article generators. Article generators scrape the internet looking for highly-ranked content. It takes bits and pieces of this content from one website to another to create a new article. The problem with this is if the content is not rewritten, the webmaster is breaking copyright law by using it. Of course, the black hat SEO optimizer using this technique doesn't care about the law, or their visitors' experience. For this reason you'll find that most scraper sites are laden with ads or serve as doorway pages to other sites.

Don't think that article generators are all bad. In fact, they can be a helpful tool in creating content. The key to remember is that what they show is a source of research only. You don't own the copyrights to the content they create, which is why they need to be rewritten. If you use an article generator, use it to find ideas, rather than something that can write content for you. In fact, I view them as elaborate keyword analyzers.

ONLINE RESOURCE

You'll find content generators listed on the accompanying membership site at www.jonrognerud.com/optimizationbook.

Hidden Links. To create hidden links, webmasters do the same thing as they would for hidden text; they make the background the same color as the text. This gives the appearance of a lot of outbound links and even reciprocal links. You might be wondering how they could have reciprocal links if they're hiding the links. Doesn't the process of getting reciprocal links require that the other webmaster's links be visible on the page? Well, what a webmaster could do is initially show the webmaster they're doing a link exchange with the links shown visible and that their website/links have been posted. But after a few weeks, they'll assume the webmaster won't be interested in seeing the site anymore, so that's when they change the color of the text to render it invisible.

Sybil Attack. According to Wikipedia, a Sybil attack is a black hat SEO optimization technique in which a webmaster takes over the reputation system of various types of networks, whether they are message boards, blogs, or social networking sites. They create dozens of IDs, using each one to help improve the reputation of one main ID. With this high reputation, they then start posting their ads, hoping that they don't get noticed because of their reputation.

A variant of the Sybil attack is when webmasters create a lot of sites that link to one another. Many of these sites offer nothing relevant, and some may even be spam blogs.

Spam Blogs. Spam blogs, also called splogs, are the blog equivalent of link farms. They post links to hundreds, maybe thousands, of sites, in hopes that they get rated high in search engines. The content, if they offer any, tends to be plagiarized content from article generators. Whether they have content or not, they extensively promote any affiliate programs of which they are a part. The splog may also use other techniques discussed here with the false hope that they can get listed even higher in search engine results.

Spam in Blogs. Keep in mind the keyword for spam in blogs is the word "in." They aren't the same as spam blogs. In fact, the blogs themselves usually are legitimate. The problem comes in the comment section. What webmasters do is make spam comments to help promote their websites or affiliate programs. They hope they get the advantage of traffic and a one-way link. What's more likely to happen is that they'll anger the blog owner, who will ban them and remove the spam comment. If a search engine finds out about this, they could end up as many black hat sites do: banned.

Wiki Spam

Introduced in the late '90s, wikis are a special kind of site that lets users post and edit websites as they see fit. They're most commonly used for informational purposes, with Wikipedia.com being the most popular example. In terms of wiki spam, Wikipedia puts it in five categories: article spam, link spamming, source soliciting, spam bots, and canvassing.

Article Spam. While writing articles about your website can be an excellent white hat SEO tactic, it can become black hat when they're placed on inappropriate websites. Wikis not geared for advertising are an example. If a spam article is found on Wikipedia, it can be deleted with the {{db-spam}} command. A person could also use Wikipedia's proposed deletion option or list it on Wikipedia's "Articles for Deletion" section. However, sometimes Wikipedia leaves the article up to be rewritten in the more encyclopedia-like tone that Wikipedia uses. Note that Wikipedia doesn't discourage articles about companies; they just have to be written properly. You'll learn some tricks you can use to meet Wikipedia's guidelines so you can promote your site. You won't be able to promote affiliate links, but you can talk about a general, top-level domain website. You should write for Wikipedia; it can get you great traffic, even though the links are "no-followed."

Wiki Link Spamming. In the case of Wikipedia, there are two places where links could be allowed: at the end of the article where a person would list the sources they used and in the section to the right of the article in a grey box that shows contact information. If a link is listed anywhere else, it's considered spam. If a website is listed in the right place yet doesn't relate to what is being talked about, it's still spam.

Another type of link spamming that has become popular is *video spamming*. Webmasters create a video promoting their site and on the video blatantly advertise their URL. While this isn't wrong to do, placing it on an informational wiki is wrong. Informational wikis are not for self-promotion but for information and resources.

As wikis are user-generated and may depend on volunteers, it may take a while for all of their spam links to get lifted from the website. So this leaves the potential that webmasters might see the links before they get removed.

Source Soliciting. Source soliciting is when webmasters go on "article talk pages" to solicit editors to use their websites. They make the claim that their website could offer more content to an article. Following are a few guidelines that wikis use to determine a legitimate post from solicitation:

- If the solicitation is made anonymously
- Whether the solicitation was made through a template or a category
- Previous discussion on why the suggested source should be used

- Whether the source is controversial
- Whether the source appears commercial

Spam Bots. Spam bots are used to collect emails from various websites on the internet or can be used to post spam on various sites. In the case of wiki spam, the spam bots place advertising links on articles it finds. The purpose is not advertising but the hope that search engines see that they have several one-way links from popular web pages. Wikipedia is fighting back against the spam bots through sysops, which is another name for Wikipedia administrators. They block any spam bots that they find. Of course, webmasters may face even more consequences as the use of spam bots is against the law. If spam bots make any edits, legally it can be considered a defacement of another person's property. It makes no difference that the property is virtual rather than hard content. If spam bots are consistently used, sysops may complain to ISPs, which could lead to prosecution.

Canvassing. Canvassing is the process of sending messages to Wikipedians in hopes of starting discussions. It is not considered solicitation because the initial message may not have the tone of an ad. The canvassing techniques used by spammers include friendly notices, cross-posting, campaigning, vote-stacking, and forum shopping.

Friendly Notices. Friendly notices are messages that on the surface seem to be focused on genuine interest in improving a discussion. However, the webmaster's true intent is to advertise its website.

Cross-Posting. Cross-posting is the act of posting the same message to multiple forums, mailing lists, or newsgroups. Editors solicit discussions outside of the Wiki by emailing other users. This can be considered a form of email spam. Wikipedia suggests that contacts should only be made on related WikiProjects and only a limited number of legitimate friendly notices should be used.

Campaigning. Campaigning is emailing editors who have "predetermined" points of view on an article. The correspondence may seem legitimate, but it's only a front to draw the editors into a spam advertisement through their email box.

Vote Stacking. Vote stacking is similar to campaigning and is the process of sending several "talk messages" to editors who have a definite opinion on a certain subject. Rather than spam in their email inbox, it comes through the wiki's internal chat or talk message system.

Forum Shopping. Forum shopping, also known as "asking the other parent," is when users ask for several opinions of fellow visitors until they get one they like. For example, if their spam article was blocked, and an internal review indicates that the block was proper, it is overall not ok to ask for yet another review. Forum shopping can be considered internal spam, and you can be permanently blocked. With forum shopping they get an additional opportunity to promote URLs or affiliate links. This technique is viewed as spam since there are more appropriate steps a webmaster can take place if they think a legitimate article got unfairly blocked.

Page Hijacking

Page hijacking is a black hat technique that can be scary, especially if it's done on sites where people freely give their private information. In this case the webmaster copies a legitimate website that later redirects visitors to malicious websites. In fact, even the hijacked page itself could be malicious. For example, it could ask for important information such as passwords, social security number, and credit card information. People give them out because they think they're visiting a legitimate site. Usually they get to the phony site by a spam email saying that their account is in jeopardy if they don't verify it. They are further fooled because the webmaster uses cloaked links to make them think they're clicking through to the real site. Thankfully, spamming technology has not progressed enough that the black hat webmaster can get to the top-level domain of a website they're hijacking. They may have similar domains, but not the top-level one. Additionally, people should be aware that companies that store their personal information won't use email as a medium to ask them to update their accounts.

Referrer Log Spamming

When you click on URLs of other sites on your own, the server that hosts the other site keeps track of the specific web page that was used to click to the other site's URL. Note: Google recently announced provisions for opting out of Google Analytics tracking and also search by SSL (secure search), which removes the referrer string. It will not be a large adoption, but for you geeks out there, it's an option. Webmasters using black hat SEO use robots to hijack these logs and update them with inappropriate information. This information would be the web pages associated with the spammer's site, not the original one. The problem in all of this is that search engines search logs help determine the link popularity of websites. If the log contains inaccurate information, the wrong person gets credit for the linking arrangement because search engines use link-counting for improved search rankings.

Miscellaneous Black Hat Techniques

1. *Mirrored website*. This process involves hosting websites with content that's the same but uses different URLs to fool the search engine into thinking it's different. This is not URL redirecting, which is pointing various URLs to the same website. With URL redirecting there is only one website. With mirrored websites there are several websites, each with different URLs.

2. *Cloaking.* The cloaking involved with black hat SEO is not the legitimate cloaking that you learned about earlier in this book. With legitimate cloaking you "hide" affiliate links or cumbersome URLs in place of hyperlinked text. With black hat cloaking methods, you're not involved at the link level, but rather at the site level. Black hat webmasters create a website that's designed to rank high with search engines but it is cloaked in favor of a more normal-looking website. Cloaking is sometimes called IP-delivery.

THE CONSEQUENCES OF BLACK HAT SEO
How to Create a Healthy, Non-Spammy Website

When Google excludes certain pages from appearing in the results pages, those pages left out and with low PageRank are shown in what Google used to call the "supplemental results." (It created too much confusion in the marketplace, so they dropped the name. Flavors of it still exists, so I'll use the name "supplemental index" for purposes of discussion.) Pages in the supplemental index may show up in search results, but pages in the main index are always given priority. With Google being the most powerful search engine, getting into its main index and out of the supplemental index should be one of your top priorities.

There are many reasons why your web page might end up on Google's supplemental index. You may not have enough content on your page to justify putting the page in the main results. Too much duplicate content can also hurt your chances and land you in the supplemental index. Too many query strings in the URL of your site can make finding your page difficult for Google's crawlers.

Also, orphaned pages, pages that aren't linked to any other inside your site, can hurt you. Avoid having your titles and descriptions the same on every page as this can land you in the supplemental index as well. This can cause problems with the crawlers, as they see just another form of duplicate content. If you plan and develop content that builds trust, you are thinking right!

Your website's incoming linking structure can also get you into the supplemental index. If all you have are reciprocal links, with potentially bad neighbors, this increases your chances of getting dumped into the supplemental index. Check to see if a page that no longer exists has an old, cached version of itself in the supplemental listings. That can drag the rest of your site down as well.

Should your website be afflicted by any or all of these problems, fear not. There are ways to get out of the supplemental index and back into the main results. If you're in the supplemental index, you are being crawled. Google does know you're there. But you'll have to take action to get into the main index. The Google webmaster tools will prove invaluable in diagnosing the situation. Sign up today; it's free.

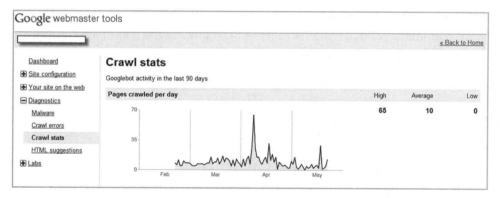

FIGURE 7–1. Google webmaster diagnostic tools.

Eliminate all duplicate content issues on your web pages. This is most likely your greatest concern and should be dealt with as soon as possible. Google wants every result to be unique as users get frustrated dealing with the same information page after page. Keep every page on your site as unique as possible. Also, improve the content you already have. Check to see how often your "cached" date is updated (click the cached link in the SERPs), and review the web crawler statistics inside the Google Webmasters tools area.

Shorten filenames for static websites and pages, use canonical references, or decrease the number of folders used as this decreases the complexity of your URL. Applying URL rewrites may work in your favor (httpd.apache.org/docs/2.0/misc /rewriteguide. html). Give each page a unique and descriptive title as well. This keeps the crawlers from finding more duplicate content in your pages' titles and descriptions. Simply using the company name or website name on every page won't help the search engines specify the content subjects and topics on each page.

How to Improve Your Website Architecture

Every site you want to have indexed (pages/content saved to their databases) by search engines should have links to it. Use a sitemap to make sure there's a link to every page. This might not be enough, so make sure you use links all throughout the site, whenever relevant. If you have no links to a particular page because you'd like that page not to be found, put that page in your website's "robots.txt" file. This tells the search engine to ignore that site. Adding an XML sitemap may help, but don't rely on it as the sole reason for indexation.

Google considers how far a page is from the homepage, i.e., how many clicks, and how deep the site structure. Although this is impossible with larger websites, a good rule of thumb is that all pages should be accessible from the homepage in two clicks or less. Look for relevant pages that can link together. Use links in the text of articles and at the end of articles to related pages. The sitemap also works well here. You can also logically group sitemaps for easy viewing.

Get Listed in Directories Google Trusts

Yahoo! directory, Open Directory Project, Business.com, and Botw.org are all good examples. If you found a directory for a specific niche, and it's vetted via an editorial process and in combination with a fee, it's likely trusted. You could start a blog and link to a different inner page every day, or write and submit articles with links to different inner pages. If you trade links with other websites, do so only with relevant, non-spam sites, and encourage them to link to your inner pages. Also, make sure that your content hasn't been stolen, as Google might be ranking the plagiarized content instead of yours. You can check this by copying key phrases from your page and putting the whole text (50 words, for example) into Google with quotes around it.

If all else fails, there are more drastic measures you can take. You can rename all the pages in the supplemental index and save them as new pages, with new URLs. Link to these "new" pages prominently on your site, and use a 301 redirect from the old URLs to the new ones. This takes a lot of work and should be a last resort. Finally, tell Google what's going on (google.com/support/webmasters/bin/answer.py?hl=en &answer=35843). If you feel you've exhausted every option, use the sitemaps to send your URL directly to Google. Also, be patient. Google isn't known for quick responses when webmasters push to have their pages put back into the main results index.

You now are aware of most of the major black hat SEO techniques used by webmasters. What would happen if you decide to use these techniques for your website? Well, initially, you may get positive results. The search engine would temporarily be fooled into thinking that you've initiated a legitimate link-building campaign and/or your site contains highly relevant content. Of course the keyword here is temporarily. You might get a high ranking for a couple weeks, but when the search engine finds out what you're doing, you could 1) lose your page rank, 2) get removed from the search engine results, or 3) get your site permanently barred from the search engine.

So, you might be thinking, if you can get indexed high initially, why not take advantage of that and risk the consequences later? After all, can't you create another website if you get banned? There's a problem with that strategy. First of all, if you create a website with irrelevant content, it's not going to do well with your web visitors. They'll see it once and never visit your site again. This is not what you want. You want your site to be designed so well that a visitor decides to bookmark you and visit your site again. They won't do this if your site is only an elaborate advertisement. Things are even worse if you use more blatant black hat SEO tactics, such as content keyword stuffing that makes your site look like it's not legitimate.

What would happen if you used black hat SEO tactics on a legitimate site? You may get a few leads or sales, but you do so at a great risk: getting banned from search engines and potentially getting reported to your ISP for spam. If you're reported to your ISP, you could in extreme cases be barred from the internet, period, at least through that ISP. You might even suffer legal consequences since ISPs can lose their reputation by members who spam. Another consequence is getting banned by your affiliate network or pay-per-click program forever. The ends do not justify the means.

Do not be fooled by the growing subculture of black hat webmasters who use black hat SEO techniques and are proud of it. There are several message boards and even books promoting black hat SEO techniques. There was even one website that talked about the "myths" of white hat vs. black hat SEO. Be aware that there are no myths with white hat SEO. White hat SEO is what you're supposed to do. It may take a while to get the results you want, but you have nothing to feel guilty about when you use white hat SEO tactics. You also have nothing to hide because you followed all of the appropriate guidelines when embarking on a search engine optimization campaign.

GOOGLE GUIDELINES

Each search engine has guidelines for webmasters. It's worth the effort to read them so you don't inadvertently commit a prohibited action. Google has an entire webmaster console with tools to help you drive traffic, manage analytics, and more. There's also a blog with frequent updates on Google developments. For your convenience I've copied the guidelines from Google below (google.com/support/webmasters/). Note that they are frequently updated, so it's always a good idea to check online for the latest information.

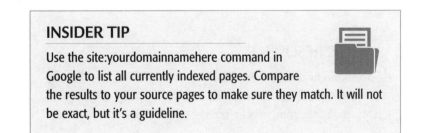

INSIDER TIP

Use the site:yourdomainnamehere command in Google to list all currently indexed pages. Compare the results to your source pages to make sure they match. It will not be exact, but it's a guideline.

Webmaster Guidelines

Following these guidelines will help Google find, index, and rank your site. Even if you choose not to implement these suggestions, we strongly encourage you to pay close attention to the "Quality Guidelines," which outline some of the illicit practices that can lead to a site being removed from the Google index or otherwise penalized. If a site has been penalized, it may no longer show up in results on Google.com or on any of Google's partner sites.

You can review design, content, and technical guidelines, as well as quality guidelines, at google.com/support/webmasters.

When your site is ready:

- Have other relevant sites link to yours.
- Submit it to Google at google.com/addurl.html.
- Submit a sitemap as part of your Google webmaster tools. Google uses your sitemap to learn about the structure of your site and to increase coverage of your web pages.
- Make sure all the sites that should know about your pages are aware your site is online.
- Submit your site to relevant directories such as the Open Directory Project and Yahoo!, as well as to other industry-specific expert sites.

Best Practices Design and Content Guidelines

- Make a site with a clear hierarchy and text links. Every page should be reachable from at least one static text link. If you are using images, consider formatting them with CSS to make them text links instead.
- Offer a sitemap to your users with links that point to the important parts of your site. If the site map is larger than 100 links, you may want to break the sitemap into separate pages. Usability is a factor across everything you do.
- Create a useful, information-rich site, and write pages that clearly and accurately describe your content.

ONLINE RESOURCE

Scroll down to about the middle of the page, and find out what Google says about quality content: http://chaosmap.com/services/content-publishing/.

■ Think about the words users would type to find your pages, and make sure your site actually includes those words and unique phrases that they might use. Be careful not to use industry jargon alone.

■ Use text instead of images to display important names, content, or links. The Google crawler doesn't recognize text contained in images.

■ Make sure that your TITLE tags and ALT attributes are descriptive and accurate.

■ Check for broken links and correct HTML. Search for XENU links in Google. (A free tool to help you.)

■ If you use dynamic pages (i.e., the URL contains a "?" character), be aware that not every search engine spider crawls dynamic pages as well as static pages. It helps to keep the parameters short and the number of them few.

■ Keep the links on a given page to a reasonable number (fewer than 100).

Consider These Important Technical Guidelines

■ Use a text browser such as Lynx (http://www.yellowpipe.com/yis/tools/lynx/lynx_viewer.php) to examine your site, because most search engine spiders see your site much as Lynx would. If fancy features such as JavaScript, cookies, session IDs, frames, DHTML, or Flash keep you from seeing all of your site in a text browser, then search engine spiders may have trouble crawling your site.

■ Allow search bots to crawl your sites without session IDs or arguments that track their path through the site. These techniques are useful for tracking individual user behavior, but the access pattern of bots is entirely different. Using these techniques may result in incomplete indexing of your site, as bots may not be able to eliminate URLs that look different but actually point to the same page.

■ Make sure your web server supports the If-Modified-Since HTTP header. This feature allows your web server to tell Google whether your content has changed since it last crawled your site. Supporting this feature saves you bandwidth and overhead.

■ Use the robots.txt file on your web server. This file tells crawlers which directories can or cannot be crawled. Make sure it's current for your site so that you don't accidentally block the Googlebot crawler. Visit http://www.robotstxt.org/faq.html to learn how to instruct robots when they visit your site. You can test your robots.txt file to make sure you're using it correctly with the robots.txt analysis tool available in Google webmaster tools. IMPORTANT: Be careful using this tool, or you may completely exclude your pages from search engines.

■ If your company buys a content management system, make sure the system can export your content so that search engine spiders can crawl your site. WordPress is a great solution. Visit wordpress.org for more information.

■ Use robots.txt to prevent crawling of search results pages or other auto-generated pages that don't add value for users coming from search engines.

QUALITY GUIDELINES

These quality guidelines cover the most common forms of deceptive or manipulative behavior, but Google may respond negatively to other misleading practices not listed here (e.g., tricking users by registering misspellings of well-known websites). It's not safe to assume that just because a specific deceptive technique isn't included here, Google approves of it. Webmasters who spend their energies upholding the spirit of the basic principles provide a better user experience and therefore enjoy better ranking than those who spend their time looking for loopholes to exploit.

If you believe that another site is abusing Google's quality guidelines, report that site at www.google.com/webmasters/tools/spamreport. Google prefers developing scalable and automated solutions to problems, so it pays to minimize hand-to-hand spam fighting. The spam reports it receives create scalable algorithms that recognize and block future spam attempts.

Quality Guidelines Basic Principles to Start With

Make pages for users, not for search engines. If users like it, search engines will, too (assuming you don't have obvious technical issues). Don't deceive your users or present different content to search engines than you display to users, which is considered cloaking.

Avoid tricks intended to improve search engine rankings. A good rule of thumb is whether you'd feel comfortable explaining what you've done to a website competitor. Another useful test is to ask, "Does this help my users? Would I do this if search engines didn't exist?"

Don't participate in link schemes designed to increase your site's ranking or PageRank. In particular, avoid links to web spammers or "bad neighborhoods" on the web, as your own ranking may be affected adversely by those links.

Don't use unauthorized computer programs to submit pages, check rankings, etc. Such programs consume computing resources and violate terms of service. Google does not recommend the use of products such as WebPosition Gold™ that sends automatic or programmatic queries to Google.

Quality Guidelines—Specific Guidelines

■ Avoid hidden text or hidden links.

- Don't use cloaking or sneaky redirects.
- Don't send automated queries to Google.
- Don't load pages with irrelevant keywords.
- Don't create multiple pages, subdomains, or domains with substantially duplicate content.
- Don't create pages that install viruses, Trojans, or other malware.
- Avoid "doorway" pages created just for search engines or other "cookie cutter" approaches, such as affiliate programs with little or no original content.
- If your site participates in an affiliate program, make sure that your site adds value. Provide unique and relevant content that gives users a reason to visit your site.

Chapter 8

How to Build Fresh Link Love

Bob continued working on his real estate client's site. He had some success with keywords but the site rankings were still very low. Naturally, he was not seeing much traffic. Bob began reviewing successful sites in the real estate industry as well as top-ranked sites in other industries.

Bob noticed that most of the top-rated sites had quality (related and relevant) inbound links. He had always written them off as "internet marketing garbage," but it was clear he had been wrong about their importance. He contacted a few relevant site owners to ask about linking but didn't receive any responses.

With a little more research, Bob found that there were a few guidelines to follow when asking for links, which he wanted to start with. He also discovered that he needed to carefully check the sites he wanted to link with to make sure their practices were in line with the search engines' guidelines. He started checking links with Yahoo! Site Explorer, and gained a lot more insight into what he could do. His first action item was to go where his competitors were receiving links from.

To get an understanding of why links are important, a background and position is necessary. Success in search engine optimization comes from continuously focusing on and achieving three things: content, link counts, and link reputation. To help understand a web's link graph and how links are positioned, a study done by IBM, AltaVista, and Compaq several years ago shows that the "web is a bow tie" (www.nature.com/nature/journal/v405/n6783/full/405113a0.html). A large number of tightly connected linked pages exist in the center, and with fewer incoming and outbound links. This simply means that the left side may influence the PageRank to move up, while the right side may influence the PageRank to move down. Acquisition of incoming, topical links whenever possible is better than outgoing ones, but a balance should be considered. More information can be found on www9.org/w9cdrom/160/160. html—the study of the web as a graph.

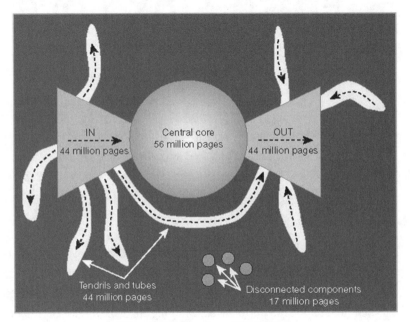

FIGURE 8–1. The Bow-Tie Theory.

The three link essentials are referred to as "the SEO tripod." It includes:

1. Optimized content and architecture
2. Link popularity (how many links point to your website and pages)
3. Link reputation (what those links say about you with anchor text) Note: Social "signals" are becoming progressively more important as well.

Activity is a new measure that adds to this tripod as well. And, as mentioned, make sure you have a well-established infrastructure.

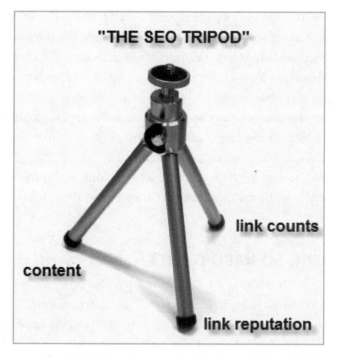

FIGURE 8–2. The SEO Tripod expanded (now with "social signals").

If you're selling shoes and somebody links to you with "buy red shoes" in the anchor text (the blue underlined text) on an outside, high-quality, related web page, you're being smart about your linking and search optimization.

If your destination page is created with up-sell messages and easy navigation, you're moving in the right direction.

When these three legs are balanced and working together with high relevancy and structure—both internally and externally—you're creating a solid foundation for high search rankings and traffic. Quality beats quantity. This is why you'll see some sites/pages outrank others with a higher link count. Domain strength, domain diversity for links, will be very important as well. Don't focus on PageRank; that's old school.

Internal structure and link profiles are important, and getting links from authority websites and avoiding technical problems (like a JavaScript redirect) are top goals.

While most of the text in this book speaks about Google, this tripod model works for all search engines. However, Bing and Yahoo! seem to favor content more. A recent site I tested ranked very well for Google by using a link program I initiated, but until I added more content, Yahoo!, Bing, and Ask were trailing behind. However, Google provides 64 percent of search engine traffic, so it's important to get rankings there.

For more competitive keywords, it's easier and faster to get listed in Bing and Yahoo! (in that order) by creating solid content and using complementary long-tail keywords. These lower searches can help build your traffic and click stream data while building out toward Google. However, don't think about one search engine in particular. Get your keyword strategy and content right, build links, and you'll win everywhere. If you are in a competitive marketplace, you may want to start with "chunky middle keywords," or long-tail phrases to start receiving traffic more quickly. Continue to build for the top "head" keywords.

The "expanded" part of the tripod is the inclusion of social media. The opportunity to affect search results and/or click-through (Google+ and authorship) activity must not be missed.

WHY IS LINKING SO IMPORTANT?

Google is big on links. It is a major foundation for search engines and pages discovery. The linking algorithms sit as a core element of its search engine. According to Matt Cutts, "Google is getting better at understanding the properties of link quality. The search engines optimize results by counting quality editorial votes as links and they help to influence their relevancy algorithms" (mattcutts.com/blog/indexing-timeline/).

As you've seen, we talked about the importance of the web in the introduction of this book. In that section, we also learned about the rise of the new search engine by Google in 1998 and how it was able to beat out AltaVista (the best search engine at the time) and Microsoft.

When Larry and Sergey (referred to as the Google Guys) wanted to "download the entire web to their desktop," it was no small feat and required a grand vision that could not stray. This drive and vision to create the most relevant search engine was found almost by accident, and developed into a white paper, "The Anatomy of a Search Engine" (infolab.stanford.edu/~backrub/google.html). The paper offers insight into how Google manages links. It says: "We assume page A has pages T1 . . . Tn, which point to it (i.e., are citations). The parameter d is a damping factor which can be set between 0 and 1. We usually set d to 0.85. There are more details about d in the next section. Also C(A) is defined as the number of links going out of page A. The PageRank of a page A is given as follows:

$$PR(A) = (1-d) + d\ (PR(T1)/C(T1) + . . . + PR(Tn)/C(Tn))"$$

Here's a Google fun fact (and potential *Jeopardy!* answer): PageRank was the brainchild of Google founder, Larry Page, hence the name PageRank.

PageRank is now "marketing spin" and creates controversial discussions in thousands of search forums. Most search marketers mention that it's outdated and

KING OF THE SEARCH WORLD

Did you know that Microsoft (Bill Gates) said it was going to take the search world by announcing a catalog of over four billion websites? Well, the day (in 2001) of that announcement, Google informed the world that it had indexed eight billion websites. Google's scale is amazing, and via intelligent, home-grown computer systems and software, it not only has provided huge infrastructure cost savings to the company but also has built a proprietary system that some say is the true "search engine secret." Google was providing 100,000 million searches a day in 2001, and as of December 2012, is providing 114.7 billion searches (http://searchengineland.com/google-worlds-most-popular-search-engine-148089). What was its biggest problem? Not its search engine algorithm—but power (electric). More specifically, figuring out how to run hundreds of thousands of servers (est.) worldwide and not consume all the power from the entire city of New York! Check Google's server gallery: http://www.google.com/about/datacenters/gallery.

doesn't get updated often (every three months as of last count) and that other pages will rank high on the search engine, even with a lower PageRank.

The paper is a quality background read, and you should note that the PageRank and TrustRank (Yahoo!'s web spam model, en.wikipedia.org/wiki/TrustRank) remain as important today as they were then.

We have not yet discussed TrustRank. The TrustRank algorithm was created by Zoltán Gyöngyi and Hector Garcia-Molina, both from Stanford University, and Jan Pedersen from Yahoo! In their abstract, "Combating Web Spam with TrustRank," they conclude:

> Search engines are today combating web spam with a variety of ad hoc, often proprietary techniques. We believe that our work is a first attempt at formalizing the problem and at introducing a comprehensive solution to assist in the detection of web spam. Our experimental results show that we can effectively identify a significant number of strongly reputable (non-spam) pages. In a search engine, TrustRank can be used either separately to filter the index, or in combination with PageRank and other metrics to rank search results.

Rather than focusing on "on-page content" (content on a page) and meta tags and internal structure (very important), the Google Guys decided to pursue the "citation" model from their academic world. In this model, white papers, theses, and special reports would be referenced in "footnotes" as citations by professors and engineers, authors, and speakers. Brin and Page decided that testing for "links/refs" would also be a good way to build "votes of confidence" for any subject matter—and it would be related and have a high vote of confidence.

INSIDER TIP

If you get links from 100 to 200 sites with low confidence or relevancy to your site, you should instead try to go for 10 to 20 highly trusted links. If you were able to get one link from CNN, it would outweigh many other poor-quality links! That's why you see certain sites or pages that outrank others with much higher link counts. Relevant, quality links are what you want.

As this work grew from the now-infamous garage in Silicon Valley into a full-blown project close to Stanford University, it became apparent that the "link citation" theory was more than valuable—it worked very well (usatoday.com/tech /techinvestor/ corporatenews/2007-07-04-google-wojcicki_N.htm?csp=34).

I mention this background and the tripod model because it's the way you need to look at your optimization—a complete model of not only links and backlinks but also of content and site architecture.

So, now that you know why links are important and have more background on search engines and the 200-plus factors that make up the Google search engine, let's talk about how to structure sites and get links.

Beginner Link Advice

To get high search engine rankings, you should provide quality inbound links to related, quality page contents. Make sure to always build links—we talk about the various types below—and the more you can get (without spamming), the better. Use the competition in your niche to figure out which links are high-quality and where they link to/from. Studying the competition will help you get a higher ranking faster, and you won't be doing it blindly. Make sure to also look at page structure, content, and so on.

Make sure to follow the list of top directories. Here is a list to start with:

- dmoz.org

- yahoo.com (dir.yahoo.com)
- business.com
- joeant.com
- gimpsy.com
- botw.org

As with all things on the web, this list can change by the time this book is printed, but quality directories that include editors or fees are likely something to invest in. Many free sites are switching to paid submission only or have closed free submissions. The list is simply a guideline to get you started. If a directory (and especially one you have never heard of) offers special incentives that seems spammy, don't do it. Google has come down hard on the directory addition strategy for search. If you think it helps your audience and is relevant within the directory, it may warrant a deeper look.

INSIDER TIP

Research the competition and get placement in vertical directories for your business. The resources section on the member site contains massive lists, and is updated there. See www.jonrognerud.com/optimizationbook and join the discussion of what has worked for you.

The results in Google will show a slightly different display after installing the SEO for Firefox plugin. You may see listings that has a lower PageRank, but is shown before a PageRank 6, for example. It's important to know that other metrics like overall traffic, user behavior, domain age, recent cache date, total links to site and individual pages help weigh the ordering of results.

Next, you would dissect the link profiles on the top ten (five shown here) and develop a matrix of variables in Excel to find out their top ranking secrets.

You'll use other tools for link management as you've seen. Note: local search uses other signals to help local websites rank, but links are important, no matter what. As you'll learn in the local SEO section, "local" links, citations, and reviews will be very effective here.

Some paid directories are created not only to make money for their creators but also to provide a firewall to protect them from spam. Google and others also value these directories as providing better-quality links, and if you can afford it, it's wise to belong to them.

Vertical Directories and Lists

- ISEDB.com (http://isedb.com/html/Web_Directories/)
- Searchengineguide.com

Quality directory links can be good for your traffic and ranking, and strongly elevate your brand. The assumption is that if somebody has the money and is willing to pay then it's not likely a spammy site. Some of these insist on company names, not keywords, but don't try to trick the system. You can establish unique domains with keywords to it with a redirect, but it's considered tricking the system. Better to do it right.

In Chapter 1 we talked about social search and user-driven content. We also introduced you to tagging and bookmarking. In your marketing efforts, it's important to take advantage of the social web to build links and your brand. The list below is by no means comprehensive, but a sample of social media sites to consider in your marketing efforts.

- Digg
- delicious.com
- Facebook
- Flickr
- 43Things
- LinkedIn
- MySpace (still)
- Newsvine
- Ning
- Reddit
- Squidoo
- StumbleUpon
- StyleHive
- Technorati
- Twitter
- Wetpaint
- WikiHow
- Wikipedia
- Yahoo! Answers
- YouTube

ONLINE RESOURCE

The Strongest Links (strongestlinks.com/directories. php) website has a listing of directories along with its Alexa and PageRank rankings, saturations, and fees. As you consider which directories to list in, this site is a good resource to help you prioritize. However, Google recently went after directories and wiped many of them out. As you know, changes happen all the time, and for Google, it's daily. Think long term, and don't get caught in these Google Slaps or worse, a seemingly permanent penalty.

Yahoo!

Yahoo! is one of the most complicated. Go to yahoo.com, select the "More Y! Sites" link, and then click on "All Products" link. You'll see everything in the Yahoo! world. Then, select the "Directory" option. You are now in the directory (dir.yahoo.com).

To locate the best place for you to list in the directory:

1. Locate a competitor; type in the name.
2. Click on it, and you'll see the breadcrumbs link to where it's located.

Yahoo! search has nothing to do with the directory. You have to enter the directory to see your listing. Think in terms of alphabetical listings. If you're deeply nested in the tree, it may not be the best place for you. Once you've typed in the competitor's name and found your place, click "Suggest a Link" to sign up for Yahoo!.

ONLINE RESOURCE

Use a tool like Onlywire.com to get your content updated to several Web 2.0 locations quickly. Hootsuite.com is a powerful addition, and it has a free and paid option. Use knowem.com to get social sites set up quickly (paid).

Directory submission is $299 annually and does not guarantee inclusion. Adult sites are charged $600. Your next step is to accept the terms of service—print, read, and understand them. Once you're in, there are four steps to update your listing:

1. Understand the cost.
2. Submit the site—you don't need to get the keywords in each link, don't sell in the description, be factual—no sales pitch. Look at some existing listings.
3. Credit card info—Visa/MasterCard and billing address.
4. Submit the actual content via a review and confirm.

Wait at least seven business days for a response. It's not immediate.

ONLINE RESOURCE

Use RoboForm.com to save your info securely—great time saver!

Don't forget that many people do a local search for businesses and services in their area. You should also build local and regional links from sites such as Yahoo! Local and Google Local, and through local organizations such as your chamber of commerce.

A Good Link Strategy: Link In, Link Out

You should link out as well as work on getting links in. In my business dealings with clients, I often come across a "not me" attitude. Website owners feel that linking out to somebody else they don't know is a mistake. Imagine if this were the case in the social network platforms and the blogosphere!

Exchanging links with other, related websites is a good practice, and try to get links where the competition is getting them, too. However, I would not pursue an automated link program for reciprocal links. It's not highly valued, and if not done right (lots of research needed), you could end up in an FFA (free for all) network, among other things.

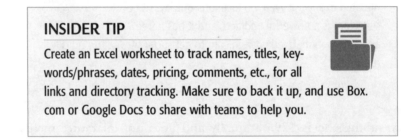

INSIDER TIP

Create an Excel worksheet to track names, titles, keywords/phrases, dates, pricing, comments, etc., for all links and directory tracking. Make sure to back it up, and use Box.com or Google Docs to share with teams to help you.

If you're a local merchant or provide services locally, you should submit to your niche, local directories. Adding yourself to the local search engines Google Local, Bing Local, and Yahoo! Local is a start. You can also try paid services like Neustar Localeze (http://www.neustarlocaleze.biz/directory/index.aspx) or Local.com.

I recently visited a local chamber of commerce. Becoming a member and engaging there is a great way to create online and offline visibility (especially if you go to all the events and promote yourself and your services). Your local chamber and other trade organizations are intelligent options to include in your marketing strategy. Go to some of their mixers and luncheons. Some of them will let you introduce yourself and your company. It is a great way to develop personal connections, get leads, and find customers or clients.

I have also talked about research that can help you get links from hub sites.

When links are coming back to you, instruct (kindly) the webmasters to use keywords for which you are trying to optimize. Make it natural and mix it up—link to

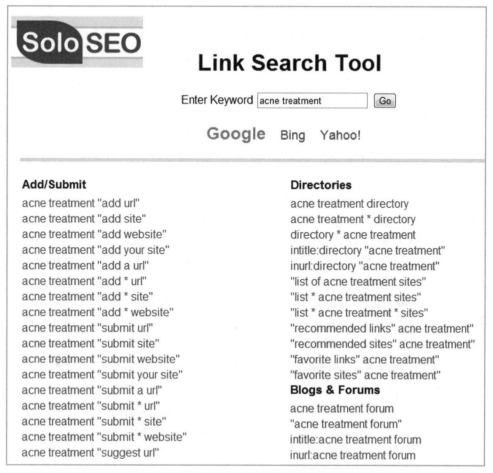

FIGURE 8–3. Solo SEO: Great way to find Link Opportunities in Google.

the homepage, inner pages, and deep/lowest pages in the website structure. Make sure the relevant links point to the correct pages; don't make the common mistake of just linking to the homepage.

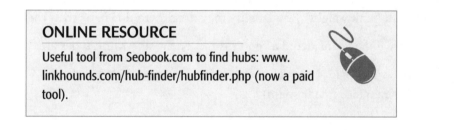

ONLINE RESOURCE

Useful tool from Seobook.com to find hubs: www. linkhounds.com/hub-finder/hubfinder.php (now a paid tool).

TYPES OF LINKS

- PageRank: natural link equity; people enjoy your site
- Links by "aggression": somebody might not like you
- Contextual and navigation
- Bartered links: as a favor in exchange for something
- Link exchanges
- Paid links: pay for a directory listing, links from partner and commerce sites. Be very careful with these. Google is out to get you if you don't do this correctly, and consider using the nofollow tag on incoming links.
- Manufactured links
- Automated links such as link exchange programs. Use with caution. I don't recommend these at all.
- Ripped-off links: spam comments on blogs, automated form posts, black hat strategy

The goal of linking is to build relevant links. Links are like "votes" for your site, as each link functions as a "recommendation" from another site to check yours out!

So, now for the important question: What can search engines do with links?

- Easily identify the links as two-way or three-way links
- Adjust or apply metrics and weight to those links
- Determine the type, the source, the target, the age of the link, a combination of things
- Although it isn't an exact science per se, search engines can spot paid links
- Filter by source (reputation passing and PageRank via outbound links, Google-specific)

The search engines also know a great deal about your site, and the technology continues to advance. The search engines know:

- Age of site, domain name, history
- IP and address history
- Easy-to-find one-, two-, three-way links
- Trust and authority
- Topic and type (commercial/informational)
- Default "link weight" (low quality may drag them down, or treat them equally)

Not every link is considered a "good" link. The weakest link types are:

- Link farms
- Link spam (comment spam)

- Web spam
- Forums and blog commenting with the idea of just getting a link
- Paid links (we'll discuss this later)
- Run of site: more links on many different sites/pages than on one site; this includes heavy use of Footer links

Remember that you're aiming for long-term success and not a one-time or short-term benefit. Choose quality over quantity. You're not simply building links for search engine position, but always keeping your customer in mind. Good links will bring you long-term success, so opt for authority and trust. Base your links on merit and editorial voting.

One-Way Links

One-way links are those in which another website advertises your URL without requiring that you link back. Google places more value on one-way links because they show that other websites truly see worth in the information you're offering. This is all in theory, of course, since there are websites on which you can post your URL for payment. However, you'll want to take advantage of both free and paid one-way linking situations.

Free One-Way Linking Opportunities: Online Writing Portals

Online writing portals are communities to which you can submit articles to be read by other members of the portal or by the general public. There are also sites that allow you to pay to have your content submitted to a network of directories (such as Isnare. com). Many online writing portals offer payment along with exposure. Some that offer payment do so in what is known as AdSense revenue sharing. For those portals you must first have an AdSense ID number, which you obtain by signing up at google.com/AdSense. You then provide your AdSense ID to the writing portal. You write an article, which you submit into the network. AdSense ads are shown alongside your article. Depending on how the revenue sharing system is set up, you'll receive revenue a certain percentage of the time when the AdSense ads alongside your site are clicked on. For example, if you write for an online writing portal where it offers revenue sharing 50 percent of the time, your ads will be shown half of the time, while the ads of the portal will be shown the other half of the time. If the ads showing during your half of the time are clicked on, you receive revenue, which shows up in your AdSense account. However, the portal receives the revenue for any clicks that occur during its half of the time.

Other examples of writing portal payments include payments based on the number of views your article receives and upfront payments. Some, such as publishing portal Yahoo! Voices (formerly Associated Content), allow for both. Generally, these types of portals offer a higher potential to profit from your content. With revenue sharing you have to get clicks in order to make a profit. In fact, you could have 100,000 views, but if no one clicks the AdSense ads during your allotted time, you won't make any profit. Compare this with sites that pay per view: 100,000 views for maybe $.01 per impression (the exact cost depends on the portal, keywords, and content you're using) would yield $1,000. Upfront payments are even better because you get compensated for your writing as well as exposure to your website. Yet you need to be careful that you're not writing an advertisement when you write articles for writing portals offering upfront payments. You also aren't allowed to promote affiliate links (at least in the case of Yahoo! Voices). So make sure that when you're writing your articles, you direct the visitor to a top-level URL instead of an affiliate link or a subdomain.

There are also online writing portals where the only compensation you receive is a traffic boost to your website and the potential for even more one-way links. These sites are known as free article directories. How they work is simple. You start by writing an article for them. Since they aren't offering payment, you advertise any link you want, whether it's a top-level domain name, a subdomain, or an affiliate link. However, many have a limit to the number of links you can include in the article body. Some may only allow a link in the resource box (information at the bottom of the article that contains your name, brief bio, and contact info, such as your email or website). You write your content and submit it to the directory. Some sites such as EzineArticles (one of the largest), require you to sign up (membership is free). Others like GoArticles or ArticleCity simply require you to post and submit your article. Many of these once very powerful article directories have been downgraded by Google. Do your research before blindly pushing your content into these directories. Article marketing is certainly not dead, but the mass distribution of low-quality grade content is.

Each site has guidelines regarding content, hyperlinks, and word count. Read the site's guidelines before submission to prevent your article from being rejected (you can

---

INSIDER TIP

Years ago, I started bringing traffic to my site via article writing, and it was a preferred choice for quality traffic. Do your research, but consider adding guest blogging and personal connection outreach to relevant communities instead. Write with quality in mind. Your ultimate goal is to have webmasters publish and consumers reference and even re-use your content, adding attribution back to your page or offer (!) in this expanded, syndicated way.

fix the error and resubmit). Once your article is posted, your content is offered to other webmasters as public domain. (Some sites give you the option to opt out of your work being used without permission; read the guidelines). This means they can post it for free on their website. Yet don't think that you are giving away your writing work, because there is a catch to this. The catch is that in order for webmasters to legally post your work, they must keep the article intact. They cannot alter it in any way. Do you see the advantage? Basically, they're required to advertise your URL (which is in the resource box most often). So when they get traffic, their visitors will be exposed to your URL, which they are free to click on if you're advertising an offer that interests them. In terms of one-way links, you get the one-way link to the free article directory along with any one-way links that could occur when webmasters decide to post your article on their website.

The other benefit to writing articles and blog posts is that it gives you more ways to appear in search engines. Don't forget to post your content to your own site—and spend a little time making changes to avoid duplication issues.

What's the best way to write articles for online writing portals? Should you write differently for free network sites vs. the paid networks? The answer to the latter question is no. The reason behind this answers the first question: online writing portals are interested in the same thing you are—search engine optimization. They need to rank high so they can get AdSense revenue or get exposure to their own services, products, or affiliate advertisements. A good tip to follow is to offer your best materials, always. Do not write artificial keyword-stuffed articles for the sake of driving traffic. Writing articles does more than boost your search traffic; it can also boost your credibility with potential buyers. Every eyeball on your article is a potential customer. Give them useful information and demonstrate your value in your field. Be helpful first. Think about a problem they are facing, and try to write to that.

Write for the customer first. But of course you still need to do your keyword research. In the case of paid online writing portals, if you can write an article on a more popular keyword, you might be able to make more money since a popular keyword equals more clicks. For free article directories, writing for a popular keyword means you'll get more webmasters interested in promoting your content.

The only restrictions you need to keep in mind are that you can't plagiarize and you can't use private label content. You could, however, find many good ideas and themes from PLR content. You might be wondering why you can't use private label content if you legally own the rights to the writing. This is because with most private label content, you're not the only one who owns the rights. There are exceptions. If you buy content with full rights from networks such as Constant Content or, of course, from ghostwriters, you can be assured that only you are getting the article. In cases like these, you could submit the article to online writing networks without penalty (unless

MORE ON LINKS

Many of these sites only allow one or two links back to your site, and only from the resource box. A relevant link that cites your website in the middle of the page content, within text that supports the anchor text/URL, is a highly qualified link! Google uses latent semantic analysis (LSA & LSI), defined in Wikipedia as a technique in natural language processing, particularly in vectorial semantics, to analyze relationships between a set of documents and the terms they contain by producing a set of concepts related to the documents and terms. See en.wikipedia.org/wiki /Latent_semantic_analysis for more.

another webmaster has plagiarized the work, which you can find out through services like Copyscape). However, most private label situations are not like this, especially in the case of memberships (which is the most popular way private label content is sold). What happens is the content gets posted elsewhere by other people who also own the rights. Some may even try to post it on online writing networks themselves. Since the content is viewed as not being original, doing these things could ban a webmaster from any type of online writing portal.

What you can do with private label content is use it to get ideas on how to write your own articles. If the private label content is in Microsoft Word format, you can use Word's AutoSummarize feature to highlight key points in the article. These highlights can appear in the article or in a separate document. Regardless, you can use these key points to form the basis for a new article. This method is preferable to rewriting the content, because you're less likely to borrow exact phrases from the original content. Of course, if the private label content has an identifiable author, you could put the phrases in quotes and cite them at the end of your article. This method is acceptable to most online writing portals since they realize you may still need to do research to write your content. However, if the content does not have an identifiable author, you need to avoid borrowing phrases. Maybe one or two here or there won't get noticed, but doing it too often could make the portal you submit your works to classify it as duplicate content. This means that your content is found on other sites, making it invalid for submission.

There are thousands of article directories and publishing portals in addition to the few mentioned in this section. In the past, it was common to mass distribute these article into directories. To create the best leverage of your content, you ought to pick five to ten sites that work for you. These will attract visitors and trust over time, and you can use them as references, too. Don't get sucked into mass-distribution!

To get you started, here are a few:

- EzineArticles
- Searchwarp
- Goarticles
- Buzzle
- ArticleCity
- Articlesbase
- PromotionWorld

Classified Ads

Online classified ads work just like print classified ads. They allow people the opportunity to post advertisements for things they are selling, business opportunities, or jobs. Most online classified ads offer free submission, but if you upgrade to their paid packages, they make your ad more prominent. For example, they might bold your ad, allow you to include pictures, and, depending on the site, allow your URL to be clickable. These things don't matter much for link building, though they increase the chance that your URL will get viewed by visitors.

ONLINE RESOURCE

Craigslist.org still has good visibility with search engines, but has also been victimized by spam. Great for local targeting. Use the local, national, and worldwide websites to look for opportunities, ideas, and potential exposure.

Message Boards and Online Groups

Message boards, which are sometimes classified as a type of group, are forums in which a group of members exchange text messages. These messages are put in different categories called threads. While most message boards leave communication on the board, some allow members to receive new posts through their email (this is an option popular with Yahoo! Groups). Members are free to talk about anything they want, and usually they can post links to their URLs. However, it's important that if they advertise, they follow the guidelines set forth by the webmaster of the message board or group. Some webmasters don't care if you're advertising, just as long as it relates to the thread

FIGURE 8–4. Socialmention: real time search and analysis.

at hand. Others allow you to advertise only in a special section of the message board. The downside to these types of sites is that your ads are clearly shown as ads, which tends to draw people away from wanting to see them. This is a big disadvantage if you want to get your site seen, but in terms of link building, it doesn't matter. You get the advantage of a one-way link just by posting your URL.

However, if you want the advantage of one-way linking and traffic, consider joining message boards exclusively designed for advertising. You could use a search engine to find these boards, or you could search the three main sites offering groups. These are Google, AOL, Bing, and Yahoo!. Many folks on these message boards are internet marketers, so keep that in mind when you post your message. They tend to be more responsive to ads promoting business opportunities, cheap advertising, or free advertising. They may also be interested in link exchanges (which are discussed more when we cover ways to get paid one-way links).

Finally, some networking sites offer opportunities for free exposure. For B2B interaction, consider LinkedIn and topical groups where you can post answers to questions posted by other LinkedIn members; that includes engaging with that community at large. Be a resource, be helpful. You should do the same and open up a group after you have built some visibility. You can demonstrate your expertise in your

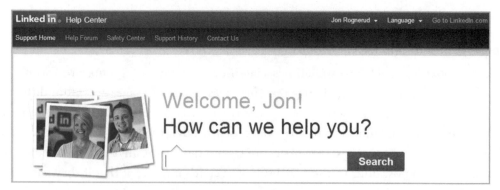

FIGURE 8–5. LinkedIn Help Center and Forum Search.

> **INSIDER TIP**
>
> Check out Yahoo! Groups and Google Groups, and depending on your topic, set up your account to email you when topics change. Good for research and feedback.

specialty by answering a question. All your contact info is visible so those interested in knowing more can send you an email or visit your site.

Free Online Press Releases

A press release is a public relations announcement distributed to the news media and other targeted publications. Online press releases unfortunately are overused and abused. Many barely pass as readable and are hyperbole disguised as a press release. However, a well-written, targeted release is still an effective marketing tool. To get an idea of how press releases are written, visit the press or media room of any large company. All are written in the same journalistic style—they start with a compelling, descriptive headline, then a nugget that introduces the story and tells the "Who, What, Where, Why, When, How" in summary. That's followed by the body, which provides detail, and the release ends with a close and information about your company. With online press releases, you also want to optimize using keywords. Optimize the headline and the body of the copy. When posting your press release on a free online press release site, you get the advantage of one-way linking and traffic. In this case, it's both traffic to the free press release site and any traffic that might be generated if your press release is chosen to be promoted elsewhere. You can also pay for online press release distribution. Good PR portals are BusinessWire. com, MarketWire.com, EmailWire.com, and PRWeb.com, which offer additional services, such as RSS feeds, SEO, videos, images, audio (Social Media Press Release options), choice of geographic distribution, and more. Many online marketers don't realize that you can submit your press release directly to targeted publications and media. You can hire a PR specialist to put together a targeted media list for you, use online software (such as that offered by Mass Media Distribution), or put together your own list. Please note that Google has publically announced that Press Releases for SEO don't work anymore.

Controversial, Free One-Way Link-Building Methods

Controversial one-way link-building methods include banner and link exchange networks, autosurfs, and safelists. Banner and link exchange networks are those in which members submit their sites in exchange for viewing other people's sites within

> ### INSIDER TIP
>
> I recommend building press releases into your market-ing plan. However, for search—the rules have changed. Don't do this for SEO, but only if you have something worthwhile and interesting to say. Read more on this from my article on http://soloprpro.com/press-releases-and-google-what-pr-professionals-need-to-know-to-promote-without-penalty/.

the networks. Autosurfs are similar to banner and link exchanges, except that they pay their members to view the material. Safelists are websites where members post their links with no obligation to view other people's ads. All of these networks may offer a credit system in which the more ads you view, the longer you can show your ad in their network.

Why are these methods controversial? And if they're controversial, why are they still being listed as white hat SEO tactics? First off, they're controversial because of those who abuse an otherwise ingenious marketing approach, for example, sites that don't pay. Additionally, many internet marketers don't like them because they feel the traffic isn't genuinely interested in what is being advertised. However, does this mean there's anything ethically wrong with them? Most people joining these networks know what they are getting into. It's not like they're being thrown advertisements against their will, as they would be if their email inboxes were being spammed or if they received pop-ups. So ethically, I don't see a problem with them, which is why I still list them in this section.

Directories

Webmasters who own directories allow one-way linking because not only do they get a moment when their ads are seen by those submitting their links, they also get the advantage of outbound links (discussed earlier in this book).

As we talked about earlier, directories are an important tool in your SEO efforts. The top directories are Yahoo! ($299 per year) and DMOZ (Open Directory Project). DMOZ is free, but it typically takes a long time to get approved and listed. In addition to the ones already listed, there are other paid directories that may require payment or reciprocal linking (discussed in the next section). If you do reciprocal linking, you don't get the advantage of having a one-way link, which is what search engines prefer to see. And if you pay for a link, you are using a paid method of one-way link building. Check out the next section to learn how you can determine whether it's worth your while to pay for a listing in a directory. In my opinion, adding random directories is not worthwhile and certainly not for link/spam techniques, but if the directory follows the guidelines set forth in the next section, it might be.

Paid One-Way Link Building

Paid one-way link building involves buying advertising space from a website. Unlike free one-way link building, the paid version allows you to get one-way links that better match the keywords found throughout your website. Because you are paying for the link, the provider ensures that the keywords are a perfect match to your requirements. This section explains in detail the process to go through to determine what sites you should use for paid one-way link building. You also learn about how to find paid one-way link-building opportunities.

We talked about link spamming and the fine line that must be walked when building your links (build quality links and build gradually). Your strategy should include both paid and free links. Paid links are fine, as is regular advertising, but Google recommends using them only with the "rel=nofollow" parameter. This values the link from an advertising perspective, but not a "PageRank citation perspective," which it considers deceptive. Keep this in mind as we go through the next section. Search engines aren't perfect, but they typically can detect paid links in the right or left columns of your site. They can also detect the number of paid links. It's far better to have links in the body of your site content rather than on a sidebar list or the bottom of the page. Of course you'll want to integrate the links with relevant content with good anchor text.

Microsoft Research, several years ago, presented the VIPS model—vision-based page segmentation algorithm. As you can see from the infographic in Figure 8-6 on page 216, it becomes easy for search engines to figure out where your links are and determine value from position and links/content around it.

What You Should Look for in Sites Offering Paid One-Way Link Building

1. *Linking Format.* Make sure that the site where you plan to advertise offers its linking format in HREF code. HREF is a special HTML tag that creates hyperlinks. The syntax for HREF is:

   <a href="yoururl">Your Desired Keywords, brand name or blended
   phrase or call to action</a>

   As you can see, HREF can help you create keyword-centric links. Place your URL where you see "yoururl" and the text to describe your link in the section where

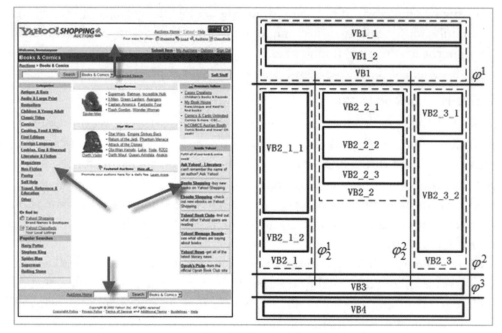

FIGURE 8-6. The VIPS Model—Microsoft.

it says "Your Desired Keywords." To find out if the site you want to advertise on uses HREF format, use "View Source" from your browser. Right-click on the page your link will be advertised on, and select "View Source." Note: This command might be worded differently, depending on the browser you use.

From there look for HREF coding. A quick, easy way to locate this would be to go to "Edit" and select "Find" within the program. That opens after you select "View Source." Type "HREF" in the text box at the bottom of the program. The program then highlights any instance it finds of HREF.

But, don't think that because you see HREF, you're home free. There are other elements that you need to look for when looking at the HTML coding of the website you intend to advertise on. These elements are explained in more detail below:

- Make sure there is no coding that indicates redirection, as this has a negative effect on your site's page rank.
- Make sure that JavaScript isn't used. The difference between linking with straight HREF and linking with JavaScript is that the word JavaScript is listed as one of the HREF properties.
- Make sure that the HREF property "rel=nofollow" isn't used because it lets a search engine know the link being advertised has not yet been approved by the

webmaster or is a paid link. When a search engine sees this property, it ignores the URL, and spiders don't follow any URLs that are listed this way. It's up to you if you decide to pay for it when it has less of an effect. You'll get traffic, but not link juice (Google frowns on this). For paid links, use "rel=nofollow" to stay within the guidelines.

■ Make sure the "robots" property associated with meta tags on the page doesn't have the attribute "noindex" (or "Disallow" in the robots.txt file on the server). The "robots" property communicates to search engine spiders or robots what you want to get indexed in search engine listings; "noindex" indicates that you don't want the URL following it to be indexed and therefore not shown in the search engine results. Don't be alarmed if you see the "robots" property, because it's not "robots" that's the problem, it's the "noindex" property. If you see "index, follow," your URL will be included for search engine indexing. Keep in mind that capitalization of the tags or properties doesn't matter. I see many websites with "index, follow." This isn't really needed, and since it's especially powerful and easy to change, I don't include it.

■ Professional webmasters may use the robots.txt file: a special search engine instruction file found under the root of the site. You can check to see what has been included/excluded by going to domainname.com/robots.txt. (Substitute your domain name for "domainname.com." If you get a 404 error, that means robots.txt is not in place). These techniques should assist in link discovery and help you find out where they may be deceiving you.

2. *Number of Backlinks Associated with the Site.* Simply defined, backlinks are the links that advertise a particular website. They could be one-way links or reciprocal links. There are a number of easy-to-use tools to check the number of backlinks a site has, including OpensiteExplorer, Majestic SEO, and inside the Google Webmaster tools. Alternatively, you could other tools like Ahrefs.com. If the site has a lot of backlinks, you'll want to advertise with it. Don't necessarily discredit sites that don't have as many backlinks, especially if they offer affordable advertising options. You would still get the advantage of a one-way link, which search engines prize. This is even better if the website you're advertising on directly relates to the keywords used throughout your site. Keep in mind what you read before: the number of backlinks (quantity, popularity) is important but so is the relevancy (quality, reputation) of the site and pages.

3. *Check the Site's PageRank.* As discussed, PageRank is a relevant measure. To find PageRank, use LinkVendor.com or install the SEO toolbar in Chrome or Firefox.

INSIDER TIP

A quick way to check search engine inclusion is to take a string or sentence from the web page and put "" (quotes) around the expression and Google search. If listed, it will show up. Be sure to include enough words to make it unique. To check your own website, just type the name with the extension + text directly into Google.

4. *The Website's Alexa Rating.* Alexa.com is a website that shows the traffic rankings of websites. However, alexa.com is unable to distinguish between "legitimate" and "non-legitimate" traffic. For example, if a site "buys" traffic, this would be included with its alexa.com results. The problem with buying traffic is that you don't know for sure if you're getting real visitors. Sites that use expired domains tend to get real visitors, so their type of traffic is legitimate. However, there are many more sites that use bots to generate false traffic. Since you don't know if a site's traffic ranking has been affected by this type of traffic, don't get too excited if the website you want to advertise on has a high Alexa rating. Alexa is most often used by technical people and so the data is demographically skewed. Although it's better than nothing, use it with caution and follow the other guidelines set out in this section for determining whether you want to spend your money advertising on a particular site.

5. *Check to See If the Website Is Listed on Google or Other Search Engines.* This guideline might be obvious, yet it's very important. Type in keywords that relate to the site and see what pops up on the major search engines. Look through the first 50 listings (although it's optimal that the website appear in the first ten listings). If the site isn't there, you don't want to advertise with it.

6. *Make Sure the Cached Version of the Web Page Contains the Links.* Cached web pages are backups of the regular page. According to GoogleGuide.com, they are "snapshots" of the original website. They're just as important as the regular version of the web page because they show when the regular web page is unable to show. GoogleGuide.com says the situations in which this could occur include congestion on the internet, an overloaded or very slow website, or a webmaster removing web pages from its site. If advertising links don't show in the cached version of a web page, you're not getting the most advertising value for your dollar. This is a disadvantage to both you and the site owners, since outbound

links increase the chances that the site will get a higher ranking in search engine results.

7. *The Relevance of the Site in Relation to Your Own.* With free one-way linking situations, you don't have the advantage of determining whether the site best reflects the keywords you might be promoting. You only get the advantage of showing search engines that you at least have some one-way links. However, if you're paying for advertising, you want to make sure that the site relates in some way to your keywords, especially your primary ones. Relevancy should be a priority consideration.

How to Find Paid One-Way Linking Opportunities

The quickest way to find paid one-way linking opportunities is to type in your primary keyword and see what websites come up in the first ten listings. I know this might seem to be clichéd advice, but hey, don't underestimate it. How can you lose if you advertise on a site that you know ranks high on a search engine? The only downside to this method is that, depending on the keyword you're promoting, the websites that rank higher may take advantage of their position by charging outlandish advertising fees.

Another thing you can do to find paid one-way linking opportunities is to use SiteScout.com (formerly AdBrite.com), Google AdPlanner, or services like it. SiteScout is a service that allows people to sell advertising space. You can buy text links, banner space, full-page ads, a special type of pop-up known as an inline ad, and video advertising. When you're more established, you might want to look at the other advertising options. For now, since you're mostly concerned with search engine optimization, go for the text links. Don't forget to go through the previous steps mentioned on how to determine whether or not you should advertise with a particular site. Just because SiteScout lists a site doesn't mean it's the best one for you. Alternatively, you can find websites to advertise on through eBay.

Lastly, don't rule out advertising on some of your favorite websites. If they aren't visibly offering an advertising opportunity on their website, email them and ask if they would be willing to sell ad space. You can also do this to initiate a link exchange, which is the focus of the next section.

ONLINE RESOURCE

On the member site at www.jonrognerud.com/ optimizationbook, you'll find more information on websites to peruse.

Reciprocal Linking

Reciprocal linking is when a website links to you in exchange for your linking to it. Reciprocal links aren't as valuable as one-way links in the eyes of search engines because there's always the chance of people abusing the system with them. However, they count enough that you shouldn't overlook them. It should follow a natural, non-spammy path—much like you would interact at a business luncheon or cocktail party. You "connect" with a few.

Many webmasters will not look at you if your PageRank is not at least 3. The truth is, it's an over-rated number. However, take a look at some of the guidelines specified in this section even if you haven't yet achieved this page rank. Why? Because there are a lot of webmasters like you who are interested in reciprocal linking but don't have the advantage of a high PageRank. Remember, linking to someone, even if the page rank is low, can be good and will potentially grow over time and have more links.

That being said, you're ready to learn what to do to prepare your site for reciprocal linking. First, you need to have a web page on your site that says "Related Links" or "Resources." Avoid the temptation that many webmasters fall into of saying "Sponsors," "Affiliates," or "Links." If the webmasters you want to exchange links with are savvy, they'll realize that titling their link sections this way makes them less likely to get their URLs seen. This is because people don't like being advertised to. Most visitors have no reason to visit a "Sponsor" or "Affiliate" page. However, they may be curious about "Related Links" because they think they might receive more content that relates to what they're looking for.

Next, make sure that your "Related Links" page is as optimized as it can be with keywords related to your site. You should even place keywords in the advertising descriptions of the sites you're posting. If possible, include content on the "Related Links" page. The best approach for creating keyword-optimized content on your "Related Links" is to include detailed descriptions of the sites. Since these sites should relate to your keywords anyway, it shouldn't be too hard to come up with keyword-rich content that accurately describes the purposes of these websites. The people linking with you will appreciate this as well because by providing a description, you're offering a way to convince visitors that they should look at the sites listed.

A "link to us" HTML code can be provided as a custom solution, but don't include it right on your site. TIP: This is a good idea for infographics or custom widgets that you have made available. People can easily place the code and resources on their pages. It's recommended to send this code upon agreement, and only as a suggestion. To initiate a "Link to Us" code, say something like "Easily link to us by using the following code," then provide the necessary HTML linking code. This syntax of this code is:

<A HREF="http://www.yoursite.com"> Your Primary Link Target, Natural Keyword Selection></A>

Enter a short description using your primary keyword to tell what your site is about. Ultimately, it's up to the receiving party to use it in that manner. Collaboration is key so that all benefit.

Does this look familiar? It should, because it's the HREF tag discussed earlier. This is the general tag you need to link to websites, at least if you're doing it through HTML coding.

Manually review other sites that you think may have some benefit for you. Do not make this your only activity for link building, however. It should be considered another tactic, that's all. To find them, use the methods discussed in the section "How to Find Paid One-Way Linking Opportunities," as the principles outlined there also apply to reciprocal linking. After that, you should see if the webmaster of your selected website is interested in a link exchange. Some sites let you submit your site instantaneously, so you don't have to email the webmaster asking permission to embark on a linking exchange. Others require an email (even those that may have a "Link to Us" code). To email the webmaster, look for a "Contact Us" section on the website, and try to show him where (what page) and why (a complimentary, useful resource) he should connect with you. If a "Contact Us" section isn't provided, you can use a Whois utility, which can be found through domain name services, to determine his email address. All you need to use these utilities is the domain name of the person you want to contact. Try www.whois.sc.

ONLINE RESOURCE

Visit the member site (www.jonrognerud.com/optimizationbook) to see more information on how to use link building tools, from manual approaches to software and browser-enabled tools and related techniques.

Following are a few suggestions for proper email etiquette when requesting link exchanges.

- *You should want to link to a site.* I know . . . you might be thinking, why link to a site if you don't know for sure it will link to yours? The answer is because by linking to their site first, you're showing intent that you are genuinely interested in a link exchange. Some webmasters won't be interested in a link exchange if they see that the person emailing them hasn't started the link exchange first. If in the end you find that the person doesn't hold up his or her end of the bargain, you can always remove the link from your website.

- *Let the webmaster know clearly in the email subject line that you intend to link to his or her site.* It could be as simple as RE: editorial comment/question on your page about XXX." By doing this you are stating your intention, which saves the webmaster valuable reading time. He or she is also more likely to open up your email. Try to direct it to the person in charge. Do not just "blanket" email webmasters from WHOIS information

- *Make sure your writing style is friendly and personal.* Show that you have genuine interest in the person's website and describe the benefits of linking to your site. Talking about how much traffic you get is a big plus (if you get a lot of traffic). You might want to include a screenshot of your traffic (most web hosting programs have options in your account manager that let you track your traffic). Alternatively, you could find your site through Alexa.com and provide the specific URL that would show your Alexa.com rankings. If you don't get too much traffic, try to sell yourself by explaining more about the audience that you intend to market to. Webmasters are interested in promoting themselves in niche markets, and if they think your site is going to be popular in a niche market, you may be able to win them over and get them to participate in a link exchange.

- *Don't threaten to delete their links from your site if they don't respond within a certain time.* Link exchanging with another site is a privilege, not a right. If webmasters are interested, they'll respond saying they'll exchange links with you. If this is the reply you get, give them some time to put your link on their sites, about a week. If they don't do anything, email them again asking if they're still interested in the link exchange opportunity. Hopefully, they'll reply saying "yes" and put your link on their sites. If they aren't, then delete their links from your site. As a side note, you can email directly and ask for a link, but not place a link on your site. Many will add yours (if done professionally, as described above)—without requiring a link from you.

- *Keep your email condensed.* You should have no more than two short paragraphs of three to four sentences. Make sure that it's grammatically correct, because if it isn't, the webmaster might get the impression that your website isn't worth linking to. Most email providers have a spell checker. Take advantage of it. Wiep.net outlines a simple but powerful approach to personal connections in the Ultimate Link Building Template for emails. See the sidebar on the next page. However, you should not just use a static template, customize and test (carefully).

- *Only send one follow-up request.* Bombarding a webmaster's email is annoying and could be considered spam. In fact, some people may even report you to their ISPs if they think you're spamming them. This could ban you from doing email marketing with anyone else using that ISP. Remember, most webmasters respond to the first email if they're interested in a link exchange. The few that don't will definitely respond on the second email. If they don't, assume they're not interested and move on.

- *Don't use this as an opportunity to advertise affiliate websites you might be a part of.* Yes, it might be tempting to tell a webmaster about the latest server that's out there and collect a hefty commission, but forego the temptation. Trust me, if their sites are up, you can be assured that they already made their hosting or server decisions. If you must refer to an affiliate link, add "(aff)" at the end of the link as an indicator. Be totally honest and transparent, and be personal. Try to help them first. How about asking to add value by writing an article or blog post for them first?
- Use commonly accepted email etiquette. Be professional and concise. Avoid using words in the subject line that may tag your email as spam (such as "free").

On the upside, you're getting a chance to get your site advertised to that many more people. If your site just happens to relate to things that webmasters are interested in, then you might get a lead or sale from them when they visit your site to consider doing a link exchange with you. Let the site do the advertising for you, not your email. The average response rate is about 1 percent. So if you send out 1,000 emails to webmasters asking for participation in a link exchange, that's a possibility of ten sales. OK, maybe it sounds desperate, but as far as I'm concerned, all types of traffic count. Tools like buzzstream.com can help you automate this process.

THE ULTIMATE LINK BUILDING TEMPLATE

(wiep.net/talk/link-building/link-request-email-template/)

Greetings, {Friend}:

{Opening/ Introduction}

{Explanation of why your website is relevant to the one you're contacting}

{Include WIIFM (what's in it for me) for the person you're emailing}

{Close},

{Your Name}

Do you have all eight of those suggestions in mind? Good. Now you're ready to learn how to automate this process, if you have the money. The wonderful little program that helps you to do this is called SEO Elite. The program scours the web looking for possible reciprocal websites based on the keywords you provide for it. You can also use the program to find keywords. The program has a built-in Whois utility to help you figure out the email addresses of webmasters who don't post them on their websites. Once the program collects the email addresses, use it to send an email to all of them. If you want to get more advanced, try a tool like Buzzstream.com. You can multiple users log in to help you. Think about outsourcing some of this work once you have a process is place.

As you go through the process of acquiring reciprocal links, there are some other things you need to keep in mind. First, remember that search engines want to index sites that would be of real value to a visitor. When their bots encounter reciprocal links, you want to give the impression that you exchanged links because your website and its contents are that good for the other webmaster. So, if you are obtaining an abnormally high number of reciprocal links, your site may not get indexed as high or may even be penalized because it's seen as trying to cheat the search engine's algorithm. This is why you want to build your links gradually.

Search engines think of this as "velocity," how fast are you going with these new links? For example, you suddenly build 1,000 links a month (and only one kind of links) for a site that had a much lower, natural, diverse acquisition of links. Watch out as search engines may consider this link spamming and may filter you. Not every case is the same, but it's a helpful guideline.

If you are a big brand, there is a lot more flexibility. If we use news powerhouse CNN as an example, it most certainly receives many more than 1,000 links per month and it's not penalized. That's because history, patterns, and marketplace are also factors, and not simply "the rules."

Also make sure that you offer some variations in your linking code. This is because search engines don't want to see that your website is linked to hundreds of other sites with the same code and description. It doesn't see this as being a natural link-building method. Use different primary keywords, or even secondary keywords, along with different descriptions. Make sure you think about using "call to action" keywords as well, even the phrase "click here."

Additionally, you should make sure that not too many links on your site are reciprocal. Keep this at a minimum, and use an organic, personal approach when and where it makes good business sense, ultimately thinking about the visitors. Remember when I said earlier that one-way links are what search engines prefer to see? Do you also remember I said that reciprocal links have lost some of their emphasis because of the potential for abuse? This is why you want to keep your percentage of reciprocal links relatively low.

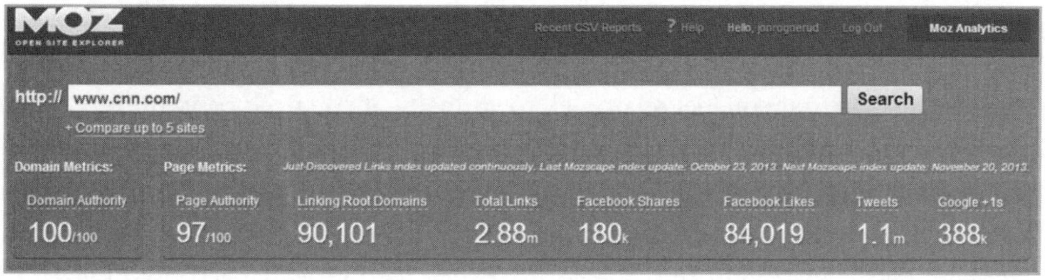

FIGURE 8–7. CNN trust and authority built—almost 3 million and growing.

In terms of where the reciprocal links point to, avoid the temptation to always have it be the homepage. First of all, from a marketing standpoint there are situations where the more specific content is provided on a subtopic web page, the more value it would have for a website visitor. Secondly, search engines don't like to see it. When it comes to natural link building, you're not always going to want to provide links to your homepage, as you would want to promote other web pages as well. Search engines are leery when they see otherwise. Remember the silo approach discussed in Chapter 3? This also applies to how you build your links. Group the links by like content to create relevancy, and you'll be rewarded with higher search rankings (and happier users!). When you think about what keywords are assigned to what pages, think of links in the same way. This will help support your entire SEO strategy, keyword research, traffic targeting, and increased conversion opportunities.

Outbound Links = Be Helpful = Google Love

Outbound links, as you've learned previously, are links that you post on your site that point to other sites or pages. These can be provided through webmasters who decide to pay you for ad space or simply because you think a website has relevant material. Google doesn't penalize you for getting outbound links from advertising, though you want to make sure the links relate to the keywords featured on your site.

So, what are some ways of finding outbound sites to link to? We'll get to that shortly. You may also want to have an "Advertise Here" section on your website. In this section you can create a form for webmasters to fill out to automatically send you an email request. You can create forms in any website creation software or use HTML if you're more technically inclined. Alternatively, you could show your email address, though make sure you don't use your main email address. This is because spammers often collect email addresses posted on websites to do their dirty business. In fact, even when you vie for traffic exchanges you should probably use a separate email address, though it's not as essential.

To find more sites to link to, you can do a keyword search (<your keyword phrase> + "forum," "blog," "directory", etc.) in Google and subsequently link to, and initiate requests to the sites that you feel relate well to your site. If you need content for your site, you could create outbound links by linking to articles from the free article directories talked about earlier in this book. If you use content from article directories, make sure you include the attribution back to the author(s). The downside to free article directories is that there is the possibility that the content may have already been used by another webmaster. If it has been and you post it on your website, Google could flag you for duplicate content, making you rank lower. If used responsibly, however, mixed in with your own, and with a unique, compelling introduction paragraph, you should be fine.

In Figure 8–8, you can see the example of an extract of keyword phrases from the original article on EzineArticles, and how others picked them up and used it for themselves.

So copy and paste a few words of the article into the search engine text box. See how many results come up. If a lot of webmasters are using the content, reconsider using the actual content. However, this doesn't mean the link the content is promoting isn't of any value. In fact, if that many webmasters are putting it on their sites, the

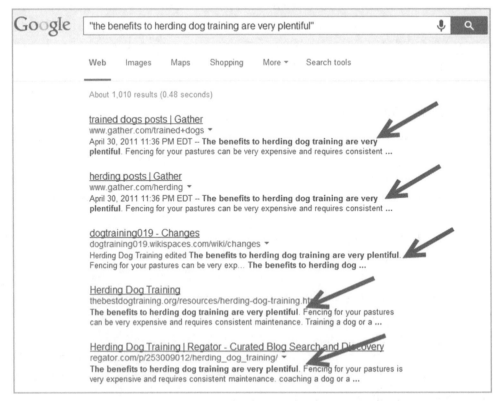

FIGURE 8–8. Content—duplicate check—usage check.

INSIDER TIP

The number of outbound links on a page should not exceed 100 as a general recommendation. Google looks at the total counts on a page, and that's true for your own site as well as others that link to you. The idea is that if it's drastically more than that, it could be considered spammy and not as valuable. Trusted brands and websites (i.e., CNN) can do what they want. You might not be able to do it, or get away with it. Ultimately, ask this: Is the content or link valuable to your visitor?

links probably are valuable. Create your own article (using the free article as a guide), and place the link on your website. Of course, if an article submitted to a free article directory is new, then you can go ahead and put the article and the link on your own website.

How to Legitimately Post on Wikipedia

It's important to keep in mind that Wikipedia and sites like it are informational in nature. Self-promotion is prohibited, but giving general information about a business, product, or service is acceptable.

Make sure your articles have an encyclopedia-like tone. Wikipedia offers some guidelines you should follow when writing for its site:

- *Know your intentions.* As an internet marketer, your natural urge is to advertise, advertise, and advertise even more. Don't do this if you want to take advantage of Wikipedia. In fact, since you know you might be biased when it comes to your own site, consider having a ghostwriter write the article. It won't cost much to get a ghostwriter to write one article, plus you will be able to get a viewpoint that's less subjective. Refer to your competition and others in your marketplace that may already have content submitted and sticking to the site.
- *Use cited text in place of links.* Wikipedia frowns on redirecting visitors to other sites. This is why when referring to another site, it's better to paraphrase what the site says than cite the reference at the end of the document. And you definitely shouldn't use affiliate sites as references, as this could be seen as advertising.
- *Don't put ads in the references section.* References are what a writer has used to help create an article. In other situations you could use an affiliate link as a reference, but article writing for Wikipedia is not one of them.
- *Don't make your article sound like an endorsement of your website.*

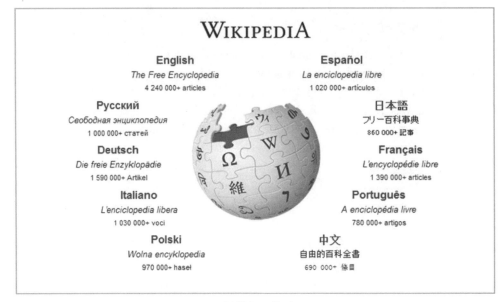

FIGURE 8–9. Wikipedia homepage.

- *Avoid spam radar.* A few things that could set off the spam radar are links at the top of an unordered list, putting more emphasis on one product over another when listing links, adding too many links mentioning the same product or service, and adding the same link to other articles.
- *Use the talk page.* It's OK to ask editors if a potential article meets Wikipedia's requirements. However, only do it once and don't put in anything else that could be construed as an ad.
- *Don't use external links in your signature.* While doing this is fine for many message boards, don't do it when writing for Wikipedia.
- *Look at other Wikipedia articles.* Yes, this might be another obvious suggestion, but how else are you going to determine what Wikipedia likes if you don't do this?

INSIDER TIP

Wikipedia is an authority site, but there was too much spam being injected, so Wikipedia implemented the rel=nofollow attribute, which quickly removed spammers. It's still valuable as a source for traffic and reference. (You have probably noticed how often listings show up with Wikipedia at the top in Google results.)

Do searches on some famous companies as well as smaller ones. Pay particular attention to how the articles for the smaller companies were written, since it can be a lot harder to get an article about a no-name company accepted over one that has already been talked about before.

■ *Use rejection as a learning experience.* If your article is rejected, don't be discouraged. You can use the experience as a learning tool to figure out more of what Wikipedia wants.

CHECKLIST FOR SUCCESS

Now that you know the ins and outs of linking, you're well on your way to building a brand and making money online. Below is a list of what SEO pros consider necessary in order to consider linking with a site. It's also a handy comprehensive reminder of how to build links the right way.

■ Build links from related or complementary websites—in other words, topically related.

■ Don't worry about PageRank (ask me why at contact@jonrognerud.com).

■ Links should contain varied, targeted keywords/key phrases as text hyperlinks.

■ Some reciprocal links are fine, but make sure you offer readers value and the site isn't a link farm. Don't do this as a norm, it tends to raise flags quickly.

■ Links optimally should be followed by a short description of the target website also containing related keywords. Top links are contained within the body of the page using keywords/text to help describe the link.

■ Don't build all the links on the same day (or within a short time period); avoid any penalties and avoid "run of site" links showing up on all pages. If using badges or widgets for link acquisition, consider adding rel=nofollow, especially if fast growth is seen. (Remember: users first, search engines second.)

■ Links should not be from framed pages.

■ Links should not be through a JavaScript or redirect scripts.

INSIDER TIP

To see the "rel=nofollow" links and who uses them and where, install the SEO for Firefox plugin by Aaron Wall (see my membership site for "firefox plugins"). Once installed, refresh the pages, and the links show up highlighted in red. Visit www.jonrognerud.com/optimizationbook.

- Get links from top-valued directories, and research categories. Use dmoz.org and dir.yahoo.com as research tools.
- Build quality links from trusted sites. Avoid bad neighborhoods. If it's obvious to you, it'll be obvious to the search engines.
- Links should not be on Flash sites or pages.
- Links should generally not include a "nofollow" tag or any other robot tags (unless it's a paid link).
- Don't link with penalized or banned sites. Use common sense.
- Avoid link farms, link exchange sites, and link clubs.

Link Terms

anchor text: The text associated with a hyperlink.

one-way link: A hyperlink that points to a website without a reciprocal link; thus the link goes "one way" in direction.

link: A citation from one web document to another web document or another position in the same document.

link baiting: Targeting, creating, and formatting your content or information in a way that encourages your target audience to point high-quality links at your site.

link building: The process of building links. Can be inbound or outbound.

link burst: A rapid increase in the quantity of links pointing at a website.

link churn: The rate at which a site loses links.

link equity: A measure of the strength of your site based on inbound link popularity and the authority and quality of the sites providing the links.

link farm: A website that links to other sites without regard to content or relevancy. Free For All (FFA) pages are examples of link farms.

link hoarding: Keeping all your link popularity by not doing outbound links or only linking out using JavaScript or redirects.

link popularity: A measure of the quantity and quality of inbound links pointing to a particular website. This feature is used by search engines for positioning of web pages in their indexes.

link reputation: A measure of the quality of inbound links—"what the link says about your page" (defined by anchor text as one important metric).

paid links: Links purchased for advertising.

reciprocal links: Links exchanged between two sites.

Link-Building Resources

The following sites are great resources to add to your arsenal of tools.

- ericward.com/articles/index.html. This site offers great articles by Eric Ward, one of the web's very first link builders. He worked on the first link requests for Amazon.com. I have worked with Eric. He's a very busy man, so make sure to book far in advance.
- wolf-howl.com/category/link-development. Michael Gray writes with humor and intelligence on link development. He likes to challenge Google directly at search engine conferences!
- stuntdubl.com/category/link-development. Todd Malicoat, known as "Stunt-dubl" online, provides heavily researched and highly valuable discussions on link-building practices.
- seobook.com/archives/cat_seo_tips.shtml. Aaron Wall's SEOBook is one of the most respected websites on the subject of SEO.
- copyblogger.com. Brian Clark's Copyblogger is an excellent site for learning how to write great content, a critical part of successful link building.
- wiep.net/talk/category/link-building-strategies. Awesome link-building strategies from our link-building friend in Europe.
- toprankblog.com/category/seo/link-building. Lee Odden's Online Marketing Blog, read by many. A great resource on how to acquire links.
- linkspiel.com. Debra Mastaler is a prolific writer and expert link builder. She writes about complex link-building topics in simple English, and has a big following in our community. She's always ready to help.

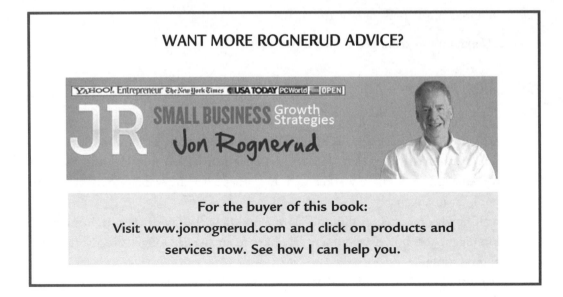

Chapter 9

Get Ready to Launch Your Website

I n this section, you'll learn about how to get your website and pages found by search engines. You'll learn the differences between submitting to search engines and self-discovery of web pages, where search engines naturally find you. You'll leverage all the critical pieces for an optimized website.

Adding your site to directories, blogs, and related websites and making your website search-engine friendly will be important in your SEO process. It will get your pages seen by search engines as well as indexed and stored in their vast databases.

Furthermore, analyzing your logs for traffic and user movement can help you to "tune" your pages. This way, you'll get more user engagement and stickiness (they stay around longer).

HOW TO SUBMIT YOUR SITE TO SEARCH ENGINES

 Bob had been told that the search engines would "find him" if he optimized his site correctly. However, after four weeks he was beginning to wonder if the search engines had taken a wrong turn.

Frustrated that he was still not receiving much traffic, he turned to the experts for help. Bob found out that it was actually not inaccurate that the search engines would find him, but there was action he could take to become more visible in cyberspace.

Bob listed the directories, blogs, and article syndication sites, and began submitting his site, beginning with the Yahoo! Directory. Within less than two weeks Bob started to see results from his efforts. Finally, he felt like he was making progress. He continued to track his keywords in Google Analytics, and traffic was on the move upward.

This section talks about how you can submit your site (and if you should) to Yahoo!, Ask, Bing, and others. You will also learn how to submit to the Open Directory (DMOZ). It's not a search engine, but it is helpful in getting you noticed by search engines. You also learn why you shouldn't use submission services or submission software.

Best Opportunity for Fast Indexing

Search engine indexing is how information is collected, parsed, and stored in search engine databases to facilitate fast and accurate information retrieval. Back in 2010, "Google Caffeine" was introduced, to allow for this process to happen faster than before (googleblog.blogspot.com/2010/06/our-new-search-index-caffeine.html). The search engine index design uses interdisciplinary theories from linguistics, cognitive psychology, mathematics, informatics, physics, and computer science.

Search engine and website optimization are about creating a site that meets search engine criteria and, ultimately, supports the visitors' needs, and that you receive quality visitors and conversions.

Automatic vs. Manual Submission

Search engines don't like automatic submissions. They get millions of attempted automatic submissions each day and, as a result, go to great lengths to try to stop them, such as requiring passwords and/or fill-in details before the submission is accepted.

Automatic submission software is banned by many search engines and directories because it can't always place links in relevant categories. Whether you hire a directory submitter or use submission software yourself, you are setting your site up for failure. Getting too many incoming links too quickly or submitting the same site to the major engines repeatedly can be seen by search engines as spamming and get your site banned.

There are few benefits to using a paid submission service, although the promotions tout that these services know of places to submit that you are unaware of. (You should not be super-concerned about it though. The Big Three, Google, Yahoo!, and Bing, will provide most of your traffic from search.) The best submission services take the time to educate their clients on submission with the expectation that they'll be able to do the job themselves next time.

Submitting your site manually gives you control over where you'll be listed. Automatic submitters may list your site with an engine you've never heard of outside the United States. Or, worse, they could be associating your site with sites that you find objectionable, such as pornographic sites. When you submit your own site, you decide what category to list in. You don't want your site to end up in the general directory or the miscellaneous category where it may never be seen.

Every site should be marketed differently, and submitted to different vertical engines and directories depending on its intended audience. Automatic submission doesn't do this.

Manual submission is the only way to choose the descriptions and keywords that you think will be most effective in promoting your site, as most engines and directories allow you to choose your own.

Common Myths of Search Engine Submission

Here are some common myths about submitting your site manually.

- Search engine submission requires enormous research.
- Almost every search engine and directory has a link labeled "Add a site" or "Submit URL," which takes you directly to its submission form. All you have to do is follow the rules and enter your information carefully.
- Websites should be listed in all search engines.
- If you do not submit to search engines, they will not find you. The lower tier search engines will not find you either. (Not true. Create a blog post or article and submit it to start. Then share via your standard social channels [Twitter, Facebook, etc.]).
- Websites should be listed on a weekly or monthly basis. Continually submitting your site can be classified as spamming and result in your site's banishment from a search engine's database. As a general rule, don't resubmit a new version of a page.
- Good submission is costly. The truth is you don't have to pay a submission service to submit your site to the search engines. Submission to most major search engines is free. Do not get caught up in this, and do not pay for submission!

Search engines and directories that you may consider submitting to

- dmoz.org/
- dir.yahoo.com/

- joeant.com/
- skaffe.com/
- botw.org
- goguides.org/
- gimpsy.com/
- wowdirectory.com/

How Long Does It Take to Get Listed?

For the top search engines, you can get seen within hours, but most commonly a few days

How often should you resubmit? Don't. Once your site is indexed, simply keep adding search and user-friendly content and there's no need to resubmit. You should, however, be familiar with your site statistics.

Look at your website statistics for robot visits.

- Google (weekly, monthly)
- DMOZ (two months and "good luck")
- Review logs and web analytics (daily, weekly, monthly)

Robots.txt

The robots.txt is a simple text file that is placed in your root directory. It directs search engine robots (*bots*, *spiders*, or *crawlers* are interchangable terms).

- It saves your bandwidth. The spider won't visit areas where there is no useful information.
- It gives you a very basic level of protection. It keeps people from easily finding stuff you don't want easily accessible via search engines. Some webmasters also use it to exclude "test" or "development" areas of a website that are not ready for public viewing.
- It cleans up your logs. Every time a search engine visits your site it requests the robots.txt, which can happen several times a day. If you don't have one, it generates a 404 Not Found error each time. It's hard to wade through all of these to find genuine errors at the end of the month.
- It's good programming policy.
- Webmaster pros have a robots.txt file in place. Amateurs don't. What group do you want your site to be in?

This last is more of an ego/image thing than a "real" reason, but in competitive areas or when applying for a job, it can make a difference. Some employers won't consider hiring a webmaster who doesn't know how to use one, on the assumption that he may not know other, more critical things, as well. Search engines work the same way; it's sloppy and unprofessional not to use a robots.txt.

HTML Code vs. Text

Your website is like an iceberg: You only see the top bit in your browser. Search engines look at your whole source code. Search engines are constantly spidering the web and indexing pages for search data.

You need to consider your HTML code-to-text ratio. How much of your web page is HTML markup and how much is text that the search engines will read? This is important because search engines only read and index the text of a page and they only go so far into a page to read either HTML or text. So if your web page is mostly written in HTML code, the search engines might not read all your text, and certainly not the "valuable" things (keywords, for example).

So what is the desired ratio? The higher your text content, the better. Thirty percent or more is not bad. However, as you've learned—each marketplace is different. Look at your competitors. If your top ten (first page listings of Google natural) list is using a lot of content/pure text, and your ratio is lower—a good signal to fix it—get to work. How much your ratio affects your overall rankings in search engines may never be known. But it's another important factor to consider when optimizing your website.

W3C Standards

Adhering to W3C Standards helps your sites maintain code that's clean and more easily spidered and indexed by the search engines. Often when a search engine spider encounters bad code, it leaves the page or doesn't perform a deep spider. This area is a bit controversial in the SEO community. There is no doubt that clean code will serve users and search engines. If building from scratch, you should at least be aware of the obvious.

The World Wide Web Consortium (W3C) develops interoperable technologies (specifications, guidelines, software, and tools) to lead the web to its full potential. W3C is a forum for information, commerce, communication, and collective understanding.

> ### ONLINE RESOURCE
>
> Search for W3C standards, and use its CSS/HTML check tools, validator.w3.org/, and content ratios at seochat.com/seo-tools/code-to-text-ratio/.

Information related to this organization can be found at www.w3.org. And, remember to see what your competitor's websites are doing in this regard.

Let the Spiders Do the Walking

Like search engines, directories can aid your web visibility. Following is a list of directories and your options for submission.

Yahoo! Directory

The first thing to do is submit your site to the Yahoo! Directory. This website contains a detailed compilation of websites that can be browsed by visitors through certain categories. Unlike Yahoo!'s search engine, Yahoo! Directory is powered by editors rather than robots—all the more reason to be sure your site has followed all the white hat techniques outlined earlier in this book.

What connection does the Yahoo! Directory have with the Yahoo! search engine? It's generally accepted that you have a greater chance of getting your site listed higher if you submit to the crawler-based Yahoo! search engine. This isn't a guarantee, but either way you have nothing to lose by submitting to the Yahoo! Directory.

To submit to the Yahoo! Directory, use its "standard" submission service or its "Yahoo! Directory Submit," which charges a fee. The standard submission service lets you submit your site in general categories at no extra cost. You're not allowed to submit to commercial categories. If you try to submit your site to a commercial category using the standard submission option, it won't be allowed. Instead, Yahoo! Directory will force you to upgrade to Yahoo! Directory Submit.

How does Yahoo! Directory Submit work? First, you must pay an annual fee of $299, for general audience sites and $600 for mature audience sites. What you get according to Yahoo! Directory is an "expedited review" of your website(s)—that's right, you can submit more than one, though you have to pay $299 or $600 for each submission. You'll get a response within seven days indicating whether or not your site is accepted. If it's accepted, you'll have to pay $299 or $600 once a year to keep your listing in the directory, at least if it's a commercial site (noncommercial sites aren't charged the recurring fee). The upside to the paid submission is that your site gets reviewed quickly; with the standard submission service you may not get your site reviewed at all. The downside is that you're paying a lot of money for a service that can't guarantee you placement (although if you're promoting a business you must use the Yahoo! Directory Submit).

In terms of getting your site accepted, what matters is relevant content. When it comes to the standard submission option, you want to ensure that your content is not commercial in any way. For example, if you're running an online clothing store, more

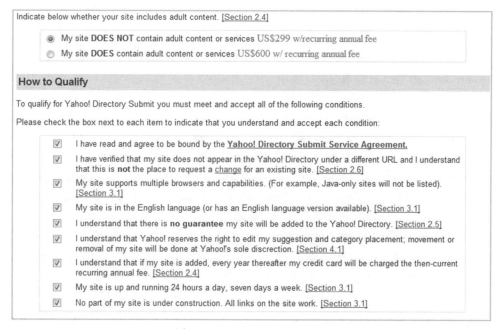

Indicate below whether your site includes adult content. [Section 2.4]

- ◉ My site **DOES NOT** contain adult content or services US$299 w/recurring annual fee
- ○ My site **DOES** contain adult content or services US$600 w/ recurring annual fee

How to Qualify

To qualify for Yahoo! Directory Submit you must meet and accept all of the following conditions.

Please check the box next to each item to indicate that you understand and accept each condition:

- ☑ I have read and agree to be bound by the **Yahoo! Directory Submit Service Agreement.**
- ☑ I have verified that my site does not appear in the Yahoo! Directory under a different URL and I understand that this is **not** the place to request a change for an existing site. [Section 2.6]
- ☑ My site supports multiple browsers and capabilities. (For example, Java-only sites will not be listed.) [Section 3.1]
- ☑ My site is in the English language (or has an English language version available). [Section 3.1]
- ☑ I understand that there is **no guarantee** my site will be added to the Yahoo! Directory. [Section 2.5]
- ☑ I understand that Yahoo! reserves the right to edit my suggestion and category placement; movement or removal of my site will be done at Yahoo!'s sole discretion. [Section 4.1]
- ☑ I understand that if my site is added, every year thereafter my credit card will be charged the then-current recurring annual fee. [Section 2.4]
- ☑ My site is up and running 24 hours a day, seven days a week. [Section 3.1]
- ☑ No part of my site is under construction. All links on the site work. [Section 3.1]

FIGURE 9–1. Yahoo! Directory entry and verification.

likely than not this won't be acceptable with standard submission. However, if you submitted a site that talked about how to be fashionable with a certain collection of clothes, this would be accepted, even if the article provided a link to your website. Yahoo! Directory would choose the latter site because it's seen as being informative and more helpful than the actual store.

If you do use the Yahoo! Directory Submit and you choose not to pay the renewal fee (if it applies to you), your listing will be dropped by Yahoo! Directory. However, this may not have a negative impact on search engine crawlers. If you get an initial boost from the Yahoo! Directory, there's greater potential that others will want to link to you. This is even truer if you follow the link-building specifications laid out in this book. This may be enough to keep your high ranking with the other search engines, including Yahoo!. If it isn't, you can always submit your site again through Yahoo! Directory Submit.

To submit a site to the Yahoo! Directory, you need to visit dir.yahoo.com. If you want to use standard submission, select the "Suggest a Site" link at the top right corner of the non-commercial category page you want your site to be indexed to. Note: You'll have to look closely, since "Suggest a Site" is in a smaller font. You could use the same method to use Yahoo! Submit, or you could use the homepage. The category you choose doesn't matter as much, because the editors working for Yahoo! Directory choose the category for you.

Yahoo! Search Engine

With your site submitted to the Yahoo! Directory, you're ready to submit your site to the Yahoo! search engine. If you performed your quality link-building work, Yahoo! should be able to pick you up automatically. Otherwise, you can use its URL submission form, which can be accessed by going to search.yahoo.com. Enter the URL you want to submit. You'll probably want to submit only your homepage, though you can submit individual subtopic pages as well. When you submit the web page, be sure to include the whole URL including the "http://www." If you don't include http://www, the page will prompt you to enter the proper URL. Also, make sure that you don't submit your site twice because you may get penalized. And, as stated before, this is an option, but you are better off creating content, building links, and setting up your server and website to be search friendly. Yahoo! will find you.

Yahoo! also offers Search Submit at http://search.yahoo.com/info/submit.html. With Search Submit you must pay an annual subscription fee in addition to payment-per-click. Don't confuse this program with Yahoo! Sponsored Search, which lists your site in certain commercial categories. The monthly fee for Sponsored Search has different price ranges. Look it up for the latest pricing, as they will change based on market conditions. These are pay-per-click programs that show ads on the right side of search listing results. You pay when visitors click on your ads. With Yahoo! Search Submit, your site is shown just like other normal search engine listings. However, you do have to pay for it. If you run out of money, you might lose your listing, though sometimes you won't.

Is it worth using Search Submit? It is in the sense that you can get your site indexed immediately. However, it offers no benefit when it comes to your ranking. The payment structure for this program is not as attractive as other pay-per-click programs, since in addition to PPC you also have a subscription fee. For this reason you may prefer to spend your money on Yahoo! Search, BingAds.com, or Google AdWords. In fact, these are a great way to test the advertising value of your keyword, at least if you want to see results before your site gets indexed.

Ask

Ask doesn't offer a free URL submission page nor does it offer paid submission.

However, the search engine periodically crawls the web, indexing sites on the basis of how many times they appear on other sites. So, again, there's value in building valid links.

Bing

Bing Search accepts submissions at http://www.bing.com/toolbox/submit-site-url. It uses its bot, BINGBot, to crawl the web in search of relevant sites.

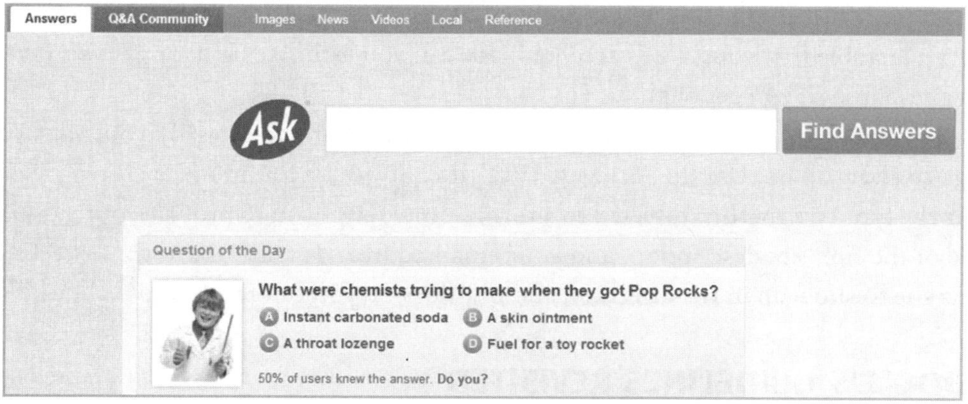

FIGURE 9–2. Ask.com homepage search.

FIGURE 9–3. Bing homepage search.

AOL

AOL Search is powered by Google's search engine technology. So once you submit your site to Google (which we talk about in the next section), you also get your results shown in the AOL Search listings.

The Open Directory (DMOZ)

The Open Directory is a special directory built by volunteers that serves as a guide to the internet. The Open Directory is now owned by Google.

Many of the most popular search engines, including Google, pull results from and point to the Open Directory, so trying to make your website a part of it definitely doesn't hurt. Plus it's free. The only major problem with the Open Directory is that you won't get a guarantee that your site is accepted, nor can you estimate how long it will take to get a response (if you get one).

To submit to the Open Directory, you need to select the category you want your page to show up on. Use the "Suggest URL" link; it can be found on the category page near the top. You are then directed to a form that requires you to provide your site URL, title of the site, site description, and your email address. It takes about three weeks for your site to show up in the directory, and if it doesn't, you can resubmit.

GOOGLE'S GUIDELINES REVISITED

Meet Google, the "coolest kid" on the cyberblock!

Google is popular, but its engine can be easy to get in to. Just build some links; read more about that in Chapter 8. You should know about the guidelines you must follow to ensure that not only does your site get listed but that it also doesn't get banned. You also learn about elements of your website that Google won't look at.

Using Keywords Early, Often, and Naturally

Google's bots may read your web pages from the topmost corner of the left side of your website to the bottom right, but new software and code structure has changed that behavior. The use of CSS is an example. Absolute CSS positioning is a way to help place content and keywords easily on a page. Content may be placed higher in the code, but the users see it further down on the page. Most SEOs agree that getting your keywords in early and often can help your position, but remember, all activities and best practices should help your ranking. Don't rely on just one or two techniques. CSS is a powerful hand to assist in the optimization of content, styling (H1, H2), and the implementation of easy-to-follow (for bots and users) CSS menus and links. However, many sites are designed with all of the links on the left-hand side and content on the right side. The problem with this design is instead of your content being seen first, Google may see the links first (again, depending on the coding and design). Your links may not be seen to be as optimized as your content, although they are very important for search, users, and the information architecture.

One solution is to use three panes rather than two. Keep the normal left and right panes, but add an extra pane at the top left of the layout. Don't put keywords in this extra pane. With this area "blank," when the Google bots read the site, rather than going for the links as they normally would, the bots see that a portion where the links are is "blank." This then forces it to read the content first, which is more keyword rich than the links.

Note that not all search engines read sites this way, which is why this guideline was provided in this special section dedicated to optimizing for Google. You could be on the safe side and use the layout anyway.

Your best option is to hire a CSS/HTML expert if getting into this level of detail. A search-friendly blog may be all you need. Think of giving search engines the content early, no matter what you do. But I must make this clear: Think of your users first, search engines will follow. If using tables in this manner, they are not hard to create. Most word processors and even WYSIWYG HTML editors provide them, so take advantage of that. Take the CSS tutorial at W3Schools.com/css/—and do it right.

Things That Google Ignores

There are some HTML attributes that Google pays no attention to when it goes through its crawling process. While you won't get penalized if you use these attributes, why waste your time with them if they're not going to count anyway?

Of course, there are exceptions to these rules, as noted in the numbered list below. There are also some elements listed that you will choose not to include.

1. *The keywords\meta tag.* Google ignores this for ranking (googlewebmastercentral. blogspot.com/2009/09/google-does-not-use-keywords-meta-tag.html). Remember that this list is what Google ignores, so it does not negate my earlier advice. The keywords and description attributes are still read by other search engines. However, the boost you get from having them isn't as great as if you follow the other techniques, such as proper link building. If you submit to Google only, you may not want to include the keywords attribute, but focus on a smart "upsell" or "positioning," "branding" of your message in the description attribute instead. Some say include them (keywords tag), but I don't.

2. *The <!—comments—> tag.* The comments tag is an optional tag designed more for the website designer than for search engines or browsers. You use it to make personal notes related to what the upcoming coding does. It's especially useful if other webmasters are working on web pages that have been started by someone else. Still, it isn't a necessary tag, so you can omit it if you want.

3. *The <style> tag.* This tag has attributes that specify what your site will look like. This deals with styling of your page (CSS). If you're using extensive CSS, include the file as an external reference. Google can detect spammy CSS, so be careful (like x,y positioning of keywords in negative space, etc.).

4. *The <script> tag.* This tag lets the browser know that a block of JavaScript code is about to be initiated. While Google ignores the information in this tag, it's still useful if you want to take advantage of JavaScript. You would use JavaScript when

you want to run applets, special programs that run in a separate browser window. Use of this tag may or may not be optional, depending on what your site is for. Google is now, more than ever, starting to read and use/translate JavaScript from 2010 and forward.

5. *Duplicate links.* If you have duplicate links to the same page, Google only counts the first one.

6. *Interlinking to points on the same page.* Interlinking involves picking a point on your web page called an anchor that you want another anchor to link to. This practice is commonly used when websites present very long copy on the same page. Readers can click on links throughout the document to jump to other parts of the document. It's very effective for increasing readability, but it's another optional device. Worst case, you could break up the copy and make more subtopic links.

7. *Graphics, animation, and video.* Google pays no attention to these types of content, but it may notice the descriptive attributes surrounding them and certainly their URLs. Image optimization should be considered since Google Image search will/can pick it up. Give them friendly names and optimize as you've learned in this book. Transcripts from videos should be used for optimal inclusion.

8. *Meta tags use.* See more on meta tags for Google at google.com/support/webmasters/bin/answer.py?answer=79812.

How Not to Link to Sites that Are in a Bad Neighborhood (and Why Would You?)

You learned a little bit about this earlier. Basically, sites that are in a bad neighborhood are those that post on link farms, splogs, or other sites using black hat SEO techniques. Stay away from these types of sites. While backlinks from spammy, bad websites cannot get you dethroned from Google (unless you link back, create an obvious relationship with them, and try to hurt yourself, then maybe), it's not a focus area for you. Even if your competitors try to build bad links to you, it will not affect you for rankings. Google will know about it, and the old "Google Bombing" is virtually nonexistent now. Can you imagine if this was possible on a regular basis? The idea of "negative SEO" (search for it) is still out there, and Google has not completely dismissed it. Of course, reputation management is another story. This is why you need to keep your eye on the sites to which you link.

One simple, but not only, way you can do this is to read the PageRank bar on your favorite browser plugin (see resources section at the end of the book). If the tool bar shows no value or "N/A", that could indicate a ban. However, don't confuse being banned with having a PageRank of 0. Just because a site has a 0 page rank, that doesn't mean it's linking to sites in a bad neighborhood. It could just mean that not enough

INSIDER TIP

See the members area at www.jonrognerud.com/
optimizationbook for more tools you can use to track
and check for potentially bad neighborhoods.

time has passed for the webmaster to get the site to rank high enough in search engines
to receive a higher PageRank. The weight of the website has not been updated to a
recognizable level. At one point, for example, there was a proxy problem (now fixed)
that erroneously showed pages with a PageRank of 0, which in fact were ranked higher.

How to Get Your Site Listed in Google Quickly

Wouldn't it be nice to start seeing your site in Google's search engine quickly? Earlier we
explained that if a site is crawled but not yet indexed, the results aren't visible to search
users.

For example, if you enter the full domain of your site with the "http://www." and
your site hasn't been listed yet, it won't show up in Google's results. When your site does
get indexed, if you enter the full URL, you'll see your site listed. This listing contains the
URL, the title of your website, and a description.

To get your site indexed quickly, you won't use Google's submission form (google.
com/addurl.html). Using this method may take one to several weeks to get your site
indexed, and remember, this is a general guideline. Most of my sites show up in hours
or days.

So, what do you need to do to get your website indexed so quickly? The first step is
to visit Google.com and enter a broad, generic keyword that's relevant to your site. You
may want to test with a broad keyword at first, then drill down a bit further. Don't worry
about trying to go for niche markets with this step, because you're going to want to have
access to sites with the highest level of traffic. (Alexa.com and Compete.com will help
you understand more about traffic.)

Once you enter the keyword, you see the Google results. Once you click into the
pages, check the site for how often the data is updated (is it a regularly updated blog, for
example) and if you think there's an option to get a link. (See Chapter 8 on link building
to learn more.) PageRank alone is not a measure for fast indexing, but I'll look at it. Visit
each of these websites, and see if they could also compliment yours, since you are already
there. But don't focus too much on it. Look for the contact information if it's listed. If
it's not listed, don't forget you can use the Whois utility found through domain name
services (or use Whois.sc). Use the same methods you learned earlier for email etiquette,

and send them an email asking if they are interested in a content piece from you. Also, don't forget that you can still purchase advertising on the resources given throughout this book.

If you advertise your link on a site that has traffic, is already indexed, and has a recent cache date, your site will likely get indexed quickly, all else being equal. These days, I use authority social media sites to help with this, including signing up and registering my websites with Google and Bing Webmaster tools.

ONLINE RESOURCE

Domaintools.com is a must-have tool to review domain information. The Reverse-IP tool will tell you if there are many sites within one IP.

Chapter 10

Food, Gas, Great Website—
Next Exit!

For a Southern California resident, traffic is a big part of many people's lives. While traffic on the interstate is a headache, traffic on the information highway is a great thing. In this chapter I look at techniques for driving lots of traffic to your website, including pay-per-click (PPC), blogs, and additional traffic strategies.

I've discussed some traffic sources in previous chapters. Listed below is a beginning checklist that includes the sources I've already discussed. For up-to-date lists and a lot more traffic ideas, visit the member site at www.jonrognerud.com/optimizationbook.

- SEO
- Multiple domains that you create and own driving links/traffic to main money site
- Pay-per-click (i.e., Google AdWords, Yahoo!, Bing, 7Search)
- Email marketing and subscription lists
- Trading traffic links
- Buying traffic links (see comments about Google's standards)
- Earning traffic links: articles, press, blogs, Web 2.0 services, etc.
- Joint venture (JV) deals
- Affiliate programs
- CPA affiliate programs

- Link bait: specialized content, widgets, infographics, WordPress themes
- Link love via other blogs
- Viral marketing: videos, word of mouth, widgets, etc.
- Offline marketing
- Banner ads
- Pop-ups
- Co-registration

In addition to selling your product or service, there are a number of other ways to make money from your website, including:

- AdSense
- Sell advertising space on your site(s) assuming you have more than one domain
- Push your own affiliate programs
- Sell your own products directly from your website
- CPA (Cost per action) networks, such as Adknowledge.com (formerly hydranet-work.com, acquired by Adknowledge.com), where you get paid when a lead is closed on your behalf.

Your site can make money even if you don't have a perfect design. Remember Bob's beautifully designed first site, which generated no revenue? Yet there are numerous examples of sites that are not "award-worthy" but generate a great deal of traffic.

We want to look to building traffic, not making a site completely perfect at first. All that will follow.

BIG TRAFFIC DRIVING TECHNIQUES

Blogs and Ways to Optimize for Traffic from Search

One of the fastest ways for you to build traffic to your site with minimal effort is to create a blog.

In this section, you'll also learn tips to optimize your blog using custom plugins. They are easy to use and very powerful.

You can start a blog for free by visiting WordPress.com, or if self-hosting (recommended), install the free (open source) version from WordPress.org. You can build content yourself or outsource the writing to a ghostwriter. The content doesn't have to be long. A short post of 100 to 200 words is acceptable to start. Try to make it useful, and link to other resources, show attribution (link) where obvious. Testing and monitoring is key.

Blogs are a great way to naturally attract search engine traffic. Most of the time, blogs already have optimized site architecture, clear navigation, and the innate potential for good linking. Intelligently linking your site to a well-created blog can increase your traffic. In fact, blogs can get so well indexed that you have the potential to show up for any number of four-word phrases relevant to your industry, if done correctly.

Try to use a keyword that gets a moderate level of targeted traffic.

If you are already inside your blog post, you can use a power tool from the makers of Wordtracker. It's the SEO Blogger tool for Wordtracker (see Figure 10–1). It installs quickly into your Firefox browser, and you launch from an icon directly on the browser. The tool will show you how many times a word is used, percentages, and more. It is easy to use.

It might not bring the most traffic, but it often brings the most profit through more subscribers and sales. If possible, narrow the scope of your blog discussion to a two- or three-word phrase that has a high yield of traffic yet little competition. Set up your blog to repeat keywords that you want to target just enough times to establish a theme. You can take full advantage of this in your post titles, category names, and the pages' URL names. Sparingly include the "moderate" keyword you selected before in your title

FIGURE 10–1. Wordtracker SEO Scout Extension blogger tool for Chrome—integrated with your browser. Try for 7-days, or membership at $69/month.

and description. All those link-backs will contain the keyword term you want the most attention for. This can work like magic, and with the updated speed of indexing (with applications like Google Caffeine), you'll likely see your post show up in search results quickly. My posts show up in minutes.

Post in a timely fashion. You can get better results by updating or sharing socially just once during one of the three best times during the day: early in the morning, at least before noon, or late at night (thinking internationally, here, as well). Monitoring when the search engine's crawlers visit your site can help as well. You can increase the number of crawler visits by blogging on the time or period they come to your site. The more you post, the more the crawlers have to go through your content. This could cause the crawler to split its job into several visits, whereupon you have even more content.

WordPress is a CMS (content management system) that allows you to also schedule posts for the future. Write your blog posts over the weekend, and schedule them for the upcoming week. Technorati (below) has stopped tracking the trends, but blogging is a key strategy to implement and deploy for personal and business use. Make sure you capture emails where you can, and learn more about optimizing from the list below.

The ultimate plugin list for maximum benefit for traffic and search friendly blogs: Just search for these in Google, and add the "wordpress plugins" to the query. Log in to your WordPress admin area, expand the "Plugins" section, and add them via the "Add New" button. See Figure 10–2 on page 251. Get more plug-ins at www.jonrognerud. com/optimizationbook.

- All-in-one SEO: must have for search-friendly SEO sites
- All-in-one Webmaster: central place to manage the top three
- Akismet: get API key from WordPress.com
- Broken Link Checker: manage/track broken links
- CBnet Ping Optimizer: manage ping systems naturally
- Google XML Sitemaps: automatically generate XML sitemaps
- Fast and Secure Contact Form: easy form for contact forms, etc.
- Simple Captcha: challenge/response test tool for varied uses
- WordPress Database Backup: say no more!
- WP Super Cache: generate static HTML pages for fast loading
- FBShare: Facebook share button
- Socialize: actionable social bookmarks to your posts
- WP Security Scan: make sure you are compliant
- RSS Footer: add small text to bottom of each RSS
- Disqus Comment System: powerful commenting system and management
- Cookies for Comments: spam checker for comments

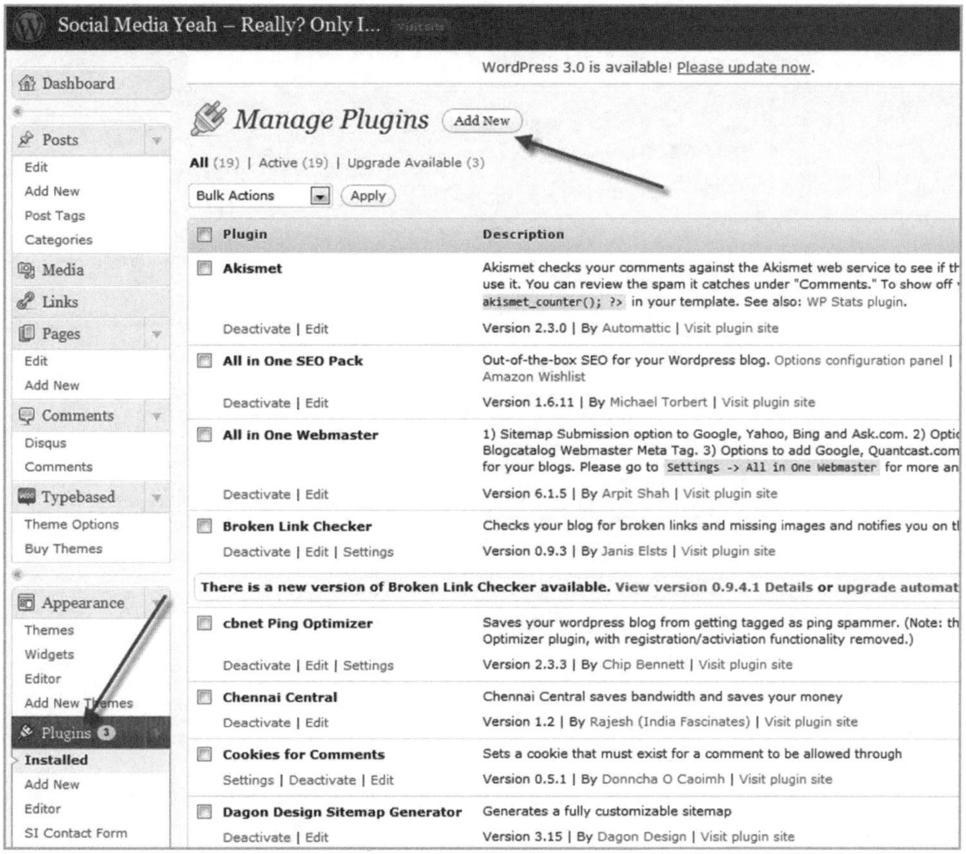

FIGURE 10–2. WordPress plugins—management.

- Google Analyticator or Ultimate Google Analytics: enabling javascript tracking for Google Analytics

You should engage in the blog communities that you are promoting within, but sharing is caring, so do not push too hard. You can also find blogs that very likely to have links that follow back (no rel=nofollow) at:

- CommentHunt.com
- FollowList.com

However, mindless blog commenting and trying to gather links without really joining the community and sharing sincerely and intelligently is a lazy person's approach. Work on quality content and quality relationships instead. Find more information about who to connect with on Twollow.com, Twibs.com, and Twellow.com (the Twitter Yellow Pages). Reach out and comment; make intelligent posts. Eventually, ask to guest post, and continue the conversation. That's what blogging and social

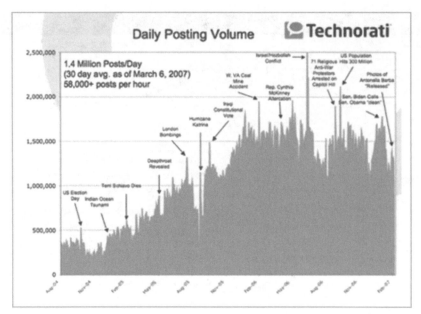

FIGURE 10–3. Blog Daily Posting Volume.

media is about: listening, engaging, and sharing. And, don't forget to track and monitor everything. Then, repeat.

Most blogs have RSS (rich site summary or really simple syndication) as a default, but make sure you set up and test your blog to use RSS feeds. RSS is a way to deliver web content that changes frequently (i.e., news sites, blogs). For more on RSS, visit WhatIsRSS.com. You'll want your blog to display headlines from other RSS feeds as well. This is because whenever a search engine bot crawls your site, it almost always sees something new, and you provide dynamic links that are relevant.

"Tagging and Pinging" refers to having your blog posts automatically tag and then ping bookmark sites to have the new blog posts automatically added. For receiving

INSIDER TIP

Start off by posting two or three times per week for maximum visibility. Many bloggers who are hyperactive post two or three times a day, every day! You can write several posts in the morning, and use the scheduling function in the blog to distribute entries throughout the day, week, or month. This is a great timesaver, and it helps if you plan to be on vacation. You can write posts in advance, and they'll be released in your absence.

FIGURE 10–4. Pingoat.net—free ping system.

high-quality, one-way links from other webmasters, tagging is not the best way to go. However, social bookmarking and tagging can be used to pick up the traffic needed to gain the attention of other webmasters, who can then see that you have great content. If you haven't posted anything new, don't ping your blog, as it'll be regarded as spamming.

Also check PingOMatic.com. These services are complimentary, and should not be overused. I recommend reviewing and including the ping listing directly from WordPress.org at codex.wordpress.org/Update _Services.

INSIDER TIP

You can configure your WordPress blog to automatically ping; see plugin tips section above.

Articles

We discussed article writing in Chapter 3. Articles are a great way to develop quality content on your website. You could publish articles written by other authors, but you'll find those articles on hundreds of other sites as well. If an article on your site only points to the website of the author, you can probably guess where traffic will head next. The author's website could possibly pick up the ranking points, and your copy of the article might be ignored.

On the other hand, should you start creating your own original articles, you might be tempted to keep them for yourself. However, your best bet is to offer your articles to other site owners. If your articles are good and contain valuable information, you will see an increase in traffic and sales. Boosting your presence on other sites can do the same for your rankings.

Make sure each article you release has a number of unique text strings. This can be used to monitor who is using, or misusing, them. Sites that don't appear in major engines may be harder to track, but they are also less of a threat.

Press Releases

Press releases are another way for you to increase your website traffic. Users will be able to easily see what's going on with your business, and will more likely be drawn in to the rest of your site. Make sure to include "For Immediate Release" and "For more information, contact:" followed by your contact information in the first lines to make it easy for visitors to find you.

Create a compelling headline to make your release stand out. Keep it short, active, and descriptive. Hook your readers with the first paragraph. Include and summarize the Five Ws: who, what, where, when, and why (and add "how" for good measure). If your readers can't easily follow your articles, they'll find another site that can explain more clearly.

Put the most important information at the beginning of your press release. Never wait until the end; doing so is a bad writing practice. Don't sell, but answer questions. Selling here is one of the biggest frustrations users experience, and will quickly turn them off to your site. Avoid saying that something is "unique," or "the best." Instead, show how people will benefit.

Getting a nonbiased source such as an expert in the field or product reviewer is helpful. Provide all possible contact information; the more users you can speak with personally, the better. Proofread everything, and don't let a single spelling or grammar error slip by. You'd be surprised how impressed visitors are by such a simple concept. Also, end your press release with # # #. This lets the editors know they've successfully received the whole release.

INSIDER TIP

It's common for press releases to show up on the first page of Google for your specific search term, and then drop off. You'll see it as part of the universal search, discussed earlier in the book. Don't get fooled by an SEO company that says that got you to the first page of Google!

Finally, think differently about your project, and don't do what everyone else does. Use relevant and original content in your press releases. You'll find them a useful means of increasing your website traffic.

Great tools to grade various online assets, are found at Grader.com from HubSpot. See Figure 10-5.

Continue to develop content and repurpose it into video and audio. The following is a list of other good traffic and contenting baiting ideas:

- White paper series
- Ebooks
- Case studies
- Industry interviews
- Infographics
- Online quizzes
- Special contests
- Giveaway/sweepstakes (using social media and Wildfireapp.com)
- Enewsletters

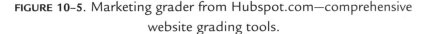

FIGURE 10-5. Marketing grader from Hubspot.com—comprehensive website grading tools.

- Community forums
- Podcasts
- Videos
- Webinars
- Teleseminars

PAY-PER-CLICK ADVERTISING

Pay-per-click is an advertising technique used mainly on websites and search engines. Advertisers bid on "keywords" or phrases that they think potential customers would type in the search bar when they're looking for that type of product or service. Usually ads are placed in order from the top in conjunction with the bid amount. The higher the bid, the better the placement. These ads are called "sponsored links" or "sponsored ads," depending on which search engine you're using. They appear next to or above the results of the original search. The advertiser pays only when somebody clicks on its ad. (See Figure 10–6.)

Bidding for ad space on popular search engines such as Google and Yahoo! can be competitive and costly. The marketplace drives the pricing. The top two pay-per-

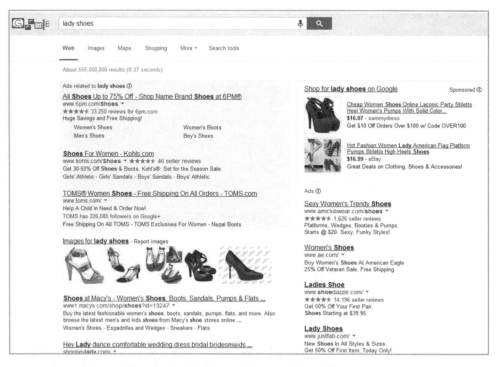

FIGURE 10–6. Google PPC ads.

Pay-Per-Click Search Engines	Minimum Deposit Required
Google AdWords	$5
Microsoft Ad Center	$5 (Bing)

This table was updated to include the top advertising platforms: Google and Bing. With Bing serving results for Yahoo!, most of the focus should be placed on Google and Bing going forward. We focus on quality traffic from the leaders in the space, so the lower tier has been removed. Google AdWords is virtually free to set up (only $5). There are coupons for AdWords, too. For more information and how to set up accounts, visit the Member Access area at: www.jonrognerud.com/optimizationbook.

FIGURE 10–7. PPC Search Engines and Deposits.

click search engines and the minimum deposits they require are shown in Figure 10-7, above.

Types of Pay-per-Click Advertising

There are several types of pay-per-click advertising. The most popular is keyword advertising. The keywords that are bid on can be words, phrases, or even model numbers. The ads will appear in the order of the amount bid, from highest to lowest. Software and other services are available to help advertisers develop keyword strategies.

Product pay-per-click advertising lets advertisers provide "feeds" of their product databases to search engines. When users search for a product, the links to the advertisers who bid for placement appear with the highest bidder appearing most prominently. The user can sort by price and click on a feed to make a purchase. Bizrate.com, Shopzilla.com, NexTag.com, PriceGrabber.com, and Shopping.com are popular product comparison engines, also known as price comparison engines.

Service pay-per-click advertising is similar to product PPC. "Service engines," such as NexTag (a comparison shopping engine), offer advertisers the opportunity to provide feeds of their service databases, which appear when users search for that particular service. As usual, advertisers who pay more are given better ad placement. However, users can sort their results by price or other methods.

Pay-per-call advertising is similar to pay-per-click advertising. Ads are listed in search engines, and directories and publishers charge local advertisers for each call they receive as a result of their listing. This form of advertising is not limited to local advertisers, as

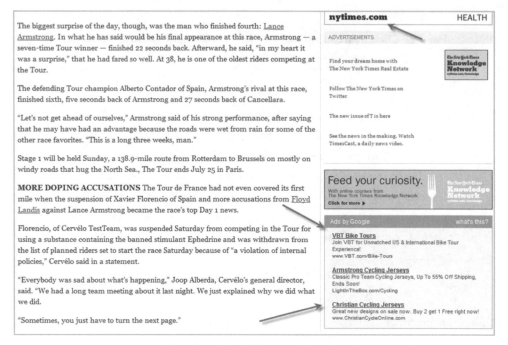

FIGURE 10–8. The New York Times—Google ads example.

many of the pay-per-call search engines allow nationwide companies to create ads with local telephone numbers. Google's content network is simply its ads shown on hundreds of thousands of websites all over the internet. You see these ads on the New York Times site as in Figure 10–8.

When conducting a PPC campaign, bidding on particular words and phrases achieves a particular position in PPC search results. The amounts of bids by competitors are displayed, and you can choose how much you will pay for a specific position. Your website needs no manipulation or changes to conduct a PPC campaign. However, every time someone clicks to your website from the ad, it will cost you.

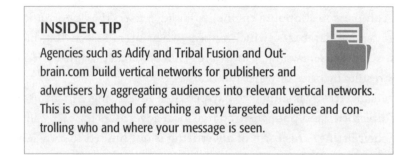

INSIDER TIP

Agencies such as Adify and Tribal Fusion and Outbrain.com build vertical networks for publishers and advertisers by aggregating audiences into relevant vertical networks. This is one method of reaching a very targeted audience and controlling who and where your message is seen.

Determining the most effective keyword terms is critical to the ROI. You need to experiment to find the most effective keywords. Refer to the "Step-by-Step Guide to Keyword Search" in Chapter 5. You can use the same tools to find keywords for your PPC campaign.

Negative Keywords

Another consideration of keyword selection in PPC campaigns is the search for words to eliminate. Due to the cost-per-click factor, to avoid paying for website visitors who have no interest in the product or service offered, certain words and terms must be excluded from the campaign. These words are referred to as negative keywords. These negative keywords must be designated in AdWords campaigns to increase conversion rates.

"Negative keywords" refers to the words, terms, and phrases advertisers would not want to cause their ad to be displayed in search results.

Suppose an online store sells chess games. The store's Google AdWords campaign has an ad group with these phrase-matched keywords:

- chess game
- chess games

The keyword research tools reveal many keyword phrases that are searched relating to chess games that aren't related to buying chess games.

For example, using the Wordtracker (free) from http://freekeywords.wordtracker. com, I see these results for another keyword phrase "cruise."

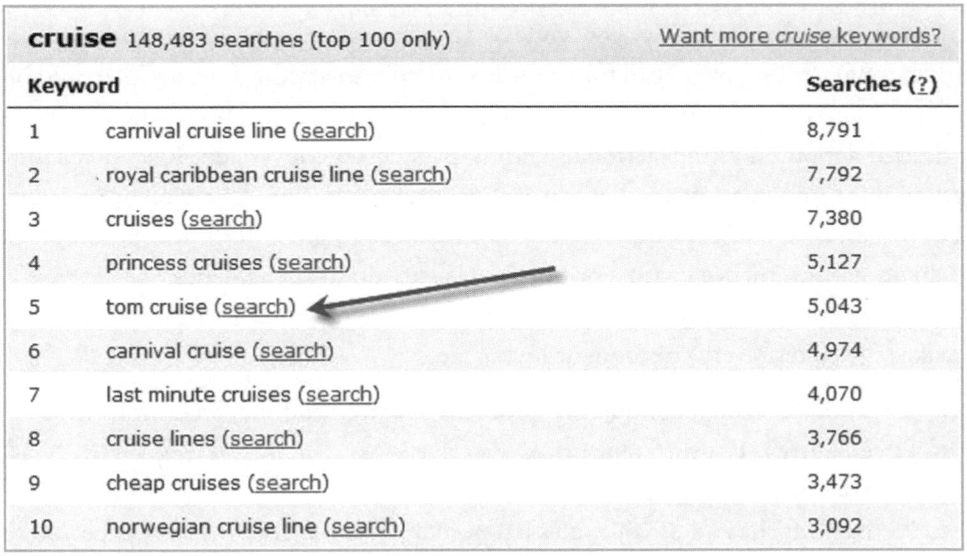

cruise 148,483 searches (top 100 only)	Want more *cruise* keywords?
Keyword	**Searches (?)**
1 carnival cruise line (search)	8,791
2 royal caribbean cruise line (search)	7,792
3 cruises (search)	7,380
4 princess cruises (search)	5,127
5 tom cruise (search)	5,043
6 carnival cruise (search)	4,974
7 last minute cruises (search)	4,070
8 cruise lines (search)	3,766
9 cheap cruises (search)	3,473
10 norwegian cruise line (search)	3,092

FIGURE 10–9. Wordtracker results for cruise.

There would likely be no benefit for the website selling cruises to display an ad in search results for "tom cruise" or "tom cruise movies" (not shown).

Once designated, if any of these negative keywords are in a search phrase, the ad does not appear in the search results.

When creating SEO or web content, these same negative keywords could be beneficial. These words and phrases are synonyms or alternatives to prevent keyword overuse that causes search engines to eliminate a page or site. You should consider running exact matching keywords for your PPC campaigns, at least initially.

Landing Pages

When developing PPC campaigns, it's a good idea to create specific pages for visitors to land on when they click the ad. This type of page is called a landing page or lead capture page. If you're running multiple PPC or ad campaigns, you can have multiple landing pages. The landing page displays content aligned with the ad. You can optimize with keywords and phrases related to the ad. Landing pages allow you to test the effectiveness of your campaigns by measuring click-through rates.

INSIDER TIP

Keep in mind, the more landing pages you add, the more you have to test and keep track of things. Start simple!

Two types of landing pages you often see are transactional and reference. Transactional landing pages call for the visitor to take an action. That action could be to sign up for a newsletter, purchase a product, or complete a form. When the visitor takes the desired action on a transactional landing page, it's a conversion. Reference landing pages present information to the visitor. For example, a domestic violence nonprofit might run an ad to raise awareness. Its landing pages might offer information on how to help domestic violence victims or how to identify domestic violence.

Check below for a list of top things to test in a landing page. It's an important study, so make sure to test every component if you can.

- Headline—a strong, compelling, problem-solving headline, relevant to topic
- Price of offer—test different prices
- Bonuses or other incentives
- PS (p.s.)—at the end of your sales letter, many will scroll down your page and read this

- Guarantees—for example, "90-day guarantee or your money back"
- Audio—test with auto-play or not
- Body copy—short and long copy, maximize use of white space, and make it short; web readers "scan" the page. Long page copy can work, too; don't just make assumptions
- Header image and/or banner—test by turning it on and off, different sizes and colors, too
- Site color/fonts—red and blue fonts work well; test it all
- Sub headers, taglines—compelling "problem solvers"
- Images, "hero shots"—personal pictures of people, then things
- Testimonials
- Videos—upload a video to YouTube, and make sure to brand it on your page
- Buttons—different colors, different text in buttons (not just "Submit," but "Yes, download the free white paper," "Gimme Now," "Immediate Download," etc.)
- Your logo—show it/don't show it; you'd be amazed what turning it off may do
- Credibility, legitimacy—VeriSign logo, BBB, Hacker Safe, Visa/MC, etc.
- Test your sign-up forms, short vs. long (short forms work better, but test this). Ask yourself: what's the least amount of information I need to work with? You can get more later, so don't try for too much up front if you don't need it.

ONLINE RESOURCE

Go to www.jonrognerud.com/optimzationbook to download the conversion tips document.

HOW TO CONSTRUCT A PAY-PER-CLICK

Advertising Campaign

1. Decide what your advertising budget is and what level of risk you are willing to take.

   · Larger search engines are less risky as they already have excellent market coverage and typically offer excellent customer service. All search engines, even the big ones, can be risky if you are not sure how to do this. I recommend reviewing some training videos and getting certified at Google. See google.com/intl/en/ads/ for more information and the global (international) training center at http://www.google.com/ads/learn/.

   · On the other hand, it's more expensive to achieve a top ranking on the largest search engines.

2. Decide which search engines you want to use.

   · Ask for recommendations from friends and business associates.

   · Do your homework. Research each option carefully.

   · 99 percent of the time I recommend starting with Google. Start with Bing/ Yahoo! if you only have a smaller budget to work with. And, with the new Bing/Yahoo! "merger" for search and combined, it will control about 30 percent of the marketplace. That can open opportunities for your business.

3. Decide which keywords you want to bid on. Do your keyword research and analyze them for traffic, competitiveness, and user intent (what is the user searching for or thinking about when entering a specific keyword phrase?)

   · There are plenty of free tools available on the internet to help you research keywords. They give you the current bid prices for certain words and phrases currently running on different search engines.

   · Pick your keywords wisely, as they can range in bid prices from $.10 to $50 and above.

   · Don't limit yourself to one keyword or phrase. Large corporations often have thousands of keywords. Focus on a set of keywords that are closely related, and match those into your ad groups, inside your campaign. Instead of using thousand of keywords, start with smaller sets, and test those against your landing pages. Look at exact match types, and move into phrases and broaden as you get more advanced.

   · Follow the keyword research steps outlined earlier in the book.

4. Pay special attention to the design of your landing page. Google favors fast loading pages, and you can test them on tools.pingdom.com/ and webpagetest.org/.

   · This page must make it clear what products you sell, the benefits of buying these products, how to make a purchase, and why your product is better than your competitor's.

   · Your business's homepage is usually not a good choice for a landing page. If visitors want to learn more about your company, they will do so on their own initiative. Google includes a quality score as a key factor for overall health of your campaign. Make sure to add content, links, privacy policy, sitemap, and generally use your SEO knowledge to make these pages stand out and receive a quality boost. This means lowered bid prices for you.

   · The fewer clicks that a visitor has to make to get to the purchase screen, the more visitors will convert into customers.

5. Begin the bidding process.

- Most search engines have automated the bidding process, so you don't have to actively participate in the process. They stop when they reach your maximum bid.
- Personal involvement is a good idea, at least at first.
- Be sure to carefully read the search engine's terms of use. Look for minimum bids required, deposits required, and what happens if you have to cancel your campaign.
- Track your data carefully, and visit copyblogger.com/landing-page-metrics/ to learn more.

PPC Monitoring and Management Services

Many companies offer PPC monitoring and management services. These companies can be an integral part of any PPC campaign. They automate many of the processes you need to perform to protect your investment. They have the added advantage of being independent of the PPC search engines and offering unbiased answers and advice. Here are some of the more popular services available and the companies that provide them.

> **INSIDER TIP**
>
> The membership site contains more examples of landing pages and conversion and PPC techniques.

PPC Management Services

- Acquisio.com
- Chaosmap.com (owner)
- Marinsoftware.com
- SpeedPPC (speedppc.com)

PPC Research Tools:

- Wordtracker
- Google Keyword Tools (Google Keyword Planner)
- Bing Ad Intelligence

Click Fraud Monitoring:

- Who's Clicking Who
- Click Lab
- Ad Watcher

CLICK FRAUD FACTS

According to *In the News*, up to 20 percent of all pay-per-click traffic delivered to advertisers originates from false sources, not from potential customers. The majority of click fraud originates from two sources: competitors and website owners. Competitors want to drain your advertising budget by producing false clicks that you have to pay for, even though they aren't viable leads. Website owners sometimes work in tandem with search engines by agreeing to feature their ads and provide their customers with more exposure. In return the website owners receive part of the revenue generated by each click. Thus, some of these website owners try to generate as many clicks as possible to increase the profitability of their agreement.

Click fraud has become enough of an issue to attract the attention of major publications, such as the *Washington Post* and *Business Week Online*. According to End ofClickFraud.com, if an organization spends $15,000 on PPC advertising distributed among the top-tier search engines, such as Google or Yahoo!, and is paying between $0.50 and $1 per click, on average they could be losing as much as $2,220 to fraud. Google is very aware of the problem, and provides a lot of information, including solutions to help the advertiser. See more at google.com/adwords/adtrafficquality/tech.html—and learn about how to track your clicks.

- ClickDetective
- Adometry

Ad Tracking

- AdTrackz Gold
- HyperTracker

THE PROS AND CONS OF PPC

PPC Advertising Cons

- It's very easy to get caught up in a keyword bidding war and spend more than you could ever recoup.
- Your ROI can be hard to measure. Some PPC search engines provide customers with measurement tools, but these aren't always accurate. Most of the smaller

PPC companies don't even provide tracking methods. AdWords provides conversion scripts, but proper click attribution can be hard to measure, as seen in Forrester's image in Figure 10–10.

- Don't waste your money on poorly organized campaigns that lack of keyword search and tracking.
- PPC advertising requires you to pay more when more traffic is generated. Natural search engine optimization lets you invest a set amount of time and money to achieve a better rank, and your cost goes down as you attract more traffic. The valid marketing data it can provide should be leveraged across your online efforts and into search engine optimization.

PPC Advertising Pros

- Pay-per-click can generate traffic immediately.
- Pay-per-click ads can be adjusted in minutes or hours in response to market behavior.
- Pay-per-click advertising can be a bargain if you choose your keywords wisely and optimize them with proper match types, negative keywords, and overall ad testing.

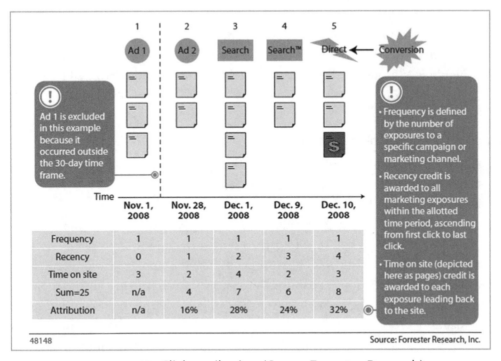

FIGURE 10–10. Click attribution (*Source*: Forrester Research).

- Pay-per-click can guarantee ad placement for a relatively small portion of your marketing budget. Lower positions will not generate as much traffic.
- Access to rich information about keywords and performance of those to "conversion."
- Use these results to push over to SEO and content build out.

Test ad impressions to find out how often keywords trigger ads. Discover the "real" search volumes.

WHAT ROLE SHOULD PPC ADVERTISING PLAY IN YOUR MARKETING STRATEGY?

Most businesses can't afford to rely on pay-per-click advertising alone. It's too expensive to keep up with the ever-rising bid amounts for advantageous keywords. However, there are certain instances in which PPC advertising can be invaluable.

If you're starting a new campaign to draw attention to a new product or service, PPC is a great way to create a buzz. You can even drive traffic to a blog or specific event on your page. Drive traffic to social media websites, article sites, and Facebook fan pages, if you so choose.

- If you sell a product or offer a service that consumers can purchase immediately upon arriving at your website, PPC is effective.
- If you can find keyword(s) that create a market niche for your organization, PPC provides cost-effective advertising. For instance, if you can generate traffic with a highly specific keyword, such as *perfectpoint pencils* instead of *pencils*, PPC may be a good option.

Google AdWords Marketing Mistakes . . .

- Not designating a spending limit. This can put you out of business fast.
- Not targeting properly at a local level (geotargeting).
- Not knowing your conversion rate. Many new marketers choose high-priced words without basing their bids on research. If you don't know the conversion rate of the product you're selling, then start slow and low.
- Insufficient keyword research. Most people use the Google keyword tool, including your competition. Expand your keyword research using all the tools mentioned earlier in the book. Jump in the car, go to Barnes & Noble, and pick up magazines for your market. What are people asking, and what specific problems do they have? What do the headlines say? What ads are they running there?
- Not writing effective ads or customizing them for each keyword.

- Ignoring daily stats and failing to track and analyze results. You need to keep daily records. Set up automatic emails to receive reports as you need them.
- Quitting too soon. AdWords takes time to learn.
- Not knowing when to quit. If you're not converting enough to make a profit, then make changes.
- Breaking the rules. Many people think they can beat or cheat the system. Others don't know better and place pop-up ads or link to inappropriate sites, thus getting their accounts revoked. If you're going to play the game, take the time to learn the rules.

WEBSITE USER TESTING AND TRAFFIC MONITORING

In the end, you want more traffic coming to your website, and you want those users to find what they need on your pages. There are many ways for you to monitor, test, and reconfigure your site to bring in quality users.

Track Your Hits from Month to Month

Then you can see if you're on the right path with your site because you can see your traffic increasing or decreasing. Also, monitor the entrance and exit pages for traffic. This shows you what page is bringing in the most visitors and which page could be causing people to leave your site.

Keep an Eye on How Long Visitors Spend on Each Page

Then you can see which pages hold their interest and which need to be modified. Watch for keyword searches as well to keep tabs on what the majority of your visitors are looking for. Watch your PageRank over time. Make sure that your trust and relevance are on the rise, and not in decline. Check your link popularity. The more popular your links are, the greater opportunity you have for visitors to see and come to your website. Enter your keywords into Google and other search engines to check the positioning in the results. This gives you a better idea how to optimize your site.

Important tracking parameters for Google Analytics are:

- Number of pages receiving organic traffic
- Number of unique keywords (Update: Google does not provide keywords for organic search, only paid search)
- Which keywords are sending the most traffic over time
- Time on site and bounce rates: not aggregate, but specific pages
- First time vs. returning visits
- Loyalty and recency

FIGURE 10–11. Google Analytics Dashboard.

- Referring domains (also international)
- Mobile devices traffic (Is your site mobile friendly?)
- Top landing pages and bounce rates
- What search engines are sending traffic: number of visits over time?
- Distribution of keywords referrals: understand the head, middle, and long-tail keywords and how they affect your site and pages. Track what keywords are moving up and what are moving down over time. Go beyond the "what"—find out the "why." (Get the *Web Analytics 2.0* book from author Avinash Kaushik.)

Overall, you want to collect search referral analytics, keyword referral analytics, engagement analytics, conversion analytics, and ROI analytics. Are you currently tracking this in your business, or are you only focusing on rankings? In fact, when you set out to measure anything, ask yourself why you want to measure it, and based on results, what you would do differently. You want to make all this data actionable. Be sure to review and account for visitors and unique visitors, but drill down into the data to find out how you measure your "real" ROI.

I invite you to join the member area at www.jonrognerud.com/optimizationbook to learn more and ask questions. I'll show you easy ways to track important data using panels inside the Google Analytics Dashboard. Google has recently made several updates to the interface.

The ultimate in using web analytics is to know the customer's lifetime value. Things like:

INSIDER TIP

Don't trust your analytics alone. Understand what's going on in your marketplace, seasonal events, etc. Use Google Trends to check if traffic trends are moving up or down.

- How many dollars were spent with your business per customer
- How many purchases on average across the period per customer
- How many referred visits (also includes activity from email campaigns)

You can then compare this against expenditure on SEO, PPC, outbound sales activity, and brand/content development. You should be in positive territory after it's all said and done.

Finally, remember to test the results of every change that you make. If your changes aren't producing positive results, abandon the technique and try something else. A free tool like Google Analytics is a good place to start; others are Getclicky.com, piwik.org, statcounter.com, Haveamint (haveamint.com), and Omniture (omniture.com/en). More advanced tools are Crazyegg.com and KissMetrics.com.

Google Webmaster Console

We discussed Google's Webmaster Tools briefly in Chapter 7. It's an invaluable resource for webmasters. The console can help website owners see exactly what on their site the Google indexing program can index and what the program has trouble with. You can also learn which searches drive traffic to your site and see exactly how users arrive there. See Figure 10–12 on page 270.

Google is always updating the console to provide new tools to webmasters. You can now view the internal and external links to your website in detail. This helps you monitor your linking strategy. You can easily remove URLs from the index, show how many people are subscribed to your website's feeds, and be provided with authenticated communication with site owners. The console includes a personal Google message center with which you can receive personalized information such as feedback or warnings, from the search engine.

To use Google Webmaster Tools, you need to create a free Google account, then have your webmaster follow the directions provided to place a small HTML file on your site, so that Google can confirm that you own the site before it reveals any statistics.

These are all very useful tools, not only in driving traffic to your website, but also in testing and monitoring exactly what that traffic does. Increasing traffic is one of the most important goals in improving your website. Without visitors to your website, you

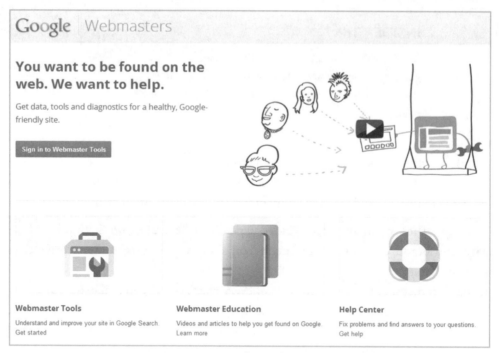

FIGURE 10–12. Google Webmaster Tools.

have no sales. In essence, increasing traffic and providing a good user experience, easy navigation, and relevant, compelling content helps your website do the job you did all the hard work for.

Bob put together a press release and blog schedule for the remainder of the year. He decided to take advantage of speaking engagements and seasonal trends to bring some publicity to his site. He mapped out topics and dates and hired a ghostwriter to do the releases and create complete posts from the blog seeds. In essence, "seeds" are the core of blog posts, but often it is built out from there. He also posted each release in the "press room" of his site. After the first release, he received instant traffic, and after the third release and the blog postings and RSS feed consumption, Bob saw a total increase in his website traffic, and it was trending upward. With little effort he was turning things around. He couldn't wait to implement the next tactic on his list—PPC advertising and social media expansion using Facebook, Twitter, LinkedIn, and YouTube. For more information on how to set this up, check the member area on www.jonrognerud.com/optimizationbook.

Chapter 11

Growth, Sales, and Conversion Strategies

Nothing moves unless something is sold. That's the key to any and all businesses, online or off. That means you need a solid sales process and to track every aspect of it. In all your daily activities, "what is the shortest path to the cash" will be an important question to continually ask.

It's fairly obvious that when you have done the work of selling the message, you need to be able to deliver when people come looking for you. If your internal processes break down, it won't matter if you have a great service or product, because you won't be able to deliver or scale up, when and if you grow.

Use the following sales process when growing a business (online or offline):

- Set your sales goals. (weekly, monthly)
- Map the sales process. (Start simple, don't get bogged down in too much detail.)
- Set objectives for key value points.
- Measure key value points.
- Identify critical vulnerabilities.
- Select your focus of effort.
- Decide on and take action on main effort.

You may notice that the process above ties back to identifying your market, researching the market and competition, and analyzing your place in it.

Measuring is an important part of your sales and marketing efforts. Measure those things that you can change, such as your message, your delivery method, and your media.

You can only measure things that move up or down, such as:

■ Delivery rates
■ Open rates
■ Unique clicks/visitors
■ Opt-ins
■ Sales
■ Up-sells
■ Cross-sells

Let's assume you're doing an email marketing campaign. If you send 10,000 emails, how many are being delivered? And, if the open rates are "good," what do you base that on? You must compare to previous campaigns, industry standards, and the overall marketplace. How many received it, or how many opened it? So, a strategic question would be: Should I increase "delivery rates" or "open rates"? If you tune the open rate and then increase the delivery rates, you will make more money just hours after sending. Building a mailing list should be one of the cornerstones of your online marketing program. Search engines change often, and if you are too reliant on one-sided marketing, you will potentially fail. Create a multichannel marketing campaign, and build real assets such as content, memberships, and email lists. One great email system is AWeber.com, my personal favorite.

Boost the numbers of emails being reviewed, and you're on your way. However, it's viewing everything, not just one or two metrics.

It's important to develop programs with a holistic view in mind. When you measure every single customer action, you improve your value and your bottom line. Likewise, you must continuously review and improve your internal processes with an eye on growth. Will the same processes work when you go from ten customers to 500? How about when you reach 10,000 customers?

Another aspect of conversion is the psychological issue. Many people may feel uncomfortable or guilty "taking customers' money." You're not taking something, you are giving them something. When you offer a product or service that has value (meets a need, preference, or desire), your customer is simply exchanging money for access to that value.

Finally, you convert customers when you continually look to improve the experience from the customer perspective. Don't continue doing something because it works, but ask, "How can I make it better?" Tracking and measuring does not only apply to what

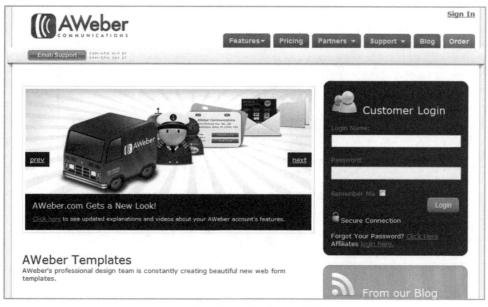

FIGURE 11–1. Email marketing—AWeber.com.

ONLINE RESOURCE

See the membership at www.jonrognerud.com/
optimizationbook site for more email providers.

your customers do but also to what you do that facilitates the relationship. If you provide value and great products, the rest will follow, all wrapped in your own business processes.

HOW TO OPTIMIZE FOR LOCAL SEARCH

Ways You Can Grow Your Local Business

This section describes the most important things you need to look at in order to optimize your website for local search. Local SEO is not different from "regular" SEO; it can be just as time consuming and competitive. The same rules apply—good content and quality links. However, the tactics are slightly different in areas. You'll learn more about this below.

Local Search Is Massive

The trends show an increase in local search and from mobile devices. By the end of 2013, predictions indicate that one out of every three searches will be mobile (http://searchengineland.com/4-mobile-search-trends-tackled-at-smx-west-2013-151657).

comScore Explicit Core Search Share Report* July 2013 vs. June 2013 Total U.S. – Home & Work Locations Source: comScore qSearch			
Core Search Entity	Explicit Core Search Share (%)		
	Jun-13	Jul-13	Point Change
Total Explicit Core Search	*100.0%*	*100.0%*	*N/A*
Google Sites	66.7%	67.0%	0.3
Microsoft Sites	17.9%	17.9%	0.0
Yahoo! Sites	11.4%	11.3%	-0.1
Ask Network	2.7%	2.7%	-0.1
AOL, Inc.	1.3%	1.2%	-0.1

FIGURE 11–2. The search marketplace (*Source*: Nielsen).
http://www.comscore.com/Insights/Press_Releases/2013/10/comScore_Releases_September_2013_US_Search_Engine_Rankings http://www.comscore.com/Insights/Press_Releases/2013/10/comScore_Releases_September_2013_US_Search_Engine_Rankings

Figure 11–2 doesn't reveal the local search numbers, but if you factor in the 1 in 13, you'll quickly realize the massive growth area of local search. Add the rise of mobile search and additional user tools such as Twitter, Foursquare, TwitHawk, and Facebook, and we have ourselves a sizable audience to satisfy! People are drawn to local activities, and it includes search. Visit www.jonrognerud.com/optimizationbook for additional tools for local search.

Where to Begin?

To learn more and to start with Google Places For Business, get a free account at www.**google**.com/business/**places**forbusiness and make sure to watch the training videos. Google Places has added a lot of new features, including power tools like the tracking of actions (how many times users showed interest in your business listing), clicks for more information on maps, driving directions, or direct clicks, as well as impressions (how many times users saw your business listing as a local search result). You can also add your images, videos, offers/promos, coupons, and more. As you'll see, it will be important to get ratings and references, too.

While much focus is placed on Google Places, don't forget to also register at:

- Yahoo! Local (local.yahoo.com)
- Bing Local (bing.com/local/)

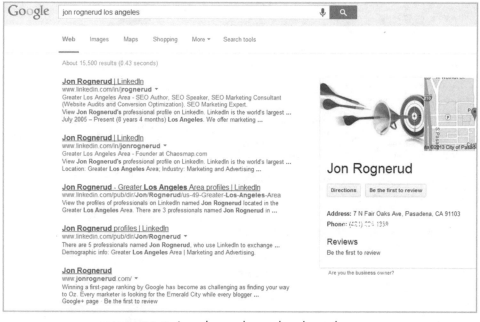

FIGURE 11–3. Local search results—brand name.

One easy way to find out if you are listed is to search for your brand name. Include the city or locale you are supposed to be listed for. Here's an example (Figure 11-3) of a search for my name in Los Angeles. Since there is no competition here, it shows a Google Local "one-box."

Eight Quick Success Steps to Local Inclusion and Visibility

1. Claim your business. Close to city center is best.
2. Verify your information. You'll be able to do this via a PIN number or postcard.
3. Select the best categories that match your business.
4. Add as much information as possible—make it complete and be specific.
5. Include your services areas.
6. Establish your profiles in local directories.
7. Establish your presence with local agencies/municipality.
8. Build out your profile and ask for reviews—don't hold back.

Claiming and Verifying Your Business

If you are not listed, that's one of the first things you should take action on. If I'm a tax attorney in Beverly Hills, California—I would search *tax attorney beverly hills*, and see the following results (not static, may differ in your origin):

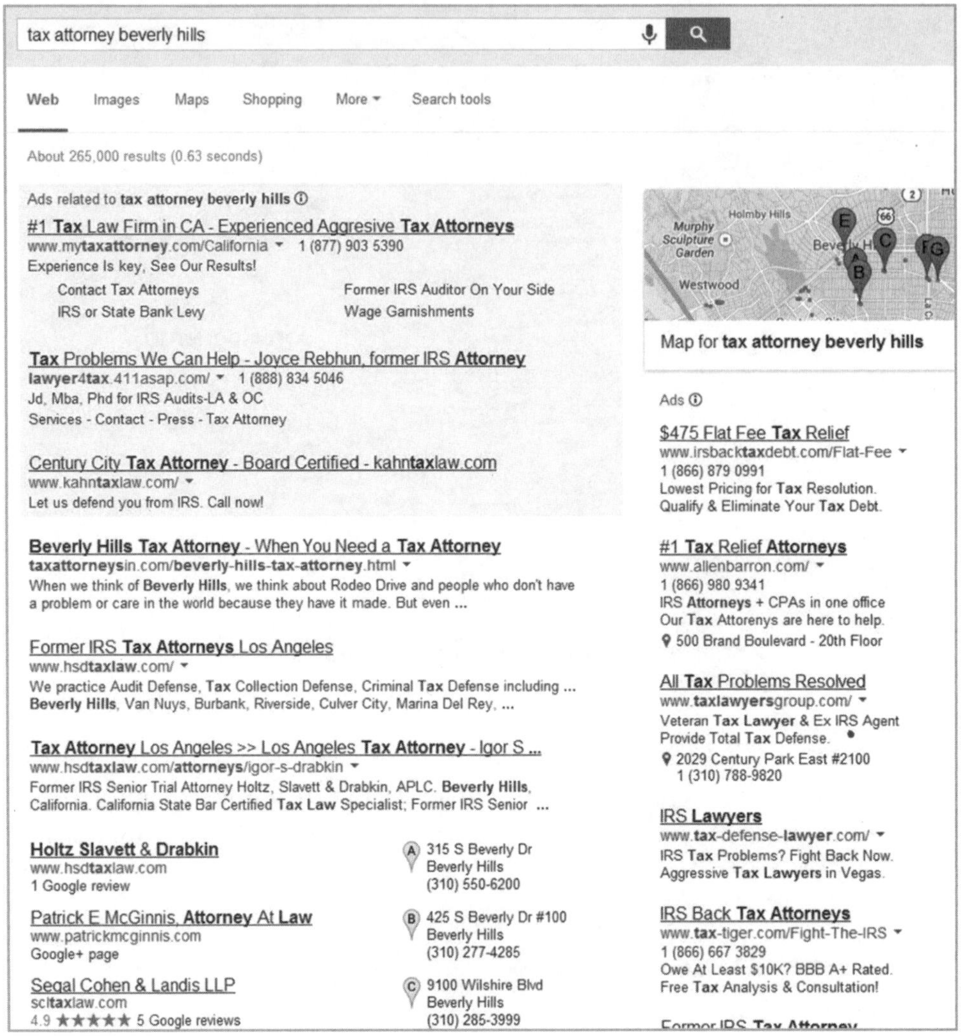

FIGURE 11–4. Tax attorney local search/map results.

As you hover over the local results—the company information changes on the right side (sometimes takes a second to load). You can quickly get a sense of how well their local meta data has been optimized by the amount of data available (photos, videos), reviews, and more. You can see further activity by visiting their local Google+ page.

Categories Selection

Select from the categories list that best describes your business (see Figure 11–5 on page 277). Before you do, make sure to review the competition also. Check to see where the top listings are listing theirs.

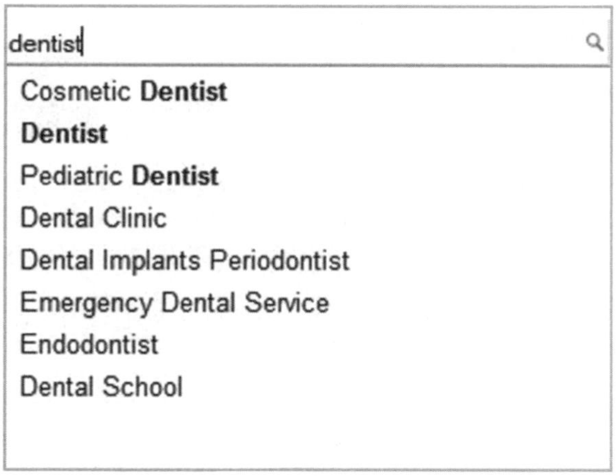

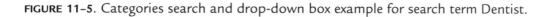

FIGURE 11–5. Categories search and drop-down box example for search term Dentist.

You can add up to five categories to describe your business. Once you start typing, the Google Places categories system will display related categories.

Continue to add as much information as possible, hours, payment types, email address, phone number, URL/web address, photos, videos, and coupons. It's all there— try to fill out each field if appropriate. Go make some videos, upload to YouTube, and link them back into your local profile on Google Places. If you install and use tools like Jing from Techsmith.com, it'll be free and easy to make an informational, useful video. Screen cam your PowerPoint presentations. You can include up to ten pictures and five videos.

Get Listed in Local Directories

Powerful citations from local business directories like Yelp and Merchant Circle is a good start. See the list of directories in the Local SEO resources section below. Make sure that all your information is correct, and keep the formatting the same across all locations.

Reviews

Reviews, citations, and links are powerful drivers to top ranking within local search. Much like external backlinks drive much of the Google algorithm for ranking, so be it for local search. Don't be afraid to ask for reviews. Offer special incentives and discounts for return visits to your office. Add a postcard or business card into your office invoice mailings, asking your customer to review the visit, and talk about the experience. Important: Don't try to spam this system, and ask all your friends to review you in a

INSIDER TIP

For a low-cost fee of $30 per year, ubl.org can list your business. It will get you listed in Google, Yahoo!, Bing, the Online Yellow Pages, infoUSA, Acxiom, and more. Review the video introduction to learn more about this service. You can also use GetListed.org for free, and it'll check to see if you are listed across Google, Yahoo!, and the top local search engines.

week! Use a solid and ethical business approach—and get references from BBB.org, chamber of commerce in your city, and the top local directories.

Using pay-per-click, you can target down to your local area (via maps). This, combined with SEO strategies from global to local, can yield strong results in traffic and targeting. Make sure you track your URLs. Google Analytics provides a power tool to do that: https://support.google.com/analytics/answer/1033867.

Local Directories Resources

- bbb.org
- brownbook.com
- businessdirectory.bizjournals.com
- citycliq.com
- cityguide.com
- citysearch.com
- dexknows.com
- insiderpages.com
- infoUSA.com
- judysbook.com
- kudzu.com
- local.botw.org
- local.com
- matchpoint.com
- merchantcircle.com
- superpages.com
- switchboard.com
- yellowbook.com
- yellowpages.aol.com
- yellowpages.com
- yelp.com

Niche Marketplaces

- Tripadvisor.com
- Chefmoz.org
- Gayot.com
- Fodors.com
- Travelocity.com
- Wcities.com
- Frommers.com
- Hotelguide.net
- Zagat.com

Local SEO Resources

Google Places User Guide

- google.com/support/places/bin/static.py?page=guide.cs&guide=28247
- https://getlisted.org/static/resources/glossary.html
- blog.getlisted.org
- davidmihm.com/local-search-ranking-factors.shtml (read this!)
- localseoguide.com
- blumenthals.com/blog
- www.brightlocal.com/blog
- screenwerk.com
- poweredbysearch.com
- searchengineland.com/library/locals-only
- searchenginewatch.com/smb-search-marketing (small business)

Additional resources for analytics and Google Web Optimizer that can help you in your local optimization and conversion efforts are:

- roirevolution.com/blog
- kaushik.net/avinash
- http://www.digitalanalyticsassociation.org/?

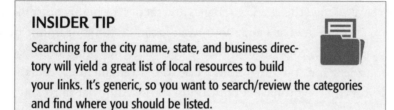

INSIDER TIP

Searching for the city name, state, and business directory will yield a great list of local resources to build your links. It's generic, so you want to search/review the categories and find where you should be listed.

■ Content Experiments integrated with Google Analytics (formerly Website Optimizer at services.google.com/websiteoptimizer)

CLOSING

Wow! You are at the end of this book. That's the good news. However, you are not finished. After learning about how to build a highly optimized website for top search engine results and awesome visitor engagement, both directly and via the social web, the work is really just getting started.

What You've Learned

You followed the thoughts and questions our friend Bob had—you've seen his approach and results. I'm sure you identified with him along the way. You saw how search came to be, and how web search works. You learned how to start a business with a new website, how to perform competitive research and finding the critical keywords to build content for your pages. You also saw how to optimize them for high performance on the internet.

Furthermore, you learned that the psychology, messaging, and positioning of your brand is extremely important for building trust, authority, and for a sense of community with your audience. At the same time, you learned what not do such as trying to "fake" your way into Google, and by building bad links only to get a temporary lift in results. You found out how to build more traffic, get conversions, and sales. That included how to optimize for local, social, as well as mobile strategies.

You now know how to build a serious, long-term business online that is growing and that can provide bigger returns than you could have hoped for. A business that you are proud of and that you can even pass along to future generations. No one can say you aren't passionate about this commitment to yourself. You became so much more during this process of learning, applying, and testing powerful strategies that actually work.

What's Next?

Now that you have learned the inside strategies and tactics for highly optimized websites, I trust that you are as excited as I am about what it can do for your online business.

As mentioned above, this is not a "set it and forget it" program. It's an ongoing process. You understand by now that while the fundamentals remain, and that people buy from people—you have a critical job to do. And that is to stay continually close to your market, competitors, and customers alike. That includes watching and understanding the complexities of the ongoing search and social changes on the web.

You have more options than ever to create, build, and keep the attention of your audience. There's always another "shiny object" that is tempting to lure them away from you. You need to stick to your core mission of offering quality, value, and service to your customers and prospects. That includes every touch-point in your organization—from the first to the last, even offline. You gain in this by continual learning, growing, and profiting and so you can invest even more into your business. It even carries over into your personal life as well.

I wish that you continue the magnificent transformation in your professional and personal life. And, if you will permit me, I'm here to answer questions when you are ready. Just shoot them over to contact@jonrognerud.com. Also, make sure to visit the www.jonrognerud.com/optimizationbook book access area where you will receive more information, demonstrations, tools, case studies, downloads, and can engage with me and our community.

Finally, I challenge you to create a whole new experience online for yourself and your community. Be not only the best you can be, but don't be afraid to step out onto the wonderful, large, scary stage of life. You'll be glad you did!

P.S.

Please connect with me on Twitter @jonrognerud. You'll find me everywhere else.

Resources

P lease visit the member section for even more information.

Affiliate/CPA Networks

- Affiliate.com
- Azoogle.com
- Clickbooth.com
- COPEAC.com
- Adknowledge.com
- Neverblue.com
- RoiRocket.com
- ClickBank.com
- CJ.com
- LinkShare.com
- ShareASale.com
- OfferVault.com (research tools)
- CBEngine.com/popular-clickbank-products.cfm
- cb-analytics.com/top-products.php

Advanced Link Resources

- AdGooroo.com/products/link_insight.php
- Conductor.com

Contextual Advertising

- http://www.sitescout.com
- Google AdWords
- Microsoft Ads Center (BingAds.com)
- TextLinkAds.com
- ADster.com
- Kontera.com

Competitive Spy Tools

- SpyFu.com
- Ranks.nl
- KeywordSpy.com
- Semrush.com
- http://www.terapeak.com/products/terapeak-for-ebay

Graphics

- iStockphoto.com
- BannersMall.com
- 20DollarsBanners.com
- Shutterstock.com
- Free Photos—sxc.hu
- Myfonts.com/WhatTheFont/
- Picmonkey.com (online graphics editing)

Product Help Software

- PHP Live—phplivesupport.com
- Zen Desk
- Kayako.com
- ACCORD5—Trellis Help desk—accord5.com/trellis

Hosting

- GoDaddy.com
- HostGator.com
- Bluehost.com
- DreamHost.com
- HostMonster.com
- Rackspace.com (higher end)
- WpEngines.com (WordPress)

Keyword Research

- KeywordElite.com
- KwMap.com
- SEMRush.com
- Wordtracker.com (also free version)
- AdWords Keywords External
- GoodKeywords.com
- AdGooroo.com (paid)
- Ubersuggest.org (free, great for "auto-suggestion" mining)
- KeywordDiscovery.com (also free version)
- Keyword Samurai (desktop trials available)

Live Chat

- BoldChat (free version also)
- Userplane
- LivePerson
- Instant Service.com (ATG Live Help)

CRM Software and Marketing Automation

- Infusionsoft.com
- Marketo.com
- Hubspot.com
- Pardot.com
- Eloqua.com
- Salesforce.com

Membership Software

- MemberGate
- aMember
- WM Wishlist (WordPress)

Call Tracking Solutions for Mobile Marketing

- HostedNumbers.com/
- Logmycalls.com
- IfbyPhone.com
- Callfire.com
- Dial800.com
- MongooseMetrics.com
- Patlive.com
- Grasshopper.com
- Ringcentral.com

Market Research

- Google Trends
- Big Boards
- Board Tracker
- eBay Pulse
- Hoovers
- CB Engine (affiliates)
- Amazon BestSellers—amazon.com/gp/bestsellers/
- eBay
- Digg Labs

Outsourcing Your Work

- oDesk.com
- Elance.com
- Guru.com
- Freelancer.com
- Scriptlance.com
- Fiverr.com

Press Release Services

- Emailwire.com
- BusinessWire.com
- Marketwire.com
- PRWeb.com
- PRNewswire.com
- eReleases.com
- WebWire.com
- Free-Press-Release.com
- PRLog.org
- i-Newswire.com

References from Chapter 1

Beal, V. (2013). *Small business mobile marketing strategies that work. ITBusinessEdge*. Retrieved June 18, 2013, from, http://www.smallbusinesscomputing.com/News/Marketing/small-business-mobile-marketing-strategies-that-work-2.html

eDigital Research, (2012). *The explosion of mobile*. Retrieved June 18, 2013, from http://assets.econsultancy.com/images/0001/7586/v2.02.png

Lely, M. (2013). *5 mobile marketing tools to reach customers on the go*. New York: Mashable Incorporation.

Martin, S. (2012, November 13). *Gain competitive advantage with mobile apps. OMG! Mobile Marketing*. Retrieved June 18, 2013, from http://www.omgmobilemarketing.com/2012/11/gain-competitive-advantage-with-mobile.html

Ofosu, K. (2012). Mobile phone revolution in Ghana's cocoa industry. *International Journal of Business and Social Science, 2* (13), 91-99.

Segal, C. (2013, June 11). *Mobile marketing helps small business thrive. Blue*. Retrieved June 18, 2013, from http://www.coxblue.com/mobile-marketing-helps-small-businesses-thrive-2/

Shopping Carts

- osCommerce
- Volusion
- 1ShoppingCart

- Yahoo! Store
- Monster Commerce
- 3dcart
- SEO-cart
- ZenCart

Survey Software

- SurveyMonkey.com
- Polldaddy.com
- SurveyGizmo.com

Web Analytics/Conversion

- Google Analytics
- GetClicky.com
- Mint.com
- CrazyEgg.com
- AdTrackz.com

Other Tools

- ClickTale—web analytics that takes a video of your users mouse/actions
- Jing—free screen capture/sharing tool
- JW Player—free flash player
- LiveFaceOnWeb.com—actor "appears" on your site
- Google Voice
- 99designs.com
- Dropbox.com
- MindMeister.com
- Google Docs
- Amazon S3

Glossary

A

absolute link. A link that specifies the website link in full rather than an abbreviated version.

above the fold. The portion of a web page that's viewable without scrolling.

ad blocking. The blocking of web advertisements, typically the image in graphical web advertisements.

ad click rate. Sometimes referred to as click-through, the percentage of ad views that resulted in an ad click.

ad clicks. Number of times users click on an ad banner.

ad network. An aggregator or broker of advertising inventory from many sites. 24/7 Media is an ad network.

AdSense. contextual advertising network from Google. Shares profits with Google.

ad space. The space on a web page available for advertisements.

ad views. (impressions). Number of times an ad banner is downloaded and seen by visitors.

AdWords. Google advertising network. Uses keywords and cost-per-click.

advertising network. A network representing many websites in selling advertising. Allows ad buyers to easily reach broad audiences through run-of-category and run-of-network buys.

address. A unique identifier for a computer or site online, usually a URL for a website or marked with an @ for an email address. It's how your computer finds a location on the information highway.

add URL. *See* search engine submission.

affiliate. The publisher/salesperson in an affiliate marketing relationship.

affiliate directory. A categorized listing of affiliate programs.

affiliate forum. An online community where visitors can read and post topics related to affiliate marketing.

affiliate fraud. Bogus activity generated by an affiliate in an attempt to generate illegitimate, unearned revenue.

affiliate marketing. Revenue sharing between online advertisers/merchants and online publishers/salespeople. Compensation is based on performance measures, typically in the form of sales, clicks, registrations, or a hybrid model.

affiliate merchant. The advertiser in an affiliate marketing relationship.

affiliate network. A value-added intermediary providing services, including aggregation, for affiliate merchants and affiliates.

affiliate software. Software that, at a minimum, provides tracking and reporting of commission-triggering actions (sales, registrations, or clicks) from affiliate links.

age. Some social networks or search systems may take site age, page age, user account age, and related historical data into account when determining how much to trust that person, website, or document. Some specialty search engines, like blog search engines, may also boost the relevancy of new documents. When "Age" is used in context of search engines, websites, and pages, "Age" is correct. It's referred to here as an "importance factor" and defines what Age means in the context.

AJAX. Method of uploading information without a web page reload.

AltaVista. Yahoo!-owned search engine.

AllTheWeb. Yahoo!-owned search engine.

ALT. Text HTML attribute that provides alternative text when non-textual elements, typically images, cannot be displayed.

Analytics Software. It allows users to track page views, user paths, and conversion statistics based on interpreting log files or through a JavaScript tracking code on the user's site.

anchor. A word, phrase, or graphic image in hypertext. It's the object that's highlighted, underlined, or "clickable" which links to another site.

anchor text. Text associated with a hyperlink.

animated GIF. A graphic in the GIF89a file format that creates the effect of animation by rotating through a series of static images.

Apache. The most common web server (or HTTP server) software on the internet. An open-source application originally created from a series of changes ("patches") made to a web server. Designed as a set of modules to enable administrators to choose which features they want to use and to make it easy to add features to meet specific needs, including handling protocols other than the web-standard HTTP.

applet. An application program written in Java that allows viewing simple animation on web pages.

ARPANet (Advanced Research Projects Agency Network). The precursor to the internet. Developed in the late '60s and early '70s by the U.S. Department of Defense as an experiment in wide-area-networking to connect computers that were running different systems, allowing users at one location to use computing resources at another location.

ASCII (American Standard Code for Information Interchange). The de facto worldwide standard for the code numbers used by computers to represent all upper- and lower-case Latin letters, numbers, punctuation, etc. There are 128 standard ASCII codes, each of which can be represented by a seven-digit binary number: 0000000 through 1111111.

Ask. Search engine owned by InterActive Corp.

ASP (application service provider). An organization (usually a business) that runs one or more applications on its own servers and provides (usually for a fee) access to others.

authority. The ability of a page or domain to rank well in search engines. Five factors associated with site and page authority are link equity, site age, traffic trends, site history, and publishing unique original-quality content.

B

B2B. Business that sells products or provides services to other businesses.

B2C. Business that sells products or provides services to end-user consumers.

backbone. A high-speed line or series of connections that forms a large pathway within a network. The term is relative to the size of network it's serving. A backbone in a small network would probably be much smaller than many non-backbone lines in a large network.

bad neighborhood. A web page that has been penalized by a search engine (most notably Google) for using shady SEO tactics, such as hidden text or link farms.

bandwidth. How much data can be sent through a connection? Usually measured in bits-per-second (bps).

banner ad. A graphical web advertising unit, typically measuring 468 pixels wide and 60 pixels tall. Usually "hot-linked" to the advertiser's site.

banner blindness. The tendency of web visitors to ignore banner ads, even when they contain information visitors are actively looking for.

banner exchange. Network where participating sites display banner ads in exchange for credits which are converted (using a predetermined exchange rate) into ads to be displayed on other sites.

baud. The rate at which bits can be sent or received per second. The number of times per second that the carrier signal shifts value; for example, a 1,200 bit-per-second modem actually runs at 300 baud, but it moves 4 bits per baud (4x300 = 1,200 bits per second).

behavioral targeting. Ad targeting based on past recent experience or implied intent. For example, if I recently searched for mortgages before reading a book review, the book review page may still show me mortgage ads.

binary. Information consisting entirely of 1s and 0s. Commonly refers to files that are not simply text files, e.g., images.

black hat SEO deceptive marketing techniques. Search engines set up guidelines that help them extract billions of dollars of ad revenue from the work of publishers and the attention of searchers. The search guidelines are not a static set of rules, and things that may be considered legitimate one day may be considered deceptive the next. Search engines are not without flaws in their business models, but it's not unethical or illegal to test search algorithms to understand how search engines work.

blog. A frequent, chronological publication of personal thoughts and web links (shortened version of web log).

blogroll. Link list on a blog, usually linking to other blogs owned by the same company or friends of that blogger.

bookmark. Link stored in a web browser for future use. An easy way to return to a website of interest.

bounce. What happens when email is returned as undeliverable.

brand. A name, term, design, symbol, or other feature that identifies one seller's goods or services as distinct from those of other sellers. The legal term for brand is trademark. A brand may identify one item, a family of items, or all items of that seller. If used for the firm as a whole, the preferred term is trade name.

broken link. A nonfunctioning link.

browser. An application used to view information from the internet. It provides a user-friendly interface for navigating through and accessing the vast amount of information on the internet.

browser caching. To speed surfing, browsers store recently used pages on a user's disk. If a site is revisited, browsers display pages from the disk instead of requesting them from the server. As a result, servers undercount the number of times a page is viewed.

browsing. A term that refers to exploring an online area, usually on the World Wide Web.

buttons. Objects that, when clicked once, cause something to happen.

button ad. A graphical advertising unit, smaller than a banner ad.

button exchange. Network where participating sites display button ads in exchange for credits that are converted (using a predetermined exchange rate) into ads to be displayed on other sites.

C

cache. A storage area for frequently accessed information. Retrieval of the information is faster from the cache than the originating source. Types of caches include RAM cache, secondary cache, disk cache, and cache memory.

cascading style sheet (CSS). A standard for specifying the appearance of text and other elements. Typically used to provide a single "library" of styles that are used over and over throughout a number of related documents, as in a website. A CSS file might specify that all numbered lists appear in italics. By changing that specification, the look of a number of documents can be easily changed.

click. The opportunity for a user to be transferred to a location by clicking on an ad, as recorded by the server.

clickthrough rate (CTR). The average number of clickthroughs per 100 ad impressions, expressed as a percentage.

client. A program, computer, or process that makes information requests to another computer, process, or program.

cloaking. Displaying different content to search engines and searchers. Depending on the intent of the display discrepancy and the strength of the brand of the person/ company cloaking, it may be considered reasonable or it may get a site banned from a search engine.

conversion rate. The percentage of visitors who take a desired action.

co-citation. In topical authority-based search algorithms, links that appear near one another on a page may be deemed related. In algorithms like latent semantic indexing, words that appear near one another often are frequently deemed to be related.

CGI (common gateway interface). Interface software between a web server and other machines or software running on that server. Many CGI programs are used to add interactivity to a website.

concept search. A search that attempts to conceptually match results with the query, not necessarily with those words.

conceptual links. Links that search engines attempt to understand beyond the words in them.

content. The information located on a web page. Includes text, images, and other information that a webmaster places on the page.

content management system (CMS). Tool that enables easy update and addition of information to a website.

contextual advertising. Ad programs that generate relevant ads based on the content of a web page.

conversion. Accomplishment of a desired goal, such as viewing an online ad.

cookie. A file on a computer that records information, such as sites visited by a user on the World Wide Web.

cost-per-action (CPA). Online advertising payment model in which payment is based solely on qualifying actions, such as sales or registrations.

cost-per-click (CPC). The cost or cost-equivalent paid per click-through.

cost-per-lead (CPL). The cost paid for each lead referred to an affiliate site.

CPM (cost per thousand impressions). Defines the cost an advertiser pays for 1,000 impressions of an advertisement, such as a banner ad, text ad, or other promotion. An impression is counted each time an advertisement is shown. If an ad appears on a web page 1000 times and it costs $1, then the CPM would be $1.

CPT (cost per transaction). An alternative to the traditional cost-per-click or cost-per-thousand pricing models, where an advertiser would pay per actual sale/transaction.

CPTM (cost per targeted thousand impressions). Implies that the audience one is trying to reach is defined by particular demographics or other specific characteristics, such as male skiers age 20 to 30. The difference between CPM and CPTM is that CPM is for gross impressions, while CPTM is for targeted impressions.

CPU (central processing unit). The main "brain" of the computer, where information is processed and calculations are done.

coverage. The percentage of a population group covered by the internet.

crawl. Same as spidering: search engines crawl links/pages and collect information about each page along the way.

crawl depth. How deeply a website is crawled and indexed.

crawl frequency. How frequently a website is crawled.

crawler. A software program that websites use to index pages throughout a site or several websites on the internet.

creative. The technology used to create or develop an ad unit. The most common creative technology for banners is GIF or JPEG images. Other creative technologies include Java, HTML, or streaming audio or video. Commonly referred to as rich media banners.

cross linking. When the owners of two or more websites interlink the sites to boost their search engine rankings. If detected, cross linking often results in a search engine penalty.

customer acquisition cost. The cost associated with acquiring a new customer.

cyberspace. Term originated by William Gibson in his novel *Neuromancer*. Used to describe the whole range of information resources available through computer networks.

D

del.icio.us. Social bookmarking website.

de-listing. Temporarily or permanently becoming de-indexed from a directory or search engine.

deep linking. Linking to a web page other than a site's home page.

demographics. Statistical data or characteristics that define segments of a population.

description meta tag. Describes the content of the web page in which it's found. Used by some search engines for keyword density purposes.

description tag. An HTML tag used by web page authors to provide a description for search engine listings.

Digg. Social news site where users vote on which stories get the most exposure and become the most popular.

direct response. The school of advertising that says, "The internet is an interactive medium. If the consumer interacts with our marketing efforts, we've done our job." Unfortunately for agencies, there's nowhere to hide with interactive campaigns, as they produce precise success or failure measurements. Same as direct marketing; relates to promotions or requests from advertiser by responding directly via email, phone, or other means.

DMOZ (Open Directory Project). The largest human-edited directory of websites. Owned by AOL, and primarily run by volunteer editors.

DNS (domain name system). The system that translates internet domain names into IP numbers. A "DNS server" is a server that performs this kind of translation.

domain name. The unique name that identifies an internet site. Domain names always have two or more parts, separated by dots. The left side is the most specific, and the part on the right is the most general. A given machine may have more than one domain name but a given domain name points to only one machine.

doorway domain. A domain used to rank well in search engines for particular keywords, serving as an entry point through which visitors pass to the main domain.

doorway page. A page made specifically to rank well in search engines for particular keywords, serving as an entry point through which visitors pass to the main content. When used in bulk they are considered to be search engine spam.

duplicate content. Two or more web pages that contain substantially the same content.

dynamic content. A dynamic web page that is often generated from database information based on queries initiated by users.

dynamic IP address. An IP address that changes every time a computer logs on to the internet. See also static IP address. AOL users show different IP numbers every time they log on, for example.

dynamic language. Programming language such as PHP or ASP that builds web pages on the fly.

E

earnings per click. Many contextual advertising publishers estimate their potential earnings based on how much they make from each click.

editorial link. Search engines count links as votes of quality. Using an algorithm similar to TrustRank, some search engines may place more trust in well-known sites with strong editorial guidelines.

email, electronic mail. Text files sent from one person to another.

emailing. The sending of email or text files from one person to another.

email marketing. The promotion of products or services via email.

email spam. Unwanted, unsolicited email.

emphasis. An HTML tag used to emphasize text.

entry page. The page from which a user enters a site.

ethical SEO. Search engines like to paint SEO services that manipulate their relevancy algorithms as being unethical. Many feel that "ethics" for search engines is not a valid term, since search engines are all software and machines and cannot hurt humans per se. Ethical SEO refers to a term and related optimization techniques that owners of search engines (i.e., Google) consider OK (compare to Black Hat SEO). It's search engine optimization that does not use trickery or tactics that are frowned on by the search engines.

exclusivity. Contract term in which one party grants another party sole rights with regard to a particular business function.

expert document. Quality page that links to many non-affiliated topical resources.

external link. Link that references another domain.

extranet. Extranet refers to a group of websites belonging to independent entities that are combined together in order to share information. For example, an organization may grant limited access to its internal network to customers or suppliers. This is in contrast to an intranet, which is a private site that is only accessible for employees of an entity.

ezine. An electronic magazine, whether delivered via a website or an email newsletter.

ezine directory. Directory of electronic magazines, typically of the email variety.

F

filter. A software routine that examines web pages during a robot's search for search engine spam. If the filter detects spam on the page, a ranking penalty is assessed.

firewall. A combination of hardware and software that separates a network into two or more parts for security purposes.

FTP (file transfer protocol). A common method of moving files between two internet sites.

FFA. Free-for-all links list: a web page that contains a collection of indiscriminate and often unrelated links. FFA pages do not qualify the links or the quality but allow you to simply add your URL. These pages are used to artificially boost link popularity and are considered spam by the major search engines.

Flash. Multimedia technology developed by Macromedia to allow a lot of interactivity to fit in a relatively small file size.

404 Not Found. The server was unable to locate the URL.

frame. A technique to display multiple smaller pages on a single display. Created by Netscape.

G

gateway. A link from one computer system to a different computer system.

GIF (graphic interchange format). A graphics format that can be displayed on most web browsers. A common compression format used to transfer graphics files between different computers. Most "pictures" online are GIF files. They display in 256 colors and have built-in compression. GIF images are the most common form of banner creative.

Google Base. Free database of semantically structured information.

Google bombing. Making a prank rank well for a specific search query by pointing hundreds or thousands of links at it with the keywords in the anchor text.

Google bowling. Knocking a competitor out of the search results by pointing hundreds or thousands of low-trust, low-quality links at its website.

Google Checkout. Google payment service that helps Google better understand merchant conversion rates and the value of different keywords and markets.

Google Content Experiments. Free multivariable testing platform used to help AdWords advertisers improve their conversion rates.

Google dance. Google used to update its index about once a month. Those updates were named Google dances. Google has since shifted to a constantly updating index.

Google Keyword Planner. Tool provided by Google to estimate the competition for a keyword, recommend related keywords, and tell the user what keywords Google thinks are relevant to a site or a page on your site.

Google OneBox. Portion of the search results page above the organic search results which Google sometimes uses to display vertical search results from Google News, Google Base, and other Google-owned vertical search services.

Google Sitemap. Program that webmasters use to help Google index their contents.

Google Sitelink. On some search results where Google thinks one result is more relevant than other results (like navigational or brand-related searches), it may list numerous deep links to that site at the top of the search results.

Google supplemental index. Index where pages with lower trust scores are stored. Pages may be placed in Google's supplemental index if they consist largely of duplicate content, if the URLs are excessively complex in nature, or if the site that hosts them lacks significant trust.

Google toolbar. A downloadable toolbar for Internet Explorer that allows a user to do a Google search without visiting the Google website. The toolbar also displays the Google PageRank (PR) of the page currently displayed in the browser. Also includes a pop-up blocker.

Google Traffic Estimator. Tool that estimates bid prices and how many Google searchers will click on an ad for a particular keyword.

Google Trends. Tool that allows a user to see how Google searches volumes for a particular keyword change over time.

Google Website Optimizer. *See* Google Content Experiments.

Google.com. The leading search engine on the internet. When people speak of search engine optimization (SEO), they're often referring to Google.

Googlebot. The crawler that Google uses on a daily basis to find and index new web pages.

guerrilla marketing. Unconventional marketing intended to get maximum results from minimal resources.

H

hacker. Originally described a computer enthusiast who pushed a system to its highest performance through clever programming. Term has since been used to identify computer enthusiasts who use their abilities to enhance and better computer systems; these hackers are referred to as white hat. Term also describes those who alter computer systems in a negative way; known as black hat.

header tags. HTML tags that outline a web page or draw attention to important information. Keywords located inside header tags provide a rankings boost in the search engines. For example:

<>This is a tag.</>
<h2>This is an H2 tag.</h2>

hidden text, hidden link. Using a text font the same color as the background color, rendering the text or link invisible or very difficult to read.

host. Any computer on a network that's a repository for services available to other computers on the network. It's common to have one host machine provide several services, such as SMTP (email) and HTTP (web).

HTML (hypertext markup language). The coding language used to create hypertext documents for use on the World Wide Web. HTML looks like old typesetting code, where the user surrounds a block of text with codes to indicate how it should appear. HTML files are meant to be viewed using a web browser.

.htaccess. Apache directory-level configuration file used to password protect or redirect files.

HTTP (hypertext transfer protocol). The protocol for moving hypertext files across the internet. Requires an HTTP client program on one end, and an HTTP server program (such as Apache) on the other end. HTTP is the most important protocol used in the World Wide Web.

hypertext. Generally, any text that contains links to other documents, words, or phrases in the document that can be chosen by a reader and that cause another document to be retrieved and displayed.

I

image map. Placing separate hyperlinks on different areas of the same image.

impression, ad impression, page impression. A single instance of an online ad being displayed.

index. Collection of data used as a bank to find a match to a user-fed query. The largest search engines have billions of documents in their catalogs.

indexing. After a search engine has crawled the web, it ranks URLs found using various criteria and places them in the database, or index.

information architecture. Designing, categorizing, organizing, and structuring content in a useful and meaningful way.

internet. A connection of two or more networks. Also the vast collection of interconnected networks that are connected using the TCP/IP protocols. Evolved from the ARPANET of the late '60s and early '70s.

internet marketing. Online marketing strategies to help a website improve its ranking in search engines. Also refers to marketing strategies that include website optimization, displaying ads or links throughout the internet with the common goal of improving the quantity and quality of visitors to a website.

internet marketing company. A company that provides internet marketing and often search engine marketing for its clients.

intranet. A private network of a company or organization that uses the same kinds of software found on the public internet, but is only for internal use. Compare with extranet.

IP number. Internet protocol number sometimes called a "dotted quad." A unique number consisting of four parts separated by dots, e.g., 165.113.245.2.

IP delivery. *See* cloaking.

IP spoofing. Returning an IP address different from the one actually assigned to the destination website. Often done with redirects. Unethical practice and a criminal offense under certain circumstances.

J

Java. A network-friendly programming language invented by Sun Microsystems.

JavaScript. A programming language mostly used in web pages, usually to add features that make the web page more interactive. When JavaScript is included in an HTML file it relies on the browser to interpret the JavaScript. When JavaScript is combined with cascading style sheets and HTML (4.0 and later) the result is often called DHTML.

K

keyword. A word used in performing a search. Used to focus a search by categorizing websites and locating specific topics.

keyword density. Keywords as a percentage of text words that can be indexed.

keyword marketing. Putting a message in front of people who are searching using particular keywords and keyword phrases.

keyword research. The search for keywords related to a website, and the analysis of which ones yield the highest return on investment.

keyword stuffing. Writing copy that uses excessive instances of the core keyword.

keywords tag. Meta tag used to define the primary keywords of a web page.

L

LAN (local area network). A computer network limited to the immediate area, usually the same building or floor of a building.

landing page. The page on which a visitor arrives after clicking on a link or ad.

link. URL placed within a web page so that when it's clicked on the browser is served with a different web page, often on a completely different website. Also a citation from one web document to another web document or another position in the same document.

link anchor text. The clickable part of the link structure. Using keywords in the link anchor text of inbound links helps the search engine rank for those keywords.

link baiting. Targeting, creating, and formatting content or information in a way that encourages the target audience to point high-quality links at a site.

link building. The process of building links. Can be inbound or outbound.

link bursts. A rapid increase in the quantity of links pointing at a website.

link checker. Tool used to check for broken hyperlinks.

link churn. Refers to the rate at which a site loses links.

link equity. A measure of the strength of a site based on inbound link popularity and the authority and quality of the sites providing the links.

link farm. One or a group of websites that link to other sites without regard to content or relevancy. Free For All pages are examples of link farms.

link hoarding. Keeping all of a link's popularity by not doing outbound links or only linking out using JavaScript or redirects.

link popularity. A measure of the quantity and quality of inbound links pointing to a particular website. Used by search engines to position web pages in search engines indexes.

link rot. When web pages previously accessible at a particular URL are no longer reachable at that URL due to movement or deletion of the page.

linking. Placing a link to another web page (usually on another website).

Linux. A widely used open-source Unix-like operating system. First released by its inventor Linus Torvalds in 1991. The inner workings of Linux are open and available for anyone to examine and change as long as they make their changes available to the public.

Live.com. Search platform provided by Microsoft.

log file. A record of the activity on a web server that tracks network connections.

login. The identification or name used to access a computer, network, or site.

long domain name. Domain names longer than the original 26 characters, up to a theoretical limit of 67 characters.

LSI (latent semantic indexing). A way for search systems to mathematically understand and represent language based on the similarity of pages and keyword co-occurence. A relevant result may not even have the search term in it. It may be returned only because it contains many similar words to those appearing in relevant pages which contain the search words.

M

mailing list. An automatically distributed email message on a particular topic going to certain individuals. Users can subscribe or unsubscribe to a mailing list by sending a message via email.

manual submission. Adding a URL to the search engines one at a time.

marketing plan. The part of the business plan outlining the marketing strategy for a product or service.

meta description. Typically a sentence or two that describes the content of the page.

meta keywords. A tag used to highlight keywords and keyword phrases that the page is targeting.

meta search. A search engine that pulls top-ranked results from multiple other search engines and rearranges them into a new result set.

meta search engine. A website that takes a search query and sends it to several search engines and directories, then summarizes the results in a logical manner for review.

meta tag. A specific type of HTML tag that contains information not normally displayed to the user. Meta tags can be seen in a page by viewing the page's source code.

Microsoft. Maker of the popular Windows operating system and internet Explorer browser.

mindshare. A measure of the number of people who think of a specific product when thinking of products in a category.

mirror sites. Identical, but separate websites on different domains. Commonly used legitimately by large websites to share heavy server loads, and by search engine spammers to generate more search engine referrals and revenue.

N

natural language processing. Algorithms that try to understand the true intent of a search query rather than only matching results to keywords.

navigation. That which facilitates movement from one web page to another web page.

netizen. Derived from citizen, referring to a citizen of the internet, or someone who uses networked resources. The term connotes civic responsibility and participation.

niche. A topic or subject that a website is focused on.

nofollow. Attribute used to prevent a link from passing link authority. Commonly used on sites with user-generated content, like blog comments.

not relevant. A result generally unhelpful to the user but still connected, however remotely, with the query.

O

off topic. Unrelated to the query.

one-way link. A hyperlink that points to a website without a reciprocal link; thus the link goes in only one direction.

online business community. Social network for business users to promote and find businesses.

online marketing. Form of website promotion completed online as opposed to offline.

opt-in email. Email requested by the recipient.

opt-out. A type of program that assumes inclusion unless stated otherwise. Opt out also means to remove oneself from an opt-out program.

organic search results. Results that consist of paid ads and unpaid listings.

outbound link. Link from one web page to another.

P

page jacking. Theft of a page from the original site and publication of a copy (or near-copy) at another site.

PageRank (PR). A proprietary numerical score assigned by Google to every web page in its index. PR for each page is calculated by Google using an algorithm based on the number and quality (as determined by Google) of the inbound links to the page.

page view. Request to load a single HTML page.

paid inclusion. Some directories that accept a URL into their database only if paid a fee.

paid link. Link purchased for advertising.

pay for performance. Payment structure where affiliated sales workers are paid a commission for getting consumers to perform certain acts.

pay-per-click (PPC). Online advertising payment model in which payment is based solely on qualifying click-throughs.

pay-per-click search engine (PPCSE). Search engine where results are ranked according to the bid amount. Advertisers are charged only when a searcher clicks on the search listing.

pay-per-lead (PPL). Online advertising payment model in which payment is based solely on qualifying leads.

pay-per-sale (PPS). Online advertising payment model in which payment is based solely on qualifying sales.

PHP (hypertext preprocessor). Programming language used mainly to create software that's part of a website. The PHP language is designed to be intermingled with the HTML that's used to create web pages. Unlike HTML, PHP code is read and processed by the web server software.

pop-under ad. Ad that displays in a new browser window behind the current browser window.

pop-up ad. Ad that displays in a new browser window.

portal. A site that offers many commonly used services. Serves as a starting point and frequent gateway to the web.

PPP (point-to-point protocol). Language that enables a computer to use telephone lines and a modem to connect to the internet. Gradually replacing SLIP as the preferred means of connection.

protocol. Usually refers to a set of rules that define the format for communication between systems.

Q

quality content. Linkworthy content.

quality link. Search engines count a link a vote of trust.

query. A request for information, usually to a search engine.

R

rank. An ad's standing in comparison to other ads, based on the graphical click-through rate. Rank provides advertisers with information on an ad's performance across sites.

rate card. Document detailing prices for ad placement options.

reciprocal link. 1) Link exchanged between two sites. 2) Link to a website placed on another site in exchange for a link back to the original website.

redirect. A tactic sometimes used to send a user to a page different other than the one found in the SERPS.

referrer, referring URL. The URL of the web page where a visitor clicked a link to come to another site.

registrar. A company that registers domain names.

relevancy. The degree to which the content on a web page that's returned in a list of search results (SERPS) matches the topic of the information that the user was searching for.

relative link. A link that shows the relationship of the current URL to the URL of the page being linked to.

rich media. New media that offers an enhanced experience relative to older, mainstream formats.

robot. A program used by a search engine to crawl the web to find, rank, and index new web pages.

robots.txt. A special file commonly used to exclude some or all robots from crawling certain files or directories on a website.

ROAS (Return on Advertising Spend). Represents the dollars earned per dollars spent on the corresponding advertising. To determine ROAS, divide revenue derived from the ad source by the cost of that ad source. Values less than one indicate that less revenue is generated than is spent on the advertising.

ROI (return on investment). ROI is trying to find out what the end result of the expenditure is, and what positive or negative results will exist. In advertising the ROI metric assesses what the advertiser received for the cost of the advertisement (see ROAS).

RSS (rich site summary, RDF site summary, real simple syndication). A commonly used protocol for syndication and sharing of content. Originally developed to facilitate the syndication of news articles, now widely used for syndication and other kinds of content-sharing.

run of network (RON). Ad-buying option in which ad placements may appear on any pages on sites within an ad network.

run of site (ROS). Ad-buying option in which ad placements may appear on any page of the target site.

S

search engine. A program that searches and indexes documents, then tries to match documents relevant to the user's search requests.

search engine marketing. The act of marketing a website via search engines, whether this be improving rank in organic listings, purchasing paid listings, or a combination of these and other search engine-related activities.

search engine optimization. The process of choosing targeted keyword phrases related to a site. Ensuring the site places well when those keyword phrases are part of a web search.

search engine spam. Excessive manipulation to influence search engine rankings, often for pages that contain little or no relevant content.

search engine submission. Supplying a URL to a search engine in an attempt to make a search engine aware of a site or page.

search spy. A perpetually refreshing page that provides a real-time view of actual web searches.

self-serve advertising. Advertising that can be purchased without the assistance of a sales representative.

SEO. *See* search engine optimization.

SERP (search engine results page). A search engine results page, or SERP, is the listing of web pages returned by a search engine in response to a keyword query. The results normally include a list of web pages with titles, a link to the page, and a short description showing where the keywords have matched content within the page.

server. A computer or software package that provides a specific kind of service to client software running on other computers. The term can refer to a particular piece of software, such as a WWW server, or to the machine on which the software is running.

servlet. Small computer program designed to add capabilities to a larger piece of server software.

siphoning. Techniques used to steal another website's traffic, including the use of spyware or cybersquatting.

sitemap. Page that can be used to give search engines a secondary route to navigate through a site.

social media. Websites that allow users to create the valuable content.

social network. A community website that lets users create profiles and find friends. Often a social network allows users to find other users based on interest, location, or name searches.

spam, spamming. Inappropriate commercial email message of extremely low value. An attempt to use a mailing list, USENET, or another networked communications facility as if it were a broadcast medium (which it is not) by sending the same message to a large number of people who didn't ask for it.

spider. Software that websites use to index pages throughout a site or several websites on the internet.

splash page. A branding page before the home page of a website.

splog. Spam blog, typically consisting of stolen or automated low-quality content.

sponsorship. Advertising that seeks to establish a deeper association and integration between an advertiser and a publisher, often involving coordinated beyond-the-banner placements.

spyware. Software secretly installed on a user's computer that monitors computer use in some way without the user's knowledge or consent.

SQL (structured query language). A specialized language for sending queries to databases.

SSI (server side includes). A way to call portions of a page in from another page. SSI makes it easier to update websites.

SSL (secure socket layer). A protocol designed by Netscape Communications to enable encrypted, authenticated communications across the internet.

static content. Content that changes infrequently. May refer to content that has no social elements and doesn't use dynamic programming languages.

static IP address. An IP address permanently assigned to a computer.

static rotation. Ads rotate based on the entry of users into a screen. Regardless of the amount of time a user spends with a screen, ads remain on the screen for the entire time and don't change.

stemming. Using the stem of a word to satisfy search relevancy requirements.

stickiness. The amount of time spent at a site over a given time period.

super affiliate. Affiliate able to generate a significant percentage of an affiliate program's activity.

T

tag. A noun or verb. As a noun, it's a basic element of the languages used to create web pages (HTML) and similar languages such as XML. Another, more recent meaning of tag is related to reader-created tags where blogs and other content (such as photos or music) may be "tagged," which means to assign a keyword.

targeted marketing. Banners or other promotions aimed, on the basis of demographic analysis, at one specific subsection of the market.

TCP (transmission control protocol). Works with IP to ensure that packets travel safely on the internet. The method by which most internet activity takes place.

TCP/IP (transmission control protocol/internet protocol). A suite of protocols that defines the internet. Originally designed for the UNIX operating system, TCP/IP software is now included with every major kind of computer operating system. To be on the internet, your computer must have TCP/IP software.

text ad. Ad using text-based hyperlinks.

text link exchange. Network where participating sites display text ads in exchange for credits that are converted (using a predetermined exchange rate) into ads to be displayed on other sites.

301 Moved Permanently. The file has been moved permanently to another location. The preferred method of redirecting for most pages or websites.

throughput. The amount of data transmitted through internet connectors in response to a given request.

title. HTML tag used to define the text in the top line of a web browser. Used by many search engines as the title of search listings.

200 Status OK. The file request was successful. For example, a page or image was found and loaded properly in a browser. Some poorly developed content management systems return 200 status codes even when a file doesn't exist.

U

under delivery. Delivery of fewer impressions, visitors, or conversions than contracted for a specified period of time.

unique visitors, unique users. Users who have visited a website (or network) at least once in a during a fixed time.

Unix Computer operating system. Designed to be used by many users at the same time and has TCP/IP built in. The most common operating system for servers on the internet.

URI (uniform resource identifier). Address for a resource on the internet. The first part of a URI is called the "scheme." The best known scheme is http, but there are many others. Each URI scheme has its own format for how a URI should appear.

URL (uniform resource locator). Synonymous with URI. URI has replaced URL in technical specifications.

URN (uniform resource name). A URI that is supposed to be available for a long time. For an address to be a URN, an institution must commit to keep the resource available at that address.

V

vertical banner. Banner ad measuring 120 pixels wide by 240 pixels tall.

viral marketing. Marketing phenomenon that facilitates and encourages people to pass along a marketing message.

volunteer directory. A web directory staffed primarily by unpaid volunteer editors. The most popular volunteer directory to date is DMOZ.

W

web browser. A software application that allows for browsing of the World Wide Web.

web design. The selection and coordination of available components to create the layout and structure of a web page.

web directory. Organized, categorized listing of websites.

web hosting. The business of providing the storage, connectivity, and services needed to serve files for a website.

website traffic. The number of visitors and visits a website receives.

website usability. The ease with which visitors are able to use a website.

whois. A utility that returns ownership information about second-level domains.

X

XHTML (extensible hypertext markup language). HTML expressed as valid XML. Intended to be used in the same places you would use HTML (creating web pages) but is more strictly defined, which makes it easier to create software that can read it, edit it, check it for errors, etc. XHTML is expected to replace HTML.

XML (extensible markup language). Widely used system for defining data formats. Provides a rich system to define complex documents and data structures such as invoices, molecular data, news feeds, glossaries, inventory descriptions, real estate properties, etc.

Index